PARTICIPATORY LEARNING AND ACTION
With 100 Field Methods

STUDIES IN RURAL PARTICIPATION SERIES

1. Participation Rural Appraisal: Methodology and Applications
   Neela Mukherjee
2. Participatory Rural Appraisal and Questionnarie Survey (Comparative Field Experience and Methodological Innovations)
   Neela Mukherjee
3. Participatory Rural Appraisal of Natural Resources
   Neela Mukherjee
4. Participatory Learning and Action: With 100 Field Methods
   Neela Mukherjee
5. Participatory Rural Appraisal: Methods and Applications in Rural Planning (Second Revised Edition)
   Amitava Mukherjee
6. Participatory Learning & Action: Monitoring & Evaluation and Participatory Monitoring & Evaluation (Second Revised Edition)
   Amitava Mukherjee
7. Speaking to Power: 27 Voice Tools Building Bridges for Participatory Learning, Action and Policy Making
   Neela Mukherjee

About the Author

Dr. Neela Mukherjee, is currently working as a development practitioner, researcher, trainer and a resource person with multiple organizations, both within India and abroad. She is associated with a Delhi-based enterprise called "Development Tracks, RTC" involved in cutting-edge research/ consultancy and training activities. Fornerly, a Professor of Economics at the LBS National Academy of Administration Mussoorie, India and an alumna of the London School of Economics and Political Science, London, her major areas of current field rescarch include participatory and sustainable development practices, community perspectives, empowerment and related issues.

Dr. Mukherjee has written extensively in her areas of interest. Her books include *Participatory Rural Appraisal, Methodology and Applications* (1993), *Questionnaire Survey and Participatory Rural Appraisal* (1995), *Participatory Appraisal of Natural Resources* (1997) published by Concept Publishing Company, New Delhi. Her book *Alternative Perspectives on Livelihoods, Agriculture and Air Pollution, Agriculture in Urban and Peri-urban Areas in a Developing Country* published in 2001 by Ashgate Publishing Co., U.K. describes community perspectives on the impact of air pollution. Dr. Mukherjee is also the editor of a series on "*Learning to Share*" PRA experience, of which, two volumes (1997 and 2000) have been published by Concept Publishing Company, New Delhi.

PARTICIPATORY LEARNING AND ACTION

With 100 Field Methods

NEELA MUKHERJEE
Development Tracks,
Research Training and Consultancy,
52/82 C.R. Park, New Delhi-110019.
India

CONCEPT PUBLISHING COMPANY PVT. LTD.
NEW DELHI-110059

ISBN: 978-81-7022-943-8

First Published 2002
Reprint 2003
Reprint 2024

Published and Printed by

Concept
Since 1974

Concept Publishing Company Pvt. Ltd.
A/15-16, Commercial Block, Mohan Garden,
New Delhi-110059 (India)
T: 91-11-41101460
E: publishing@conceptpub.com, *W*: www.conceptpub.com

IN HONOUR
OF
DR. ROBERT CHAMBERS

PREFACE

The present book "Participatory Rural Appraisal: Learning and Action with 100 Field Methods" owes its existence to an innovative, creative and stimulating world of development practice with which I am associated. In a continuous process of learning from the field it becomes important to document the lessons learnt, assimilate them and share them with others engaged in the domain of development. This book provides an opportunity to share a multitude of field lessons learnt so far. The inspiration for writing this book can be attributed to my colleagues in development practice, who in their enthusiasm encouraged me to go ahead and write this book. The book takes stock of a decade of field experience in PRA/PLA methods.

Writing a book on any aspect of development practice is not only time-consuming but also a difficult exercise. It implies concentrated focus on writing and developing chapters based on heterogeneous nature of field experience, in-situ, in different locations, culture and context. It also implies period/s of seclusion away from the field and other activities. However, the benefits generally outweigh the costs because a book on development practice has intrinsic value. It is not only a vehicle for sharing field lessons with a range of actors in the field of development it helps in developing tools for self-assessment. It can help in breaking the "cycle of isolation and anonymity and the culture of silence", be an instrument in "gaining recognition for knowledge and perceptions" of local women and men and help in raising issues for policy dialogue.

For me, opportunities to learn from the field were neither systematic nor smooth. As a development practitioner my direct involvement with a number of development projects in India and other countries were in terms of capacity-building as a trainer-facilitator, facilitating formulation of community empowerment programmes/projects, supporting planning processes and participatory reviews, setting up monitoring systems and facilitating participatory evaluation and impact assessment. Such people-oriented activities helped me in learning new and innovative methods and practices and in continuously comparing and assessing approaches, methods and strategies in different culture.

Field learning grew at an exponential rate influenced by diverse actors including a range of organizations and people adopting different approaches in different locations, having different objectives, opportunity-frontiers and challenges, having differential response mechanisms and ways of enhancing problem solving abilities. There were great variations in the organizational culture of such organizations, where mindsets and approaches varied widely. The capabilities and capacities of organizations differed markedly, so were the leadership styles and team spirit in organizations and the ethos of team/s concerned. The visions of such organization ranged from tunnel vision to focused vision and wider ones as well and some were engaged in creating vision along the way. The rural and urban local communities, which were participating, were diverse having different context and culture, resources, opportunities and constraints, influencing localized development processes.

In the midst of diverse development paths adopted by different organizations, one common lesson learnt from the field was that our capabilities as development practitioners (in the larger context) strongly influence the process of development and performance in-situ and such capabilities are intrinsically associated with our mindsets and social skills. It is often that because of our conventionally structured mindsets our capabilities remain weak thus hampering our understanding of the development process and our role in that process. Capabilities change with change in mindsets and improvement in social skills. The issue is "how" to change our mindsets and boost social skills. This is what the book is all about.

There is a host of innovations taking place in the field of participatory development. The process of open-ended inquiry has led to such innovative methods and processes. The flexibility associated with the process of participatory learning and action has helped in creating and supporting a range of innovative tools and techniques, which are field-based and field-tested. Early on, I started writing on my field experience and the lessons learnt from the field in a series of monographs on the methodology of PRA/RRA published by Concept Publishers, New Delhi. Some of my field notes were published in different issues of the "PLA Notes" (formerly "RRA Notes") of the International Institute for Environment and Development, London. Some other field lessons learnt were included for informing the World Development Report 2000/1 of the World Bank by the Participatory Group at the Institute of Development Studies at University of Sussex, U.K. Extracts and anecdotes from my field notes were published in Brock (1999) edited, "A Review of Participatory Work on Poverty and Illbeing, Consultations with the Poor". Some others were included in Narayan et.al (2000) "Voices of the Poor Can Anyone Hear Us?", published by the World Bank. Many of the field lessons and experience were also documented in the Human Development Report on Bangladesh, 1996 by United Nations Development Programme, Dhaka.

The focus of the PLA Notes and other publications as referred above, are quite different, with the former concentrating on snap-shots of PRA/PLA techniques and processes (within a word limit of 1200) and the latter on local perspectives on poverty. Hence, a range of contextual experience in methods and practices need an outlet and an appropriate framework. The options are either to publish them in journals or to put them in the form of a book. In this context it may be mentioned that publications of papers on field methods and practices are often faced with gross limitations, where academic journals of the North do not find them credible enough while appropriate journals are virtually absent in the South. This is not to undermine the growing informal literature on PRA/PLA-type field experience that has come up over the years.

Though there have been a large volume of publication on field lessons, there is a dearth of books and papers/notes in direct proportion to our requirements for changing our mindsets and adding on to our social skills. Much of published field experience stand-alone and is good as locality-based experience. A holistic framework for integrating such local level experience and lessons is essential. The present book is a modest attempt at that. It also provides a framework for appreciating participatory methods and approaches in a holistic manner. Such methods and approaches, directly and indirectly, support changes in mindsets, help in developing one's faculties, in strengthening inner qualities and analytical skills and in improving upon field-based practice and performance.

PRA/PLA is not mere casual application of field techniques at random. There is a much larger process involved. It involves preparation of mindsets for listening and learning, inculcation of values, which support listening of "unheard" and "unseen"; of skills for learning rapidly, of mental preparedness for role reversals, of managing expectations and conflicts as and when they occur. All of these do not happen within a short span of time. They happen gradually and improve with experience. The quality of mindsets improves with daily reflections and exercises in embracing errors.

In the present book the methods for PRA/PLA are not perceived as narrow tools and techniques. Rather they are looked upon as methods with broader connotation in terms of our mindsets, personal qualities and values, participatory processes, unstructured learning and personal reflections. The role of development practitioner is complex and chaotic and normally keeps changing over time depending on context and situation. A development practitioner can have alternative roles as a welfare worker, animator, activist, leader, and fieldworker facilitating, promoting and supporting local communities towards self-reliance, consulting and assisting. All these roles call for great flexibility in mental make up and a variety of skills as demanded locally. Often practitioners/ development organizations fail to differentiate between their different roles and approaches in development practice resulting in chaos and confusion. A development practitioner needs good observation power and the ability to interpret different situations, ability to appreciate one's changing role and skills to support communities, groups and individuals. Hence broadening of mindsets and strengthening of skills are essential in today's development world. Narrow mindsets and weak set of skills of a development practitioner can only harm the process and prove costly for local development initiative/s.

The chapter-layout of this book has been designed keeping in view the paradigmatic shift in development thought and practice; the changes desirable in the mindset of a development practitioner; and the enabling skills for facilitating and supporting development process at the grassroots. In this book, the participatory methods have been discussed under eight groups based on the criteria of direct and indirect support towards field participation. There are those methods, which help us in doing the background work, in preparing our mindsets and body language as individuals and there are those, which help us to organize ourselves and improve our analytical abilities as facilitators. A discussion on "verbal" methods, which help in building rapport and holding conversation, is followed by discussion on "visual" methods of mapping and diagramming. There are separate discussions on methods, which help in revealing priorities and preferences such as ranking/ scoring, those, which portray seasonality and those, which involve walking together with local women and men.

The book has ten chapters, which are briefly described below.

In chapter 1, "Development Paradigm, Community Participation and "Our" Mindsets" I have described the on-going shifts in development paradigm and how de-construction of mindsets and acquisition of social skills are important for unraveling the new vistas of learning and the emerging contours of social development in practice. I have drawn upon few important factors that have strongly influenced such shifts in development paradigm. These are "multiple perspectives" and alternate "worldview" of stakeholders of development, indigenous knowledge system, and "whose development", "ownership" factors in sustainable development and increased awareness of poor and deprived groups about human rights. In this chapter I have also distinguished between conventional and new development paradigms, the role of participatory approaches, the methodology of Participatory Rural Appraisal (PRA)/Participatory Learning and Action (PLA), genesis and description of PRA/PLA, its principles and cornerstones.

Chapters 2 and 3 contain methods for improving upon our mindsets, personal qualities, attributes and analytical skills. Our internal learning processes need to be in proper shape before we facilitate community development. In Chapter 2, after a broad description of what is a method I have discussed those methods, which influence our approach, role and responsibility in development practice and are supportive of our internal learning processes and our values. Those methods have also been discussed, which help in organizing our mental set up about mutual roles and instill a sense of responsibility associated with it. A positive outlook and alert faculties, a set of values based on PRA/PLA principles, awareness about role reversals, a helping attitude, a relaxed approach and some managerial and organizational skills help in gearing our approach towards participation, provide clarity of role and a sense of social responsibility.

Chapter 3 is meant for those of us who would like to be more analytical and would do necessary spadework before going to the field. Many of us would like to prepare a list of activities for field inquiry, select localities at random, or do purposive sampling of localities to be visited. We may find it useful to hold briefing meetings with team of external facilitators, read earlier reports, scan through secondary source/s of information, clarify objectives of field visit, evolve a list of indicators, prepare mental/written checklist of issues, hold discussions on field methods and their possible sequencing. There are activities before fieldwork and also during and post- fieldwork. Preparedness as indicated in Chapter 2 and 3 helps in better facilitation, lends positive influence on mindset and strengthens analytical skills.

In Chapter 4 those "verbal" methods have been described, which help in rapport building and holding conversation. They are easy to apply while interacting with local communities and it is important to appreciate the appropriateness of different "verbal" methods for different purposes/types of inquiry. The range of learning that can emerge from such methods is enormous and can be both at an individual and at a group level. The degree of probing tends to vary across methods.

Chapter 5 is a description of a range of "visual" methods on mapping and sketching. It includes social mapping with topical methods such as resource mapping, facility mapping, literacy and health mapping, livestock mapping and others. In resource mapping, it includes both locality-specific resources and micro-resources through microenvironment mapping. Mapping on a temporal basis is illustrated through mapping, past, present and future and children's vision mapping. Aspects of well being/poverty/wealth are also included in chapter 5 through methods involving mapping, grouping, ranking, construction of matrices and distance grouping. Participatory concept mapping, which helps in evolving local concepts from the grassroots, is also a part of this chapter.

Chapter 6 is on "visual" methods concerning diagrams and flow charts. Diagrams drawn are "visual" and provide a tangible basis for any discussion and thereby enrich the process. In this chapter different variations of "Chappati" (Venn) diagram have been discussed together with source diagram, pie chart, ratio analysis, impact flow diagram and analysis, flow chart, visual trend analysis, causal tree analysis and picture symbols. In PRA/PLA such diagrams form the basis of discussion and help in clarity and "visual" details. Physical sample method is included here, which helps in providing a physical basis for discussion based on such sample and its related aspects.

Chapter 7 is on methods revealing priorities through ranking and scoring, which provide opportunities to local people to physically rank and score items and criteria in order to reveal their priorities and preferences.

In chapter 8 the "seasonality" method has been described, which is important in showing seasonal variations in lives and livelihoods of local communities.

Chapter 9 describes methods related to "joint walk" with local groups to have a close look at areas/locations/sites, which are considered relevant for "overviews" or have special focus. The chapter explains how such joint walks constitute sessions of mutual learning by visiting areas for better understanding and comprehension. It involves physically walking to such areas and understanding the physical-ecological and socio-economic dimensions of the issues concerned.

Chapter 10 is on applications of PRA/PLA-type activities and reflections on PRA/PLA. After an inter-comparison of methods and a description of PRA/PLA-type activities in different chapters, this chapter provides an assessment in terms of the issues raised in different fields and the academic circles. Though the utility and power of PRA/PLA are well demonstrated in development practice there are accompanying issues related to field applications, capacity building of practitioners and issues concerning up-streaming, policy-making, epistemology, information and research. These points have been taken up for discussion in chapter 10.

The book is meant for development practitioners including project coordinators and managers, non-governmental development organizations, government personnel in development and field workers. The policy makers, policy advisors, donor agencies and policy researchers will also find the book useful. The book will provide an interesting reading for the rural development professionals, consultants, students of development, field researchers, field specialists, teachers/trainers in field methods and training institutions and those interested in the area of participatory development.

I am deeply indebted to the rural and urban local communities in different parts of this globe who have taught me powerful lessons in local participation. Apart from interacting with them in their localities, many of them have critically reflected on issues related to community participation in meetings and workshops at different places. They have applied PRA/PLA-type activities and have commented upon the practical aspects, the utility and the shortcomings in PRA/PLA.

It is my privilege to write this book in honour of Robert Chambers of the Institute of Development Studies at Sussex, U.K., whose path-breaking contributions to development practice has helped in reversing conventional development processes worldwide. The book is also for those development practitioners with whom I have worked directly and had the opportunity to see their commitment towards participatory development from close quarters.

On a personal note, I am grateful to my mother Indrani Sen Gupta who took the trouble of managing my household during my long absence away from home for field visits. I am thankful to my husband Amitava for the rounds of discussions that we had on the subject of 'development" and for his encouragement towards completion of this book. The book has its own share of errors and omissions for which I am solely responsible. It will be my pleasure to have comments and remarks from the readers for bringing about improvements in future edition of the book.

7 July 2001

Neela Mukherjee
Development Tracks, RTC,
Chittaranjan Park, New Delhi 110019 (India)
Phone 00-91-11-6480332 & 00-91-11-6481824
E Mail: neelamuk@del2.vsnl.net.in

ACKNOWLEDGEMENTS

The book would not have been possible without the active support and cooperation of many village/urban communities, groups, individuals and institutions. Each of them deserves mention not withstanding the long list of names, which follows.

Local Communities

I am deeply indebted to the local communities in rural, peri-urban and urban areas in different localities and countries who interacted with zeal and enthusiasm in the PRA-type sessions for different Projects and contributed towards knowledge, experience and analysis in their own way.

India

Andhra Pradesh
Village Madhapur, Ranga Reddy
Villages of Mehbubnagar District

Bihar
Village Dhobah (District Muzaffarpur)

Delhi
Alaknanda Slum, Alaknanda, New Delhi

Gujarat
Villages Bar, Vislanga, Kattarnipalli, Moti Baswani (District Dahod)

Haryana
Villages Kadhaoli, Sagarpur Uncha Gaon, Baroli, Pali Kasba, Chandawali, Jajru, Pyala, Sahupura, Sahapur Kalan, Sumper, Sohtai and Malerna (District Faridabad)

Jharkhand
Villages Jihu, Larhi, Ramgarh, Sijua, Balidih, Gobardaha and Barki (District Hazaribagh)
Villages Singhpur, Muri, Nawadih, Hasadih, Kulsadh, Lota and Banta Hajam (District Ranchi)

Kerala
Village Ulloor, Trivandrum

Madhya Pradesh
Villages Biharbadi, Debalphaliya, Naganwat Choti, Naganwat Bari, Darkali (District Jhabua)

Maharashtra
Villages Zhadgarh and Awale (District Thane)

Orissa
Villages Amligaon and Phulogarori, Konark

Rajasthan
Villages Rola, Shamlaser Koopda, Shambhupura (District Banswara)

Tamil Nadu
Village community Paraikulam, Madurai

Uttar Pradesh
Villages Chandpur, Navampura Kala, Seer Govardhanpur, Sarai Dongre, Lohta, Chitaipur, Nathupur, Tikri, Maraon, Maheshpur, Adityanagar, Karamanbir, Nuaon and Tarapur (District Varanasi)
Village Panchma (District Gorakhpur)
Village Kushiara (District Mirzapur)
Village Lolai near Lucknow

Uttaranchal
Villages Bhagwanpur- Jullon, Bhaniyawala, Signiwala and Guddi (District Dehradun)
Villages Koti, Dwara and Soura, Doon Valley Watershed, Dehradun

Village Timli, Vikasnagar
Village Chowki (District Dehradun)
Villages of Tehri Garhwal
Village Baruabagh, Haldwani

West Bengal

Villages Berapal, Kalsigeriya, Krishna Rakshit Chak, Mulbandh, Durganhari, Mulbandh, Benagariya, Tungadhua, Geriashuli, Susnigeriya (District Midnapore)
Villages Khanpur, Khoragorh and Baksha (District Hooghly)
Villages Patkita, Barasini, Golecunda, Asurgariya, Astagora, Dhadka, Latapara, Velaidih (District Purulia)

Bangladesh

Bogura - Villages Jhurjhuri, Makimpur, Daspara, Sarabpur, Chak Sarabpur, Dhangora and Makimpur

Comilla – Village Changini

Faridpur – Villages of Faridpur/Madaripur

Hathazari, Chittagong – Villages Nandi Para- Mirzpur, Laxmi Mahajan – Mehkole, Khastogerbari – Fatehabad, Gonimistrybari – Fatehadad, Nathpara-Mekhole, Madhya Pahartoli, Baruapara, Chibatoli, Magner Para, Rudra Para and West Fatika – Mirzapur

Kishoreganj– Villages Bhatgaon and Brahmankochure, Rashidabad Union; villages Barabagh, Projapathkhila and Pabankandi, Latibabad Union; villages Noyapara and Maizpara, Mahinanda Union, villages Shalpa Maria, Bagadia and Koromali, Maria Union

Mymensingh – Village Dhoopaguchina

Patuakhali– Villages Nishanbariya, Uttarpankhali (Thanas – Kalapara and Galachipa)

Savar – Village Khagan, Charabagh, Dhaka

Sherpur – Villages of Jhinaigati, Sherpur, Madhupur

Sirajganj– Villages of Tarash/Raiganj and Sirajganj

Sylhet — Villages Gourishankar, Kallogram, Islamabad, Lakhhiprasad, Jashpur, Lamni, Darbast, Muktapur, Srikhel, Kohaigarh, Changhat, Rameshwar and Haripur

Sreenagar, Munshiganj – Villages Maddha Bagra, Maghdal, Mandra Bhaggyakul, Jagannath Patti, Rarikhali – North Balashur and Bepari Para

Tangail – Village Banstaol, Mirzapur

Tangail - Commercial Sex Workers

Mymensingh – Urban Slum

Dhaka slums – Karail Slum, Peara Bag, Geneva Camp, Mahuttali Basti, Gandaria Slum, Nilkhet Babupara Slum, Mirbagh Slum, Aga Sadek Lane, Banani Wapda Slum, Wireless Gate

Dhaka city - Garment Workers
Dhaka city - Street Children
Dhaka city – Informal Traders of Dholai Khal

Botswana
Village community Nlaphwane near Francistown

China
Village communities, Honghe National Nature Reserve
Village communities, Sanjiang Natural Nature Reserve including village Qinghai
County Fu Yuan, Non Jiang Town, Sanjiang Province

Ghana
Agiya, Kumasi, Ghana

Maldives
Community islands of Noonu Atoll, Faafu Atoll and Dhaalu Atoll

Nepal
Village communities of Syangja, Nepal

Vietnam
Village community, Vo Ninh Commune, Quang Ninh Commune, Bo Trac, Quang Binh Province
Village community, Phuong Do Commune, Ha Giang Province

United Kingdom
Local community, Sparkbrook, Birmingham

Individuals

K.C.Thapliwal, S.T.S. Lepcha, Pawan Kumar, Ajay Prakash, J.B. Pandey, Bangali Babu Sharma, Ramesh Pandey, Nishi Rawat, Jyostna Sitling, Anil Bery,

Rahmat Khan, Chotelal

B.N. Yugandher, N.C.Saxena, S. P.Gupta, S.K. Ray, K.V.Sundaram, D, Bannerjee

Robert Chambers, Norman Uphoff, Nicholas Stern, Richard Ford, Max Steuer, Ed. Kuska, Daphne Thuvesson, Mary Hobley, Yvonne Rydin, Jean Dreze, Graham Chapman, David Taylor, Parmesh Shah, Meera Kaul Shah

Jules Pretty, John Thompson, Irene Guijt, Ian Scoones

Meera Jayaswal, Sudipta Ray, Bratindi Jena, Fiona Marshall, Simon Croxton, John Gaventa, Patta Scott-Viliers, Karen Brock, Nigel Poole, Dolf te Lintelo

Mitali Sen Gavai, Shakuntala Bannerjee, Sumita Roy

Neera Burra, Mithulina Chatterjee, Pravin Kaushal, Niharika and Project staff of PRAKRIYA, Rural Litigation and Entitlement Kendra, Dehradun

Indira Kohli, Hari Govind Singh, Dubeyji ('Mantriji'), R.S. Shukla, Praveen Saldana, Ratan Singh, PRADAN, V. Ratna Reddy, Asif Zaidi, Abhijit Ghosh, Gopa Pandey, Kartar Singh, Mahesh Chander

Nay Htun, Sohaib Sultan Khan, Henning Katcher

Mohammad Pournik, Saraswati Menon, Omer Zafar, P. V. Ramesh, Shyam Khadka, Gerald Gunther, Sabrina Abdullah, Sukanya Mohan Das, Meilani Razdi

Richard Bond, Keith Virgo, Steve Jones, Andrew Shepherd, Sarah Crowther, David Thompson

Ashok Kumar Mittal

Gramin Vikas Trust, Udaipur/Bhopal, India
P.S. Sodhi, V. S. Tomar, Meera Shahi, S. S. Rana, Bhartendu Singh, R.S. Bhatti, A.S. Patel, Asha Sachdev, Hansa Sakariya, Jaya Patel, Jyotika Bamaniya, Laxman Yadav, Madhura Rawat, Nagma Khaliq, Sangeeta Singh, Udai Lal Gurjer, Vijay Bhusan Nag, Yash Kanungo and Bharat Singh
Village Jankars - Kachru Lal, Kanta ben, Kanu ben, Kesar Singh, Lal Singh, Leela ben, Motiyas, Verunika ben

IFFDC, Pratapgarh (Rajasthan), India
Ashok Alambain, G.C. Tiwari, R. Jadav and Project staff of IFFDC, Pratapgarh WIRFP.

Bangladesh
Nasreen Jahan, Md. Shahabuddin, Subrata Chakrabarty, Samadbhai, Arif Mohammed, Yee Woo Guo, Michael Constable, Raj Thapa Gemini Wahaj, Dilwara Khanoum, Hasina Begum, Makshuda Akhtar, Nahid Pervin, Lena Hasle, Farah Gaznavi, Najma Sadiq, Durafshan Chowdhury, William Masolin, Nilufar Matin, Pradeep

Gain, Salma Shovan, Khorshed Erfan Ahmed, Shenaz, Shireen Akhtar Khan, Dee Jupp, Babu Bhai, Nargis Bano and Aroma Goon, A.J. Minaz Uddin Ahmed, B.K. Barua, M. A. Khaleque and Mahbubur Rehman and Project staff of Community Empowerment Projects of BRDB Sylhet, RDA Bogura and BARD Comilla.

Botswana

Bo Gohl, FAO, Botswana

Corris Sprenkels, Zwanshambee Brigade Trust, Botswana

China

Liu Guoqiang, Yan Chengao, Darell Sequeira, Wang Longfu, Lei Kun, Wu Zhiping, Zhang Xiaoyun, Wu Quong, Li Sheng, Officials of PPMU office , Heilongjiang,

Officials of WMA, Heilongjiang, Officials of Honghe Nature Reserve,

Officials of Sanjiang Nature Reserve

Maldives

Narinder Kakkar, Philippe Zysset, and Shaheem Razee, Mohammed Zahid, Aminath Lateefa, Mohammed Rasheed, Maldives

Vietnam

Ms. Thu, Hoang Hung, V. Jayaraman, Nguyen Tien Phong, Marjoline Nicod, Mr. Vu, Rab Nawaz, Hoang Van Son, Nguyen Thi Mai Huong, Le Van Hong, Lalitha Jayaraman, Ashok Saikia, Ms. Ann, Ms. Han, Ms. Yen, Ms. Biem, Mr. Lam, Mr. Sinh, Mr. Thang, Mr. Trung, Mr. Sy, Mr. Min, Mr. Do, Mr. Doan, Mr. Que, Mr. Nien, Mr. Toan, Mr. Trung, Mr. Tuyen, Mr. Yen, Mr. Hoa, Mr. Hung, Mr. Soa, Mr. Ngoc, Mr. Thanh, Mr. Cuoc, Mr. Cu and Mr. An

Institutions

Watershed Management Directorate, Dehradun, Uttaranchal, India

LBS National Academy of Administration, Mussoorie, Uttaranchal, India

International Institute for Environment and Development, London, U.K.
Institute of Development Studies at Sussex, Brighton, U.K.
United Nations for Project Services, Kuala Lumpur, Asia
United Nations Development Programme, Delhi, India
United Nations Development Programme, New York, USA
United Nations Development Programme, Dhaka, Bangladesh
United Nations Development Programme, Male, Maldives
United Nations Development Programme, Hanoi, Vietnam
United Nations Development Programme, Kathmandu, Nepal
United Nations Development Programme, Beijing, China
United Nations Development Programme, Islamabad, Pakistan
United Nations Development Programme, Gabarone, Botswana
United Nations Development Programme, Geneva, Switzerland
IFAD, Rome
Stanford University, Stanford, USA
University of California at Berkeley, California, USA
Clark University, Worcestor, USA
World Food Programme, Dhaka, Bangladesh
Food and Agriculture Organization, Gabarone, Botswana
Centre for Applied Social Sciences, Harare, Zimbabwe
The World Bank office, Ghana
Farming Systems Programme, FAO, Gabarone, Botswana
Department for International Development, London
Department for International Development, New Delhi
W.S. Atkins International, Cambridge, U.K
European Community, New Delhi, India
ARCD Project Dong Hoi, Quang Binh Province, Vietnam
ARCD Project Ha Giang, Vietnam
Administrative Staff College of India, Hyderabad, India
National Institute for Rural Development, Hyderabad, India
Rural Litigation Kendra, Dehradun, India
Gramin Matshyo Foundation, Grameen Bank, Bangladesh
PROSIKA, Dhaka, Bangladesh
Grameen Bank, Bangladesh
Rural Development Academy, Bogura, Bangladesh
Bangladesh Rural Development Board, Sylhet, Bangladesh

Bangladesh Academy for Rural Development, Comilla, Bangladesh
NOVIB, Dhaka, Bangladesh
PROMPT, Dhaka, Bangladesh
PRA Network, Dhaka, Bangladesh
PRA Network, Kathmandu, Nepal
T. H. Huxley School at Imperial College of Science, Technology and Medicine, London University, U.K.
School of Oriental and African Studies, London, UK
Health Services Management Centre, School of Public Policy, Birmingham University, U.K.
CARE India, New Delhi, India
Arthik Anusandhan Kendra, Mirzapur, Uttar Pradesh, India
Punjab Agriculture University, Ludhiana, India
Indian Council for Agriculture Research, New Delhi, India
RIS, New Delhi, India
Council for Social Development, New Delhi, India
Indian Social Institute, New Delhi, India
ICRIER, New Delhi, India
India International Centre, New Delhi, India
Ford Foundation office, Bangladesh, India and China
The British Council, London, U.K.
Institute of Development Studies, Jaipur, India
PRADAN, India
Indira Gandhi National Forest Academy, Dehradun, India
State Training Academy, Nainital, Uttar Pradesh, India
State Forest Academy, Dehradun, Uttaranchal, India
Wildlife Institute of India, Dehradun, India
Concept Publishing Company, New Delhi, India
Development Tracks, Research, Training & Consultancy, New Delhi, India

Governments

Government of India
Government of Bangladesh
Government of Vietnam

Government of China
Government of Maldives
Government of Nepal
Government of United Kingdom
Government of USA

LIST OF CHARTS

LIST OF TABLES

CONTENTS

1

DEVELOPMENT PARADIGM, COMMUNITY PARTICIPATION AND "OUR" MINDSETS

In Chapter 1, "Development Paradigm, Community Participation and Our Mindsets", I have described the on-going shift in the development paradigm, the factors influencing such shift, genesis and transition of participatory approaches and the principles and pillars of Participatory Learning and Action (PLA)/Participatory Rural Appraisal (PRA). The essence of the chapter is about the importance of de-constructing "our" mindsets for unravelling the new vistas of learning and the emerging contours of social development in practice. While explaining the shift in the development paradigm I have drawn upon certain important factors that have strongly influenced such shift. These factors are "multiple perspectives" and alternative "worldview" of stakeholders of development, indigenous knowledge systems, people-centred development, "ownership" factors in sustainable development and increased awareness of poor and deprived groups about their domain of rights.

1. THE PARADIGMATIC SHIFT

Development paradigm is in a transition phase evolving from "top-down" to "bottom-up" approaches. The following illustrates some of the dimensions of the changes taking place.

— From "command and control" system towards more decentralised approaches;
— From "positivist" framework to "constructivist" framework;
— From "closed" mindsets to more "open" mindsets;
— From "lecturing" mode to "listening" and "learning" mode;

— From theoretical approaches to more practical and field-based approaches;
— From narrow approaches to more holistic approaches;
— From pursuing "targets" to enabling participatory processes; and
— From people as "objects" to people as "participants"/citizens.

Over the past years such development paradigm has been undergoing a major shift, strongly responding to the outcomes from field inquiry. The clear message of the new paradigm is learning from the field, learning to respect and recognise field knowledge and experience, listening to alternative perspectives, appreciating other people's reality and learning through "hand on"/practice. One stimulus to change has come from field-related experience of what works and what does not work and why. Such field results have amply showed that the conventional approaches and solutions to development issues are increasingly becoming less effective and are seldom yielding the desired results. The message is that we learn best from the field, from practice, from listening to other's views and experience, from our reflections and mistakes. The quality of such learning is better as an iterative and a continuous process.

Such paradigm shift is taking place across civil societies, State institutions, donor agencies, programme/project management, research bodies, technology-development institutions and other sectors related to social development. The winds of change are on and there is a realisation in most quarters that the challenge of development lies in its relevance to the people as participants/citizens and development initiatives are best sought in the realm of people-centred development. However, the pace of change has varied considerably across institutions with the paradigmatic shift in development catching up faster with the civil societies and programme/project management at field level. This is because never before has there been any opportunity to work in such open-ended field conditions and be so innovative, have seamless learning experience and be able to critically reflect upon it.

1.2 Factors influencing Paradigmatic Shift

What factors are influencing shift in the development paradigm? We can attribute such paradigmatic shift to five important factors, as listed and discussed below:

1. That there is a whole gamut of indigenous knowledge systems lying in the people's domain;
2. There are multiple perspectives of stakeholders of development and they are often at variance with "our" perspective/s;
3. One important issue is what is this development all about?
4. Who "owns" this development and how sustainable is the process? and
5. Questions are being raised by groups excluded from the conventional mainstream development about human rights and fulfilment of basic needs.

1.2.1 Whose knowledge counts?

The conventional world of social development has been slow in recognising the significance of indigenous knowledge. Experts have been considerably reluctant in appreciating the vast storehouse of indigenous knowledge systems. Local knowledge retrieval and management has been a major omission in our conventional pursuit of development goals and activities. This has resulted in local communities appearing as a bundle of problems, rather than as plethora of opportunities. The outsiders often perceive that they have solutions to local problems. Max-Neef *et al.* (1991) wrote "we live and work within models of society that overlook the growing complexity of the real society in which we are immersed. Therefore, we watch the feverish and obsessive doings of the technocrats who design solutions before having identified where the real problems lie".

With exogenous solutions creating chaos rather than resolving problems, it is being gradually realised that such solutions are mostly not workable since they do not fit with the context of the problem, the local ethos and are not "owned" by the people concerned. Development experience from different areas shows that many of such external solutions have been abandoned, found risky and have achieved little success. In the process of adopting external solutions, local knowledge, local initiative and local experience have been discouraged. A common example of imposing external solutions from the "top" is that of providing exotic breeds of livestock to the local communities. One such experience is described below. These and other sophisticated solutions as illustrated through project intervention of an exotic breed of livestock have been rampantly experimented by experts in many parts of the world and have caused irreparable damage, considerable loss to poor communities and failure stories through unsustainable development.

Box 1.1 : Imposing Exotic Bulls

Sainath (1996) writes about the Orissa experience where the hi-breed bull scheme was introduced and how it failed miserably and led to considerable damage to local lives and livelihoods. The scheme was to create a new breed of cattle for which the livestock inspector relentlessly castrated all bulls in the area. Then the cows were done artificial insemination for hi-breed. As a consequence of mass castrations the indigenous Khariar bulls were completely wiped out while the exotic variety of livestock with low immunity vanished before long. The indigenous Khariar breed, which was made extinct, was capable of yielding 4 to 5 litres of milk per day. Prior to such extinction, the earlier pract'ce for cattle breeders from other areas was to visit this area to buy Khariar bulls. They were popular as studs and helped to improve breeds elsewhere. With Khariar breed getting wiped out cattle population in the area declined rapidly which increased the vulnerability of the poor. This was more pronounced in the lean years when they had no cattle to sell as a source of livelihood. With loss of cattle, there was local disaster all around and migration to "better off" areas increased. Such disaster arose because people were never consulted rather they were allured to raise exotic livestock through gift of land, which later turned into a farce. Eventually some NGO started a project to revive the Khariar bull but reversal of the process, slow in itself, meant hard work and money.

Source: Adapted from Sainath, P., (1996), *Everybody Loves a Good Drought, Stories from India's Poorest Districts*, Penguin Books, New Delhi.

In today's world, it is being increasingly recognised that the local communities have vast reservoirs of indigenous technical knowledge (ITK) and most often they are maintained through oral traditions. It is possible to find a minuscule of such knowledge in books and reports, however, most of it flows through "word of mouth", both at intra- and inter-generation levels. This has helped in preserving, conserving and augmenting such knowledge. Such indigenous knowledge has evolved over time based on years of experience. ethnic practices, culture and intuition. Many of such knowledge items have been processed and organised through couplets, songs, poems, practice, prejudices, anecdotes and other handy forms. It is one's "eye" for such knowledge, which helps in recognising it and learning more about it.

Knowledge can be broadly grouped into two, explicit and tacit knowledge. Explicit knowledge is that kind of knowledge that one gathers directly from reports, books, computers, etc. Such knowledge is available easily and can be replicated, if necessary. Tacit knowledge is that kind of knowledge which one can learn only by means of direct interaction with individuals/groups/communities, by creating opportunities for individuals to reveal that knowledge. Indigenous knowledge system is tacit knowledge and for accessing tacit knowledge appropriate "mindsets" and communication skills are important. It implies a learner's attitude and behaviour as one congenial factor in establishing rapport with a person who has this knowledge. Such knowledge varies across people, communities and areas and is often specific to locality, age, gender, class, caste, etc. Such ITK is important because such knowledge is contextual, includes answers to many questions, augments problem-solving abilities of both local communities and external agencies and helps in probing relational linkages between issues and causal forces from different dimensions.

1.2.2 Whose worldview is neglected?

Another factor influencing the paradigm shift of development is recognition of the fact that there are multiple perspectives of the primary stakeholders of development, e.g. the local communities, who have different "worldviews". Appreciating such multiple perspectives is crucial in determining the priorities and preferences of the primary stakeholders, who are generally excluded in the decision-making process and whose voices do not get heard in the mainstream "development circuits" and citadels of decision-making. It is being realised in development circuits that it may be a costly affair to overlook such priorities and preferences, whose "worldviews" have practical significance in terms of sustainable development. Such "worldviews" are based on local experience and knowledge and their recognition is a way of not merely informing the development process but also creating legitimate space for their involvement and enhancing their problem-solving abilities for future.

About the significance of "worldview" of primary stakeholders one common example is that of the failure story of India's rural housing scheme "Indira Awas Yojna" across different States meant for the poor households. Under this scheme the poor were not consulted for constructing houses for them. The initial set of houses constructed for the poor were mostly abandoned because they were far removed from their original habitat. Such free housing was rejected outright by the poor. Any person travelling across different States of rural India will find remnants of such ill-constructed houses, which are vacant, misused or dilapidated. Such discarded houses provide ample evidence to show how development solutions can be naïve and irrelevant to its participants in the absence of any consultation with them as primary stakeholders for consideration of their "worldview".

The same "Indira Awas Yojna" scheme when implemented through consultation with poor households proved quite relevant when the members of the poor households were directly involved in the construction of their own houses in their original homestead. Such new construction was an extension of the old structures and better suited to the needs of such households. Thus consultation with poor households and involving them in the construction of their houses made implementation of the scheme directly relevant and effective. It was a case of learning-by-doing on the part of the State machinery although the lesson learnt was a costly one. The cost was in terms of the resources such as money, machinery, labour, materials and time spent during the initial round for constructing houses for the poor, which was not acceptable as a solution for whom they were meant.

1.2.3 What is this development all about?

In the conventional world the objective of development is more about meeting targets and creating physical infrastructure. Once stated targets are achieved by a project/programme it is assumed that development objectives have been achieved for that locality/area. Actions by development agencies are in terms of meeting physical targets. The emphasis on the "human" factor is hardly there in the picture. A series of physical indicators are used for monitoring and work progress and fulfilment of yardsticks creates an illusion that development has occurred. Such emphasis is on physical targets or "objects" and not on "people" who are the real "subjects" for whom development is supposed to take place. In the context of conventional development (Max-Neef *et al.* 1991) write "development is about people and not about objects. The best development process will be that which allows the greatest improvement in the people's quality of life .... Human needs must be understood as a system; that is all human needs are inter-related and interactive."

Max-Neef (1991) suggests that at a practical level there are two challenges to meet. One is stimulating the use of non-conventional resources for achieving actualization of human needs and the other is supporting and strengthening local-level initiatives. It is being increasingly realised in different quarters that in the conventional development models there is no assessment of people and processes and absence of objective such as "human development". In the changing paradigm human development is emerging as the ultimate objective in terms of gaining sustainable livelihood, actualisation of human needs and community empowerment in the larger context.

1.2.4 Development—Who "owns" it?

The other factor influencing paradigmatic shift in development is the concept of sustainable development and issues in "ownership" and "involvement" of primary stakeholders. One lesson learnt from past project experience is that if the people do not "own" a project meant for them then such a project has a bleak future for it is difficult to sustain the development momentum. The issue of sustainability is important because a project life is limited. Once a project life comes to an end the most relevant question is whether there is any appropriate organisation to carry the work forward. The litmus test for a project is the sustainability of its development momentum beyond the project life. It is common experience in the developing world that when a project withdraws the development momentum initiated by the project collapses or withers off in no time. This is because, either the project activities were not really the felt needs of the communities involved; or the organisational setup to carry forward the momentum is either weak or non-existent.

As Valadez and Bamberger (1994) put it, there are at least three issues related to sustainability of project-propelled development. Such issues are (a) whether intended benefits are getting delivered and whether on a continuous basis? (b) whether physical infrastructure is being maintained? and (c) whether long-term institutional capacity is getting built? Continued delivery of intended benefits includes (i) provision of goods and services; (ii) stability and continuity of services, (iii) quality of services, (iv) beneficiary satisfaction, (v) accessibility of intended poor groups. It is possible that the project is not able to provide the full list of intended goods and services.

It has often been the experience that the goods/services provided by a project are, neither durable nor continuous. An asset created, for instance, a hand-pump for drinking water, may work well at the beginning but later can break down and not get repaired. On the other side, it is also possible that an asset delivered under a project may be of low quality due to expenditure cuts and cost controls initiated by the project or due to corrupt practices. As regards beneficiary satisfaction, the beneficiaries may not be satisfied with the assets delivered by a project since they do not happen to be their priority and they have not been consulted either. For example, a beneficiary group cannot make sense of a hand-pump getting installed by the project authority because their priority is an irrigation channel. Another problem regarding delivery of benefits is that the poor households are unable to access the asset created by a project concerning them. This often happens in practice where poor households face exclusion from usage of project-created assets, for example, a hand-pump for drinking water because of its remote location while the relatively better off households tend to have easy access to such benefits with their influence on decision-making.

Often the physical infrastructure built under a project does not get maintained because there is no organisation to take charge of such infrastructure once the project life is over. It can also be a case of poor maintenance where enough capacity for maintenance does not exist with the beneficiaries or the project as such. One important point is building long-term institutional capacity to continue with the development momentum once a project life is over. In case local communities are not involved in a development project from the start then institutional capacity of the community to handle post-project activities becomes weak or non-existent. In such cases, once the project withdraws there are little or no linkages to carry the process forward.

It has been realised in development circles that the aspect of institutional sustainability has been overlooked in earlier projects. The new generation of social projects generally has institution building as an integral part. Such institution building breeds local "ownership. Once local organisations are formed or the existing ones strengthened, local capacities are enhanced and the local "ownership" factor grows. If the capacity of such local institutions grows over time then managerial and other skills are developed together with a vision to take charge of the activities initiated by a project. This helps in bridging the institutional gap for carrying on post-project activities.

One relevant issue in today's development world is how to build strong institutions at the grassroots. Earlier, the emphasis was on reaching targets, mostly material targets in terms of goods produced and material assets created. The human factor was overlooked as if development was about producing material goods. The social elements of development were thought to be unimportant. Reaching ambitious targets was the priority rather than human and social capacity building. Hence even when project "targets" were realised human and social capacities remained weak for the continuation of project activities. Hence, when targets were fulfilled by 100 per cent implying that the project had built the necessary "hardware" in terms of reaching material targets, the human and institutional "software" meaning thereby the human skills and capabilities lagged behind. Hence, overlooking such social and human software made it an empty box and the biggest lacunae for projects in social development. Such a gap in human and social "software" has been overcome to some extent and many projects have undertaken different initiatives in human and organisational capacity building and innovative processes are being adopted for strengthening human skills and institutional capacities. The emphasis is on finding ways for sustaining development initiatives through building and strengthening local institutions.

1.2.5 Social exclusion and "power" relations

Today, some of those who have been excluded from the "mainstream" development implying discriminated and isolated are challenging the legitimacy of the conventional development models. Such groups in some quarters are raising their voice in different forums, formal and informal, about their "right to development and human rights". The benefits of government policies and programmes are being questioned and there is rising awareness that the conventional models of development and growth being highly skewed have worked in favour of the rich and the powerful. A part of such consciousness is due to the work done by civil societies and human rights organisations with poor women and men groups in raising awareness about human rights, right to information, right to basic needs like education and health, etc. A part of it is also being aroused by the inequities in income and wealth and the stark contrast in the quality of life between the rich and the poor.

Though some of the poor and deprived groups have started questioning the existing power relationships, many of them are unable to find ways to get their voices heard. The poor men and women often express a sense of hopelessness, powerlessness, humiliation and marginalisation (Narayan *et al.*: 2000). A lot remains to be done for creating pressure groups so that the "excluded" ones are in a position to demand their basic rights and equitable power relationships. An example of denial of basic rights as given in Box 1.2 is best illustrated from our field experience in a Dhaka slum while preparing the Human Development Report of Bangladesh, UNDP (1996).

Box 1.2 : Human Rights in a Slum

Our team approached a tenant family in Basti No.16 colony of Dhaka, Bangladesh, and while chatting with the family members we asked about their views on life, their primary concerns and how they coped with their day-to-day living. They said that they were unable to express their views because they would have to pay a heavy price if they did so. On asking "why" they replied that the previous day, a neighbouring family was evicted only because they were found speaking to outsiders on their problems of tenancy. We left that place and started looking for other families to interact with. Another family showed interest in talking to us and told us of their concerns. They said that their living conditions were miserable with tenancy problems, low sanitation and without access to basic services like potable water. However, of all the problems they refused to elaborate on tenancy conditions. Halfway through, we had to leave Basti No.16 colony in a hurry because suddenly the landlord of that colony came and rushed towards us to stop us. He told us to leave immediately and not to come back. We repeatedly requested him to be reasonable and allow us to clarify our position. He hastily left without responding, repeating his warning that we must not come back to talk to his tenants.

Source: From field notes of Neela Mukherjee for UNDP's 1996 Report on Human Development in Bangladesh.

The above example illustrates the skewed power relation between the slum dwellers as tenants and the landlord and denial of the basic right of expression. Though many such relations are deeply entrenched in the society some changes are taking place for the better as mentioned above. Even when the majority of voices have yet to gather strength and speak for themselves, the message is clear that the existing power relations need to be made fair and equitable.

1.3 Paradigm Shift—From "Positivist" to "Constructivist" Approach

Paradigms are basic belief systems and respond to three basic questions concerning the nature of reality (ontology), the nature of relationship between the knower and the known (epistemology) and the methodology involved (Guba:1990). The differences in the paradigmatic bases of social development are a key to understanding the diversities in the nature of systems of inquiry and their practice. The conventional approach to social development is based on "positivism", the basic belief system of conventional inquiry. The nature of "reality" (ontology) of positivism constitutes "reality", which exists "out there" and is driven by immutable natural laws and mechanisms. Its nature of relationship between the knower or inquirer and the known (epistemology) is based on objectivity.

The methodology of positivism is rational and scientific. Questions and hypotheses are framed in advance in forms of propositions and are subjected to empirical testing under carefully controlled conditions. Such methodology employs observation, measurement, experiment and theory building with statistics playing a major role in formulation and testing of hypotheses. Such methodology based on scientific inquiry has been the guiding force in social disciplines, which has adopted the principles and procedures that govern investigations of the physical world. Even for social disciplines we regard the scientific methodology as a sure and independent way of being rational in our inquiry.

The conventional approach to social development is handicapped by the single "objective reality" as propounded by the paradigm of positivism and the claims that such "reality" governed by scientific laws is absolute and can be formulated perfectly and replicated. The "reality" is not perceived as a challenge to be faced, but rather as a problem to be brought under control by re-applying the conventional model with greater tenacity (Max-Neef *et al.*:1991). In the emerging era of post-positivism, such claims of "positivism" are being increasingly questioned in social disciplines. The methodology of natural sciences is being questioned. It is also being realised that the social and economic theories, which have sustained and directed the processes of development, are not only incomplete but also inadequate (Max-Neef *et al.*:1991).

In early development economics the State had a key role in intervening and correcting market failures and ensuring economic efficiency, growth, macro economic stability and social development. The neo-liberal development theory saw the State as a barrier in development process. In recent years there has been a shift in development strategy from singular emphasis on market deregulation to additional emphasis on institutional reforms and social development. In development practice it is a move away from holistic theoretical approaches towards more empirically informed and inductive approaches. Together with this the role of civil society has become important for achievement of development objectives along with development stakeholders and local governance with Participatory Poverty Assessment (PPA) becoming common practice (Mohan and Stokke:2000).

In this context, post-positivism recognises that many imbalances of positivism have been allowed in the name of achieving realistic and objective inquiry. Some of them are as follows:

- The imbalance between "rigour" and "relevance", where search for "rigour" for establishing validity makes the findings less generalised.
- The imbalance between "precision" and "richness" which leads to overemphasis on use of quantitative methods and preciseness and accuracy of response.
- The imbalance between "discovery" and "verification" which leads to acceptability of few results and rejection of others since there are not many objective ways of verifying them.
- The imbalance between "elegance" and "applicability" where the emphasis is testing of formal and "reductionist" theories, which are too simplistic to capture local complexities.

1.3.1 The "constructivist" paradigm

The new approach to development is based on "constructivist" paradigm. Methodologies of such paradigm are involved in understanding the following:

- Aspects of human experience undergone as participants;
- The context of that experience;
- The naturally occurring context;
- Ways of understanding the context and experience in a holistic and integrated manner; and
- The inquirer using ordinary field methods.

The "constructivist" methodologies reject the naturalistic interpretation of the social sciences and aim at inquiring and interpreting the realm of inter-subjective meaning as constituted in culture, language, signs, symbols, etc. One contribution to the systems of inquiry from the "constructivist" paradigm is the emergence of participatory approaches to development whose framework of analysis is constructive rather than naturalistic.

1.3.2 The paradigm of "critical realism"

The paradigm of "critical realism" is another development in the era of post-positivism from which participatory approaches to development have routed its evaluation of findings. The nature of "reality" is such that it is important to be critical about findings because of human limitations regarding knowledge of "reality". Critical realism recognises that findings emerging from the interaction of inquirer and inquired will have limitations and biases. Hence it implies that the report on any inquiry needs to be consistent with the existing tradition of the field and every inquiry should be subject to peer group review.

Methodologically, "critical realism" generally looks for the critical multiplicity, which is elaborated triangulation. According to the paradigm of critical realism, it is essential that the "findings" of an inquiry be based on "triangulation" of as many sources—of data, investigators, theories and methods, place and time—as possible because of inherent human limitations of knowledge, limitations in detecting errors and overcoming biases.

1.4 Participatory Approaches and Post-Positivism

Participatory Rural Appraisal (PRA)/Participatory Learning and Action (PLA)-type approaches have become increasingly popular for participatory development. Such approaches are based on post-positivism and combine the strengths of "constructivist" paradigm and that of "critical realism". From the "constructivist" paradigm, PRA/PLA-type approaches seek to understand human experience as it is lived and felt by the participants, the context of such experience in an inter-disciplinary framework. Critical realism helps in evaluating such analysis and correcting errors and biases through multiple sources, methods, locations and other ways.

1.4.1 Origin/history of PRA/PLA (Private)

This section provides a brief account of the origin/history of PRA/PLA-type approaches. The origin of PRA/PLA-type approaches can be traced back to a multitude of approaches, which gradually emerged since the 1970s mainly due to unsatisfactory results obtained from application of the conventional methodology to rural development. In the sphere of agricultural and rural development, efforts of the "production centred" conventional development was mostly directed to increase the yield of major cereals in resource-rich, stable and homogeneous environments. The fruits of the Green Revolution got concentrated in the hands of the rich farmers and the problems of resource-poor farmers in diverse and complex environments deteriorated over the years. Such problems of resource-poor farmers being different were not attended to by the strategy of the Green Revolution, benefits of which had mostly "trickled up" rather than "trickled down".

The necessity of disaggregating economic and social data by people and geographical areas was realized so as to highlight the relatively depressed areas and people. New approaches whether through observation or through participation attempted to understand the problems of resource-poor farmers and improve the quality of information collected on them by overcoming the deficiencies of the conventional survey method. These approaches incorporated flexibility of methods and elements of the people's participation in different measures to reflect better field-level realities. Many such approaches combined elements of both quantitative and qualitative methods in different proportions.

It is crucial to understand the intricacies of socio-economic and ecological environment within which resource-poor farmers operate and their problems can then be resolved by collaborating with them according to their needs and priorities. It was to deal with this issue that the Farming Systems Research (FSR) evolved in the 1960s whose objective was to further research in the area of farming systems, analyse problems and plan research and extension activities. The form of evolution of FSR was different in agricultural institutions located in different countries. The common theme in the evolution was a field-oriented and comprehensive approach of a multi-disciplinary team undertaking repeated farm trials with some degree of farmers' participation. FSR used many traditional methods while innovating new methods to yield quick and realistic results.

The conventional questionnaire survey and its final outputs are generally time-consuming, long and tedious. It involves respondents playing a passive role in answering structured questions designed by specialists based on their worldview (Mukherjee: 1995). The disillusionment with the normal processes of the conventional questionnaire survey and their outputs had also emerged on the scene and alternatives to the questionnaire survey were getting explored (Chambers:1997). A host of field-oriented methods were evolving over time. They were relatively more efficient in yielding the same volume of information or even more in a short period of time, as compared to the survey method which is time-consuming and involves a lengthy procedure for collection, analysis and publication of data. Such methods from various sources were put together as Rapid Rural Appraisal (RRA).

RRA developed as a methodology in the 1970s influenced by FSR (Farming Systems Research) and other methods and also shortcomings of the conventional questionnaire survey method. Some of the early path-breakers of such methodology were Robert Chambers, Peter Hildebrand, Robert Rhoades and Michael Collinson who along with others met in conferences at the Institute of Development Studies in October 1978 and December 1979. Through the literature, the concept of RRA spread in different parts of the world and in the mid-1980s there was a wide array of experience from the application of RRA in different parts of the world (See Chambers:1997).

As a methodology for agricultural development RRA was developed for quick field-oriented results with the following objectives:

— Appraising agricultural and other needs of rural community;
— Prioritising areas of research for meeting such needs;
— Assessing feasibility of development needs and action plans; and
— Implementing such action plans, monitoring and evaluating them.

RRA can be described as a way of organising the people for collecting and analysing information within a short time span. It involves interacting with people in a limited manner to draw inferences, conclusions, hypotheses or "assessments" which include the acquisition of new information in a limited period of time. RRA has the flexibility to adjust to situations and can cater to different objectives because there is no standard set of methods applied in each case. The methods vary from situation to situation and are determined by local conditions, local problems and objectives at hand.

1.4.2 Other developments

There are different methods similar to RRA (Chambers:1983), some of which are "Sondeo" (Hildebrand:1982), "Informal Agricultural Survey" (Rhoades:1982), "Rapid Reconnaissance" (Honadle:1979), "Informal Methods" and "Reconnaissance Survey" (Shaner *et al.*:1982), Agro-ecosystem Analysis (Conway:1985, 1986), Rapid Agro-ecosystem Zoning (Conway *et al.*: 1987), "Samuhik Brahman" of Nepal (Mathema and Galt: 1987), "Diagnosis and Design" (Raintree and Young:1983) and "Exploratory Survey" (Collinson:1981). These methods have some common features: (i) quicker than conventional methods; (ii) applied in field situations; (iii) learning directly from people; (iv) semi-structured, multi-disciplinary approach with flexibility and innovation; (v) emphasis on understanding processes through involving people, and (vi) gathering insights on problems and their probable solutions rather than final answers and recommendations (Conway:1988). Some of the methods are described below :

— Informal Agricultural Survey,
— Exploratory Survey,
— Sondeo,
— Agro-ecosystem Analysis, and
— Rapid Agro-ecosystem Zoning.

The Exploratory Survey (Collinson:1981) or the CIMMYT methodology has three stages: (i) a standard questionnaire is used for zoning of target population groups into recommendation domains; (ii) semi-structured interviews for an exploratory survey of target group of farmers and (iii) for verification through a formal survey of a large number of farmers in the target area based on a questionnaire developed from the exploratory survey. CIMMYT has used the above stages in the field of agricultural development for analysing how better management techniques are affected by resource requirement.

Informal Agricultural Survey (Rhoades:1979) was developed at the International Potato Center (CIP). This is similar to stages (i) and (ii) of CIMMYT's methodology except that the questionnaire is not used, instead other methods like ranking of problems and transect walk are used. CIP provides a basis for (i) designing and conducting of formal survey for deeper investigation; (ii) assessing feasibility of projects in selected regions; and (iii) taking up specific problems of farms for experimentation.

Agro-ecological zones (Hildebrand:1981) are identified on the basis that conditions are similar within zones and farmers within the zone are supposed to have similar sets of problems and technological needs. Two simple techniques for facilitating agro-ecological zones are agro-ecological transect and field plotting. Field plotting is to plot a field in terms of its crop associations and observed farming practices, while agro-ecological transect by a team involves walking from lower to higher (or higher to lower) elevations. Notes are taken of natural vegetation, land-use and sketches of field shapes and crops grown. Technological features of agricultural practices are taken into account including factors like settlement patterns, distance between fields, factors determining labour or time requirements in getting to fields or transporting the harvest to market (Rhoades: 1987).

"Sondeo" was developed by Hildebrand (1982) for multi-disciplinary work at ICTA in Guatemala. It was used to familiarise staff with areas in which they work and to identify innovations, which can be tried directly with the farmers. The method can be adapted for other purposes such as natural resource appraisal, health, nutrition and social and economic change. "Sondeo" is an exercise consisting broadly of the following steps. The first is to identify a homogeneous cropping system amongst many farmers in the area. Two teams of agricultural scientists and social scientists are taken to the area for a week or so, who combine in smaller teams of two each to work and exchange experience. Inter-disciplinary teams of small size work on the site for a few days and keep sharing their experiences, changing team members and deciding on priorities. This is followed by a report written over the weekend by different team members. The team scientists working on agricultural technology use the information by "Sondeo" to make their research more field-oriented.

Agro-ecosystem Analysis (Conway:1985, 1986) is generally concerned with the agro-ecosystem of an area whose micro unit is generally the village. Agro-ecosystem represents a system comprising a set of natural conditions (climate, topography, soil, etc.) and a set of agricultural activity existing to utilize that system. In an agro-ecosystem analysis a secondary data review precedes the field visit where a set of diagrams are produced on the agro-ecosystem based on direct observation, semi-structured interviews and other visual methods of RRA. The diagrams produced through field visits are then analysed. On that basis a list is made of important factors influencing the agro-ecosystem in terms of productivity, stability, sustainability and equity. It also gives rise to a set of key questions and related hypotheses, which the group agrees to be important. This is followed by an assessment of the impact of innovations and interventions on system properties and their prioritisation through ranking. The key questions are both research and development questions where the first category leads to further research while the second category leads to development action (McCracken, Pretty and Conway:1988).

The methodology of Rapid Agro-ecosystem Zoning (Conway *et al.*:1987) consists of treating areas in terms of General Recommendation Domains (GRDs) to help in development planning. GRDs consist of individual domains or areas characterised by similar biophysical and socio-economic features on the basis of which appropriate recommendations are made regarding innovations and interventions.

1.4.3 The transition

Rapid Rural Appraisal (RRA) remained "extractive", i.e. researchers observing, writing and analysing. The methodology had great scope in terms of making the people's participation an integral part of it. One essential requirement of the new paradigm of development was to have a methodology central to the people's participation, which would enable the local people to make their own analysis. The other desirable element was to have a relatively quicker method of data collection. Hence, the tacit shift required was from "extractive" to "participatory", from "narrow-based" to "broad-based" approach in terms of greater participation and the range and nature of applications. It was a shift of emphasis from "rapid" to "participatory", which fitted well with the paradigm of participatory development and became the starting point of Participatory Rural Appraisal (PRA). Today, PRA is a widely used methodology for an interactive process of social development throughout the world. It is a way of learning from the people, with the people and by the people. It is also known as Participatory Learning and Action (PLA), a name promoted during the latter half of the 1990s by the journal "PLA Notes" (earlier called "RRA Notes") published by the International Institute for Environment and Development, London.

It is important to point out the influence of applied anthropology on PRA in terms of flexibility of field learning and richness and validity of indigenous technical knowledge; the value of participant's observation and conversation; the importance of attitude and behaviour and the emic (the local insider) and etic (the outsider) distinction (Chambers:1997). Similarly participatory action research evolving over time also influenced PRA more through normative ideas than through methods. Its contributions to PRA are that the poor people are creative and can do their own analysis and should be empowered. Professionals have roles as catalysts and facilitators and learn through committed action and should reflect critically (Chambers:1997).

In a short period of time, PRA/PLA as a methodology has attracted attention and strengthened itself through its emphasis on the people's capabilities, field-based learning and innovations. Many experts have realised that the time has come for reversing their roles as facilitators of development, where the weak, deprived and marginalised people are able to express their own views and do their own analysis in their own ways with the help of PRA process and methods. PRA/PLA has supported the paradigmatic shift in the world of development and has helped to fill the vacuum existing in the sphere of social development methodologies. This has also helped its quick spread.

1.5 Participatory Learning and Action

The word "appraisal" in PRA has a much broader connotation than its dictionary meaning as "estimation of the value of an asset/goods" or "an act of estimation/assessment of nature, quality and importance of asset". In the world of project cycle an appraisal is done to assess economic, financial and technical feasibility of a project. Once a project is identified, a preliminary assessment is followed by the technical appraisal of the concerned project. The stage of appraisal precedes that of planning and design and is normally done by technical experts. The experts calculate the internal rate of return (IRR) of a project to determine whether the project would achieve some minimum acceptable IRR on the resources invested. New dimensions of conventional project appraisal include gender analysis, social impact assessment and environmental impact assessment as done by experts. They might choose to consult different groups of people associated with the resource-flows, the final decision-making will, however, be with such experts.

In the world of PRA, the word "appraisal" has a much broader connotation than its dictionary meaning or its project cycle implications. Participatory appraisal is concerned with the local people's appraisal of their lives and livelihoods. It is the local people who assess their natural, physical, social, human and financial resources in terms of their knowledge and experience. It is they who account for the cost, benefits, strengths, weaknesses, opportunities and threats. It is they who analyse, describe, define and decide on the boundary conditions and act. "We", as outsiders to local communities, undertake the role of facilitating the process of participation by creating enabling conditions. The opportunities are local knowledge and insights, local experience, local expertise, local ways and ideas, local-level involvement and often lower costs.

PRA/PLA is an approach for learning and organising participation of local communities and groups for interacting with them, understanding them and learning from them. It helps in initiating a participatory process, in sustaining it and in opening up vistas of avenues for participation. PRA/PLA has been described as a growing family of approaches and methods to enable local (whether rural or urban) people to express, enhance, share and analyse their knowledge of life and conditions, to plan and to act (Chambers:1994). It is a means of identifying and facilitating intended groups and evoking their participation and also opening ways in which such groups can participate in decision-making, project design, planning, execution and monitoring. PRA/PLA involves participatory processes, a set of people-oriented principles, attitudes, behaviour and methods congenial to learning and participation. Such menu of methods enable local people to participate in knowledge-building exercises, investigate and analyse their problems, evaluate constraints and opportunities and take informed decisions for pursuing goals of sustainable development.

One offshoot of PRA/PLA is PRRA or Participatory Rapid Rural Appraisal, which is widely used for generating information required by external agents but expressed by the communities themselves in their own way and with their own emphasis (UNDP:1996). It is quite different from RRA, which is quicker with information gathered from one or two members of a local community, which are then interpreted by external experts in their own way and with their own emphasis. The principle of PRRA is to acquire just enough information of the poor people's own experience and analysis of the situation under consideration. Similar to RRA, it is generally a "one off" and "extractive" exercise, but differs in its emphasis on the process of participation and ensures that people themselves define their priorities. PRRA is sometimes used to provide illustrative views of community for future use in development activities. It also provides an entry point for more intensive community participation. It is important to recognise that PRRA is neither exhaustive nor conclusive. It is rather indicative and seeks to embrace the diversity of situations and diversity of the people's own experience and perceptions of such situations.

PRA is sometimes known as Participatory Rapid Appraisal where the emphasis is both on "participatory" and "rapid". The emphasis on "rapid" is in terms of its capacity for quick generation of data and not on the process of development or implementation of plans. Other names used for describing PRA are Participatory Learning Method (PALM), and Participatory Appraisal of Natural Resources (PANR). PRA as practised in the field has given rise to different schools of PRA with difference in style and emphasis (Chambers: 1991). Because of PRA having an in-built participatory mechanism, it is a lead-methodology to focus attention on people, their livelihoods and their inter-relationships with events and processes and the socio-economic, ecological and other forces.

PRA/PLA provides an alternative framework for data generation and analysis where the people generate different kinds of qualitative and quantitative data and information for their own analysis. In such participatory appraisal, both economic and non-economic factors are important, not all of which are easily quantifiable, as indicated below:

- Some factors are directly quantifiable, for example, coverage of households in a locality, say, by literacy-drive programme.
- Some aspects are indirectly quantifiable through "proxy" variables, for example, impact on children's nutrition in an area through educating women.
- Some of the benefits have qualitative dimensions, for example, improvement in mental well-being of poor households from women's empowerment project.
- Some aspects are not quantifiable in meaningful terms but are important for any assessment, for example, social impact of policies prohibiting collection of minor forest produce from local forest.

1.6 Principles of PRA/PLA

The principles guiding PRA/PLA are discussed below.

1.6.1 Listening and Learning

PRA/PLA is based on the principle of listening and learning through participatory interactions and learning progressively. The local people have their knowledge, their experience, their history and culture, their views and ideas and their priorities and preferences. Listening to local people helps in portraying their "worldview", which otherwise remains latent and not revealed. The greater the interaction with people in the capacity of a listener rather than a speaker, the greater is the learning achieved. Such learning can increase progressively. Proper learning can take place with appropriate mental and physical setup of a learner. If a learner wishes to learn, then, it is important to be mentally prepared to listen, learn and show respect towards those from whom such learning can take place.

1.6.2 Offsetting Biases

PRA/PLA aims at offsetting biases, which generally accompany a "rushed" appraisal by professionals for quick results. Professionals tend to appraise samples at convenient locations, such as roadside locations; at convenient times when the weather is favourable; consult would-be-beneficiaries (mostly men) who are generally better off; and professionally tend to look at those aspects which they think are important. In order to offset such biases, PRA/PLA, encourages relaxed listening and learning, seeking participation from people who are relatively worse off, visiting remote and interior locations and visiting local communities at their convenience.

1.6.3 Utilisation of Precious Community Time

About learning from local people, PRA/PLA is based on the principle of utilising precious community time in the best possible way. Local community members are busy in pursuing local livelihoods and it is important to keep track of their time and learn as much as time permits. This also implies that community members are requested to spare their time for interaction at their convenient time. The learning should also be focused so as to make proper utilisation of such time.

1.6.4 Seeking Diversity

PRA/PLA involves learning from diverse conditions and different actors.

In the complex maze of learning there are different events, processes and forces, which help in understanding of issues from different perspectives. For any analysis, greater the diversity, better is the understanding of "reality".

1.6.5 Cross checking

The process of cross-checking is an important principle of PRA/PLA for minimising errors and doing mid-way corrections. Since there are different sources from which information can flow it is important to cross-check the reliability and validity of the data by putting it to different tests. There exists different ways to check the validity of the data in PRA/PLA, such as changing methods, locations, timing, groups, teams, etc., some of which are described later in this book.

1.6.6 Optimal ignorance and appropriate imprecision

In order to minimise cost and time, the principle of optimal ignorance is a handy principle for PRA/PLA facilitators to keep in mind. It means knowing what is worth-knowing and knowing enough to serve the purpose and not knowing the rest or not trying to find out more. Associated with this is seeking appropriate imprecision or avoiding precision of information that is not necessary.

These principles of PRA/PLA help in making learning iterative, in facilitating participatory sessions, in making such processes interactive, innovative and informal and in making effective use of time.

1.7 The Four Pillars

The foundations of PRA/PLA are based on four pillars, where each has a critical role to play while influencing the other. The four pillars are as follows :

— Attitude, beliefs and behaviour,
— Process,
— Methods, and
— Sharing.

Each of the pillars is incomplete without the other as explained below.

1.8 Attitude and Behaviour

Such process of learning from the field and its practice hardly happens automatically. It needs to be triggered through some process or method or some event or act and also needs to be practised to make it an integral part of one's approach. This is not easy and it is for this reason that many institutions involved in development activities are still lagging behind in their mental make-up for participation. This is primarily because of their closed mindsets, which lack a window for opening up to the paradigmatic shift.

The point is that many of us cannot think beyond our conventional frame of mind and rather accept stereotyped solutions, which easily fit with our conventional experience. Our mindsets are structured in safe, secured and predictable environment and we are looking for fixed solutions and answers to our problems. We are virtually caged in a complex labyrinth of our own prejudices, biases, our limited knowledge, training and experience and the environment surrounding us. They are in control of our thought processes and we find it difficult to think and interpret differently.

1.8.1 Why change "our" mindsets?

What are we missing beyond the smokescreen of our limited knowledge and experience, our training and bias? What are we unable to see beyond the narrow confines of the "predictable" world? With our conventional mindsets, we miss out on new outcomes, new experience and knowledge, new vision and new ways of looking at ourselves. One plain and simple reason for changing our mindsets is that it blocks many opportunities for augmenting our knowledge frontier and learning new lessons, new practices and new ways of doing things. Many of us are also unaware that such structured mindsets often lead to a typical syndrome of "I know all" where real learning can become difficult. The following points indicate the importance of unshackling our mindsets and creating a win-win situation :

- It helps in increasing our learning about other people's reality. It helps us in realising that for any outcome there are multiple stakeholders and multiple views so that there is space created for them.
- With fixed mindsets we offer no better than stereotyped

solutions to ever-increasing problems. Today's problems are complex and contextual and many of them are unprecedented and not easily predictable. Any simplistic exposition of such problems runs the risk of ignoring their determinant forces, often beyond the comprehension, competency and control of "limited mindsets".

— Our stereotyped mindsets cannot gauge appropriate solutions. Imposing stereotyped solutions can only lead to future complications. With flexible mindsets we are able to create space for the people's knowledge and initiatives as an alternative resource base. Flexible mindsets help in finding sustainable ways of overcoming problems by involving other stakeholders.

1.8.2 De-constructing "our" mindsets

On the positive side, there are abundant examples to show that many stereotyped mindsets have been de-constructed both at the organisational and individual levels and a process of change has been triggered off through an organisational change and change in the mindsets of individuals associated with it. Such changes in the mindsets have been brought about in different ways such as "hands on" training, self-learning, reflecting, persistent practising, mentoring, counselling, role modelling, role reversing, exposure visits, peer group pressures, etc. All of them are ways for broadening our mindsets. The point made here is that there are different methods for influencing and changing mindsets though they may vary in their effectiveness depending on the situation and the person concerned. It is important to mention that such deconstructions of mindsets have no "blueprint", are context-specific and essentially follow the principle of "learning-by-doing".

For learning to take place our "mindset" as a learner is the most crucial factor. There are different levels of such learning process and different kinds of learners, some more eager than others, some fast to learn, some recalcitrant and others slow. The main issue in the context of participatory approaches is "are we ready to learn"? Do we have the "mindset" of a learner? Even when a learner has a "mindset" are there the accompanying social skills? These questions are directly relevant in today's context because it helps us to appreciate the fact that despite a window of opportunity created in the world of social development many of us are still in our old syndrome and are considerably handicapped to that extent.

1.8.3 Our attitude and behaviour

Since PRA is essentially a participatory methodology, one essential prerequisite is that the attitude, belief and behaviour should be such as to facilitate people's participation. There are certain kinds of attitude/behaviour which are not conducive to participation. The attitude of an "outsider" as a "giver" of benefits to local communities/groups or demonstration of "dominance" in behaviour while interacting with the participants often inhibit two-way communication. Chambers (1993, 1997) writes about "we"-"they" syndrome where "we" as outsiders think that "they" (local communities) are problems to which "we" have solutions. Our normal professionalism is handicapped by conditioning through education, training and socialisation and internalisation of normal professional concepts, values, beliefs, methods and behaviour. Our dominance is reflected in our speech and behaviour and we distance ourselves from the lower in normal hierarchy and also blame them.

New development professionalism needs to keep pace with the new development paradigm and Chambers (1993) lists the changes required as listed in Box 1.3, which are radical and practicable. Chambers (1993, 1997) writes that such new professionalism threatens the citadels of learning, their traditional textbooks, treadmill teaching, conservative curricula and assurance of timeless knowledge. New professionalism reverses power relations by putting the last first in choice of clients (poor, more deprived), professional values (readiness to learn), research methods (more field-oriented holistic approach) and role (with people as teachers). Such reversals are already happening though not enough.

New development professionalism calls for appropriate behaviour. Without appropriate behaviour of an "outside" facilitator the participants in PRA/PLA can feel left out and be withdrawn and not wish to express themselves. In such a case much of an opportunity for communication can be lost. Generally an outsider's entry in a locality raises questions and curiosity in the minds of that local community. Hence the behaviour of that "outsider" is essential in removing doubts and in building rapport with the residents of that locality, be it urban or rural. The behaviour of an outsider as a listener and learner and with personal quality of "embracing error" would reflect the true spirit of PRA/PLA. Not only is

Box 1.3: Personal and Professional Changes Required

- To question our values
- To be self-critically aware
- To look beyond simple often as optimal
- To offset our spatial and seasonal biases
- To help local communities to do their own analysis
- To stay in locality and learn from and with people
- To test and use participatory approaches
- To change methods and procedures
- To encourage decentralisation and diversity
- To put people before things
- To put poor people first of all

Source: Chambers (1993, 1997).

the attribute of listening important but learning from them and showing respect is equally important. In this case social analysts have pointed out the importance of body language showing respect, concern and a serious intention to learn from others. Non-verbal behaviour is important and one needs to be aware that body language can be quite different in different cultures and appropriately make gestures and signs. In PRA/PLA, it is important to be a good listener and at the same time ask probing questions.

Respectful behaviour can have several advantages. It can help the outsider to gain entry or acceptance in a local community. However, distorted behaviour can make for distortion of impressions in the minds of local community members, discourage them from expressing their opinions or can even distort the information required.

The beliefs and attitudes, which are supportive of participation of the local people are as follows :

- Local communities are knowledgeable and have a vast repository of experience;
- Their knowledge and experience are relevant for development purposes and are worthy of respect;
- The local communities have their own "worldview" and capacity to analyse their problems and act;
- The local communities are capable of rational decision-making,

implementing, monitoring and assessing, whether as a community, group, household or as individuals; and

— An "outsider" has an opportunity to learn from local communities about their lives and livelihoods with an appropriate attitude and behaviour.

1.8.4 Improving individual skills and performance

The issue is about improving individual skills and performance. In this context it is important to appreciate that there are different levels of learning and what a learner can do at these levels. Though each learner needs to be self-aware about individual limitation of faculties and disposition it is important to strive hard for improving one's learning abilities by moving from one learning level to another. In 1956, a group of education psychologists developed a classification of behaviour important for learning. Commonly known as "Blooms Taxonomy" it provides us a basis for classifying different types of human behaviour starting from simple to complex. The "Blooms Taxonomy" is shown in Box 1.4 in which there are at least 4 levels of learning and what a learner can do at different levels.

Box 1.4 : "Blooms Taxonomy"

Knowledge level – identify, name, list, repeat, recognise, state, match and define;
Comprehension level – explain, discuss, interpret, classify, categorise, cite evidence for, compare, contrast, illustrate, give examples of, differentiate and distinguish between;
Application level – demonstrate, calculate, operate, implement, compute, construct, measure, prepare and produce; and
Problem-solving level – troubleshoot, analyse, create, develop, devise, evaluate, formulate, generalise, infer, integrate, invent, plan, predict, re-organise, solve and synthesise.

Note: The verbs described in each category of learning provide an idea of what a learner is able to do at different levels.

1.8.5 Learning by Organisation

It is not only individuals who need to learn but also organisational learning is important for participatory approaches. In today's dynamic environment, a development organisation's ability to learn is critical to its performance. The issue is what are the characteristics and processes of an organisation, which wants to learn. In this context, we can draw upon a study done in the corporate sector in May 1993, sponsored by the International Consortium for Executive Development Research in Lexington and the University of Michigan at Ann Arbor, USA. Some findings of the study are as follows. Organisations have different styles of learning. Using three methods of research-literature review, in-depth case studies and survey of 1,359 managers from companies around the world, the researchers identified four basic types of organisational learning as shown in Box 1.5.

Box 1.5 : Types of Organisational Learning

— **Competence Acquisition** – For acquiring competence, organisation cultivate new capabilities in either teams or individuals. They continuously seek new learning to work and promote learning as a fundamental part of their business strategy.

— **Experimentation** – Some organisations experiment with new ideas. They attempt to be first to market new processes or products.

— **Continuous improvement** – Organisations aiming at continuous improvement strive to master each step in a process before moving on to the next. Their goal is to become the recognised technical leader for a particular process or product.

— **Boundary spanning** – Organisations in this case continuously scan other organisations' efforts, by benchmarking their progress against competitors' and by pursuing information from sources outside their organisation.

Source: Adapted from International Consortium for Executive Development Research in Lexington and the University of Michigan at Ann Arbor, USA, 1993.

The study has drawn some general lessons such as process-oriented "changes" go through a series of phases that, as a whole, usually require considerable length of time. Skipping steps create only the illusion of speed and seldom produces a satisfying result. Critical mistakes in any of the learning phases can have a devastating impact, slowing down momentum and negating hard-won gains. Hence it is important to take stock of the learning process and identify the shortcomings from time to time and ways of overcoming them.

1.8.6 Ways of learning

Here the will and the attitude to learn are important for any learning to take place. Our readiness to learn helps us to be good listeners. It helps us to accept weak, deprived and marginal people as teachers, to learn from them about their skills, professions, ways of life, livelihoods, coping strategies, their problems, priorities and preferences. Appropriate probing, body language, patient listening and a positive approach help in enriching such a process of learning by "breaking ice" and building rapport and trust with local communities. Respectful behaviour of outsiders tends to create positive vibes from the local people in terms of soliciting their participation. In a learning session, provoking or sensitive comments are generally avoided and transparency is maintained with minimum interruptions.

Improving upon personal attitude and behaviour through training programmes is one major way of raising awareness about one's personal qualities and limitations and acquiring new skills. Good training sessions have proved to be effective in the past for some but not for all since the mode of training has its own limitations, especially when training is one-off. Even when training is done in a sequence, it is important to create space for other ways of capacity building through other means. Slow capacity building over time with periodic reinforcement of new training inputs is desirable. Some tested ways to influence attitude and behaviour of any team in an organisation are listed in Box 1.6.

To start with, training workshops based on fieldwork can provide useful lessons for influencing attitude and behaviour. However, there can arise the need for having more than one round of training workshop since PRA/PLA-type approaches require periodic re-inforcement of behavioural inputs. When an organisation identifies potential trainees with differential needs in capacity building it is important to plan suitable ways for meeting those needs. Quality-oriented training in PRA/PLA-type approaches can initiate changes in behaviour of individuals, which can then be sustained, amongst others, through team spirit and motivation

Box 1.6 : Some Ways to Influence Attitude and Behaviour of Project Team Members

— Training
— Building teams of motivated individuals
— Periodic performance assessment by peer group
— Forming informal learning groups
— Informal discussions with other stakeholders on a periodic basis
— Holding workshops with local communities/other institutions
— Holding participatory "clinics" for resolving field issues
— Mentoring by seniors
— Counselling by team members
— Competing/collaborating in small groups
— Imitating role models
— Self-learning from field
— Incentives and rewards for good and creative work.

to improve upon one's performance. Such motivating forces can be provided by organisations from "within" through senior staff, peer groups and junior staff, other groups and field-level realities. An important message, which any organisation can bring to its team members, is that self-propelled learning from the field is a powerful way of inculcating the desired attitude and behaviour for PRA-type activities.

Organisations willing to learn can build teams of motivated individuals with multiple skills in planning and execution of developmental projects. Peer groups can be encouraged to meet for informal interactions and sharing of views. Informal learning groups, small in size, cutting across different layers of an institution can highlight issues from different perspectives and discuss them. Learning groups can cut across different members, local communities and others. PRA "clinics" for resolving issues can be conducted from time to time for flagging and resolving organisational and/or field-related issues and ways of resolving them. Such "clinics" can play a useful role in conflict resolution both within and outside the organisations and help in strengthening the process of learning.

In mentoring, a close relationship with a senior staff in that organisation with proven behaviour and skill is likely to keep a young staff open and yearning for growth. Organisations can nurture such relationship by assigning mentors to junior staff members. The mentor has to create effective channels of communication, inspire and instil values in the junior, encourage positive attitude, and discourage cynicism and negative attitude in the junior. This would increase the confidence of junior staff mentored upon, open channels of communication and influence ways of thinking and thereby create opportunities for attitudinal change.

Some people change their behaviour after observing others at work. Teams of junior and senior members of an organisation undertaking fieldwork can also help to influence behaviour in case such teams operate on the basis of democratic values. Long fieldwork and travel can strengthen personal relationships and help in better understanding and inculcation of team spirit. Sometimes incentives and rewards also provide a moral boost to appropriate behaviour.

Any learning to be strong requires opportunities for self-critical reflection. It is important to mention that activities based on participatory approaches require continuous need assessment by the participants. Though most of the generic needs are easy to identify, others crop up at different stages of planning and action. Hence, a first round of capacity building would at best be a starting point and the process can be built upon through a sequence of inputs coupled with self-awareness and self-critical sessions.

1.8.7 Role reversals of a development practitioner

With the development process moving forward, the relationship between a development practitioner and the local community keeps changing. At the beginning, a practitioner's role is more as an animator, as an activist providing leadership, and then the role is more of a facilitator and later as a consultant. There need to take place shifts in strategies and attitude. A development practitioner needs to develop keen observation power and the ability to interpret different situations, appreciate one's changing role and formulate appropriate strategies for local-level development of communities, groups and individuals.

The role of a development practitioner is complex and complicated and normally keeps changing depending on the context and situation. It is not only that of a facilitator. Kaplan (1996) writes that pure facilitative field work is not appropriate where there is no activity on the ground to facilitate. In such situations, a practitioner needs to work more as an animator, as activist providing leadership, which is lacking, providing "voice" in the midst of Freire's oppressed "culture of silence". Kaplan (1996) further writes that the same attitude of an activist will appear "paternalistic and patronising" when the local group/organisation attains a certain degree of capacity and some confidence. The same attitude becomes detrimental and tends to block mindsets as and when local development makes progress. The development practitioner generally scorns the welfare approach (which can sometimes be critical depending on the situation) and can hardly distinguish the overlaps between development, non-development and welfare approaches. It is important to recognise that there need to take place shifts in strategies and attitude and ways of interacting with local communities. There are alternative roles of a development practitioner as welfare worker, animator, activist and field worker facilitating and supporting communities towards self-reliance, consulting and assisting. All these roles call for different strategies and activities as the situation demands and often call for differential approaches. Often the practitioner and the development agency fail to differentiate between different roles and approaches in development practice. This reflects the underlying tensions in sharing of power. It is important to perceive one's role in community participation as constituting different phases of more dependence, less dependence, little dependence and no dependence. In the ultimate analysis the local communities need to take charge of their own development process and accordingly it is desirable that the dependence on development agencies reduce over time.

1.9 Process of Participation

The process of participation implies a way or ways in which participation occurs or takes place. The process of participation is important for it answers important questions such as who participates in the discussions/ activities, how such participation happens, with whom it happens, why and where it happens, how many times it happens, etc. Answers to such questions would indicate the nature, quality, breadth and depth of participation. For instance, the process and quality of particion as reflected in the following leaves much to be desired.

(a) If local community members are forced to participate by an order from the government;

(b) Only men are asked to participate in a programme and not women;

(c) Poor households participate in meetings in which they have little or no say; and
(d) Such meetings are held in locations situated in well-off areas where poor households feel inhibited to speak openly.

In (a) it is a process of forced participation; in (b) the process of participation discriminates against women and is gender-insensitive; in (c) it is a process of passive participation of poor people and in (d) there is a locational bias in the process in favour of well-off areas/groups. It is important to be aware of such pitfalls in a participatory process and to search for opportunities for mid-way correction so as to make the process more equitable and enabling for the poor, the weak and the deprived to participate.

1.9.1 Process of rapport-building

A participatory process is involved in the act of establishing communication links with local people. Such a process has its own pace depending on the circumstances. The process of rapport building is neither quick nor a short-term event. Establishing communication links can often be a slow process or it may even fail to happen. Considering that the process of rapport building is a stepping stone to effective participation, conscious efforts are required to build proper rapport with local people. It is a kind of capital investment in participation for obtaining positive results for the present as well as the future. For many governmental and non-governmental agencies, which have demonstrated weak performance in field situations, the process of "rapport building" with local communities has been a major gap.

Proper rapport building with local communities is often time-consuming for a variety of reasons. For participatory sessions, people need to be relaxed and also require a reasonable level of trust and faith in the external agencies, which are visiting them. To start with, many of them may not appreciate or be interested in participatory sessions/activities and hence may not be willing to join. Again, some local communities/groups may not be willing to participate beyond a point for reasons such as tiredness and fatigue. If stretched beyond this point participatory sessions can become unproductive. The community may lack time for interaction.

There are those social characters, for example, musclemen that are skeptical of any outsider and have a strong hold over the community and can influence public opinion, so as not to let an outsider have easy entry into that community. One such experience during the fieldwork on Human Development Report of UNDP Bangladesh (1996) is given in Box 1.7. The experience also indicates that we need to be prepared for odd incidents during field work and also try our wit in handling dominant people who tend to obstruct and disturb participatory processes.

Box 1.7 : With the Help of a Muscleman

We went to Madhya Bagra again on the second day of our field visit. While entering the village we were confronted by a young man, who rudely told us that we could not enter the village because we should not disturb the women as it was their day for paying instalments to the Grameen Bank. We suggested that some women had asked us to visit them and we would not talk to those women who had to pay their instalments. We were firmly told that this was not possible. We were taken to the man's house and asked to wait until the women returned after paying their instalments. We saw Farook standing close by, whom we had met the previous day. We immediately asked him to help us to interact with those women who were not paying instalments. He told the others that they should cooperate with us. Farook was exceedingly rude to us the previous day and had disturbed our interactive sessions, but after he observed what we were doing he was convinced that our intentions were genuine. The earlier man stopped harassing us once Farook intervened. We later discovered that Farook was a muscleman, but he was very helpful to us.

Source: From the field notes of Neela Mukherjee on village Madhya Bagra, Bangladesh, January, 1996.

Some individuals/groups may casually join for some time and then drop out or not join at all. Sometimes rapport can be built with local people only when they know that such intervention is going to be of some use to them. In case the expectation of local communities from outside agencies is high management of expectations becomes important. In case of suspicion by local people of outside agencies, the process of rapport building requires greater effort for clarifying doubts and creation of a congenial atmosphere. In any case, it is important for outside agencies to clarify objectives right from the beginning. This also helps in not raising expectations of local community members.

1.9.2 Pace of interactive process

An interactive process initiated through PRA/PLA is important in its own way and also in terms of its subsequent continuity including both interim and end-results generated by it. A range of participatory processes can be generated through PRA/PLA. The process of participation is basically a learning process and has its own pace which varies with time, communities, groups, facilitators of participation, issues at hand, ways, motivation, location, expectations, etc. Participation is relatively easy in communities, which are more equitable, relatively cohesive and smaller in size. In case a local community is not a homogeneous entity, participatory processes with community as a whole and with different groups provide clues to subsequent ways of improving upon such participation.

The people's direct participation is a basic element of PRA/PLA. Without such participation PRA/PLA is not feasible, for the outsider is not able to appreciate and understand the systems within which the local communities operate. The outsider at best can guess, make hunches, try to impute his/her values and knowledge and attribute qualifications to understanding local situations. Whether it is participation by a community/communities, groups or individuals, the greater the degree of participation the richer is the learning process.

1.10 Diverse Participatory Methods

Though attitude and behaviour conducive to participation are essential prerequisites for PRA/PLA, they are not sufficient since skills in methods are also important, so are the skills in facilitation of methods and also the role adopted by facilitators. PRA/PLA methods are flexible, unstructured, broad, innovative and continuously evolving. A range of participatory ways, tools and techniques are available for interactive participation. Some important methods in common usage are time line, participatory mapping, semi-structured interviews, seasonality, transect walk, vector scoring, matrix scoring and others. A range of such methods is dealt in detail in the subsequent chapters of this book. By moving from one method to another, the participatory methods can be sequenced where one analysis leads to another. Such combination of methods helps probe-in-depth. Use of different participatory methods depends on the kind of inquiry, objectives at hand, local analysis, the participatory process, data requirements, the resource/topic/issue in question, facilitator's capabilities, etc. As discussed later in the following chapters there are methods to improve personal attributes and qualities. Participatory methods are closely related to attitude and behaviour. For proper application of participatory methods appropriate attitude and behaviour are essential. On the other hand the participatory methods themselves can influence and change attitude. The participatory methods/tools and techniques can be grouped into different clusters as follows:

— Those supporting roles and responsibilities of outsiders as facilitators;
— Those which help in improving analytical power and better organisation of field visits;
— Those which help in building rapport, and holding conversations;
— Those which involve "visual" methods such as mapping and sketching;
— Those which involve "visual" depiction such as diagrams and flow charts;
— Those that help in revealing priorities – ranking and "scoring" methods;
— Those meant for analysing "seasonality"; and
— Those which involve physical walk.

1.11 The Process of "Sharing"

"Sharing" is dissemination of learning arising from participatory sessions and activities. Learning from local communities helps in creating a joint pool of knowledge/information, which also needs to be shared with others for further learning to take place. Such learning from individuals, groups and communities at the local level is shared with them as well as with others. Such sharing sessions in PRA/PLA enrich the learning process and help in highlighting local perspectives. It is sharing of knowledge, information, views, technology, materials, time and other resources between local communities and outside agencies; amongst community members themselves; and amongst outsiders and others associated with such participatory learning.

Sharing is an integral part of PRA/PLA. Without sharing participation becomes limited. Unless the local people are willing to share their views and time, the outsiders cannot learn from them. The more they share, the more are the opportunities to learn. Hence, as a first step, sharing is essential for learning to take place and also for its cross-checking and validation. Sharing can also take place after learning has occurred, a step, which follows learning. Such sharing can take place at community meeting places by prior arrangements where the results of PRA/PLA-type activities are presented jointly by the community members and the outside agency and key learning points are summarised. Such sharing raises new points, gives new insights, provides opportunities to those left out from stating their views, generates additional information and helps in analysis and validation of data.

1.11.1 How "sharing" helps?

The significance of sharing of learning as the fourth pillar of PRA/PLA is listed below:

- Sharing reinforces learning from, with and by local communities.
- Sharing increases transparency and understanding and reinforces mutual learning. Sharing enriches analysis and provides opportunities to clarify issues, fill gaps, highlight different perspectives of a problem, revise, add, alter and make changes.
- Sharing helps in overcoming hidden barriers to communication. It provides opportunities to those who are not self-starters to come forward and to express their opinions and ideas. Some people come forward only when they listen to the ideas which others have offered.
- It throws up opportunities for exchange of ideas, discussions and follow-ups.
- It helps in intra- and inter-group resolution of conflicts amongst local groups/communities and outsiders. Sharing helps in clarifying doubts and resolving issues.
- It helps in cross-checking of errors and omissions.
- Sharing helps in identifying areas of co-ordination and co-operation between community members and developmental agencies.
- Sharing helps in identification of local leaders/co-ordinators and other resource persons.

The participatory methods/tools/techniques have been discussed at length in the subsequent chapters.

REFERENCES

Chambers, Robert, (1981),"Rapid Rural Appraisal: Rationale and Repertoire", *IDS Discussion Paper No.155*, Institute of Development Studies, Sussex.

Chambers, Robert, (1992), Rural Appraisal: Rapid, Relaxed and Participatory, *IDS Discussion Paper 311*, Institute of Development Studies, October, Sussex.

Chambers Robert (1991), "Shortcut and Participatory Methods for Gaining Social Information for Projects", in Cernea, Michael M. (ed.), *Putting People First, Sociological Variables in Rural Development*, published for the World Bank, Oxford University Press.

Chambers, Robert (1993), *Challenging the Professions Frontiers for Rural Development*, Intermediate Technology Publications, London.

Chambers, Robert,(1994), "Participatory Rural Appraisal (PRA): Analysis of Experience", *World Development*, Vol. 22, No. 9, pp. 1253-1268.

Chambers, Robert, (1997), *Whose Reality Counts? Putting the first last*, IT Publications, London.

Conway G.R. (1985), Agroecosystem Analysis, *Agricultural Administration*, 20 (1), 31.

Conway G.R. (1986), Agroecosystem Analysis for Research and Development, Winrock International Institute for Agricultural Development, Bangkok, Thailand.

Conway G.R., Mian A., Alam Z., Yar M., and Husain T. (1987), Agroecosystem Zoning of the Hunza Valley: First Iteration - May 1987, Draft Report, International Institute for Environment and Development, London.

Conway Gordan (1988), "Editorial - What's in a name", *RRA Notes* No.1, June.

Collinson M.P. (1981), "The Exploratory Survey Content, Methods and Detailed Guidelines, for Discussions with farmers", in CIMMYT Eastern Africa Economic Programme, *Farming Systems Newsletter*, April-June.

Guba, Egon G. (ed.) (1990), *The Paradigm Dialog*, Sage, California.

Hildebrand P.E. (1981), Combining Disciplines in Rapid Appraisal: The Sondeo Approach, *Agricultural Administration* 8 (6), 423.

Kaplan. Allan, (1996), *The Development Practitioners' Handbook*, Pluto Press, London.

Freire, Paulo (1970), *Pedagogy of the Oppressed*, The Seabury Press, New York.

Khon Kaen University, (1987), *Proceedings of 1985 International Conference on Rapid Rural Appraisal*, Rural Systems Research and Farming Systems Research Projects, Khon Kaen University, Khon Kaen, Thailand.

Mathema S.B. and Galt D.L. (1987), "The Samuhik Brahman Process in Nepal: A Multidisciplinary Group Activity to Approach Farmers", Paper presented at the Workshop on Farmers and Agricultural Research: Complementary Methods, Institute of Development Studies, England 26-31 July.

Max-Neef, A. Manfred, Antonio, Elizalde and Martin, Hopenhayn, (1991), *Human Scale Development, Conception, Application and Further Reflections*, The Apex Press, New York.

Mohan, Giles, and Kristian, Stokke, (2000), "Participatory Development and Empowerment: the dangers of localism", *Third World Quarterly*, Volume 21, No. 2, pp: 247-268.

McCracken, Jennifer, Pretty, Jules and Conway, Gordon, (1988), *An Introduction to Rapid Rural Appraisal*, Sustainable Agriculture Department, I.I.E.D., London.

Mukherjee, Neela, (1993), *Participatory Rural Appraisal, Methodology & Applications*, Concept Publishing Co., Delhi

Mukherjee, Neela, (1995), *Participatory Rural Appraisal & Questionnaire Survey: Comparative Field Experience & Methodological Innovations*, Concept Publishing Co., Delhi.

Mukherjee, Neela, (1997), *Participatory Appraisal of Natural Resources*, Concept Publishing Company, New Delhi.

Mukherjee, Amitava,(ed.), (1995), *Participatory Rural Appraisal, Methods & Applications in Rural Planning*, Vikas Publishing House Private Ltd., Delhi.

Narayan, Deepa, Raj Patel, Kai Schafft, Anne Rademacher and Sarah Koch-Schulte (2000), *Voices of the Poor, Can Anyone Hear Us?* Published by Oxford University Press for the World Bank, New York.

Pretty, Jules, (1993), "Alternative Systems of Inquiry for a Sustainable Agriculture", Sustainable Agriculture Programme, International Institute for Environment and Development, London, 10th December.

Raintree J.B. and Young A. (1983), Guidelines for Agroforestry Diagnosis and Design, *ICRAF Working Paper* No. 6, Nairobi.

Rhoades R.E. (1979), The Art of the Informal Agricultural Survey, Social Science Department Training Document, International Potato Centre, Lima, Peru.

Rhoades Robert E. (1987), "Basic Field Techniques for Rapid Rural Appraisal", *Proceedings of 1985 International Conference on Rapid Rural Appraisal, Rural Systems Research and Farming Systems Research Projects*, Khon Kaen University, Khon Kaen, Thailand.

Sainath, P. (1996), *Everybody Loves a Good Drought, Stories from India's Poorest Districts*, Penguin Books, New Delhi.

Schwandt, Thomas R. (1990), "Paths to Inquiry in the Social Disciplines-Scientific, Constructivist and Critical Theory Methodologies", in Guba Egon G. (ed.) *The Paradigm Dialog*, Sage, California.

Shaner, W.W., Philipp, P.F., and Schmehl, W.R., (1982), *Farming Systems Research and Development: Guidelines for Developing Countries*, Westview Press, Boulder, Colorado.

Valadez, Joseph and Bamberger, Michael (1994), *Monitoring and Evaluating Social Programs in Developing Countries, A Handbook for Policymakers, Managers and Researchers*, EDI Development Studies, Economic Development Institute of the World Bank, The World Bank, Washington D.C.

2

PERSONAL ATTRIBUTES, ROLE AND APPROACH

Personal attribute, qualities and values are of crucial importance for PRA/PLA-type approaches. It all begins from changes brought about within one's self, in one's attitude and behaviour and set of values. There are certain core values to be imbibed within one's inner self, such as willingness to respect and learn from local communities' knowledge and experience, which can then help in bringing about "role reversals" from "expert" and "decision maker" to "learner" and "enabler". It is not only willingness to respect others but also showing it is important. Positive body language and positive approach help in showing respect to others. It is important to reflect on one's own experience and personal behaviour together with acknowledgement of errors and limitations. In short, having a deeper understanding of one's own self, one's values, approach and limitations and bringing about gradual self-development is supportive of the spirit of participation. The starting point is gradually changing one's self and inculcating core values for facilitating participation. Among personal attributes and skills, which can help in better performance are direct observation, taking walks in the locality for better understanding, taking personal notes, maintaining flexible approach and sharing field learning. A respectful attitude and a positive outlook goes a long way in making rapport building an easier task.

Some methods, tools and ways enhancing personal attributes, values and self-understanding are described below:

- Role Reversal
- Learning to respect
- Imbibing positive body language
- Reflections and embracing errors
- Code of conduct for field

— Sharing field lessons
— Learning by direct observation
— Learning by walking
— Taking Notes

2.1 Role Reversal

In a PRA/PLA-type approach, an "outsider" needs to be aware and clear about the kind of role one is expected to play. The role is that of a facilitator/animator/catalyst supporting and promoting participation. It is the approach of a learner with respect to the participants from whom things are to be learnt. It is the role in facilitating such a learning process leading to some positive action. It is the role to be played in offsetting the conventional biases of "development tourism" and traps, which outsiders generally fall into while conducting field inquiry. "Our" well-known rural development biases highlighted by Chambers are :

— "Roadside bias" (visiting those villages well connected by roads),
— "Gender bias" (generally interacting with men),
— "People's bias" (interacting with key people),
— "Professional bias" (seeing things in the light of one's professional discipline rather than in an inter-disciplinary manner),
— "Time bias" (visiting local communities at one's own convenient time rather than theirs', also visiting them when they are busy and do not have spare time), and
— "Seasonal bias" (visiting local communities in "dry" seasons and not in seasons, which are problematic, e.g. the rainy season).

The outsider's role in PRA/PLA-type of activities lies in nurturing participation of local communities, especially of the deprived and marginalised groups. The role reversal of an "insider" is that from "passive" to "active" and creative role, while the outsider's role is that of encouraging and supporting participation, creating enabling conditions and taking lessons leading to community action.

2.2 Learning to Respect

Respect is an important attribute for learning from others. Certain preconditions are necessary for proper learning to take place. It is here that respect for the knowledge embodied in the other person is an important part of the process. We cannot learn if we do not respect the person from whom we want to learn. Conventionally our respect for a person depends on many factors such as power relations, education level, articulation, knowledge, wealth, etc. More the power and wealth, pomp and show, more is the respect, which a person commands in a society. PLA is based on the principle of respecting others. Proper learning cannot take place without respect from both sides. Disrespect or lack of respect for the person from whom one needs to learn interferes with the learning process and does not make it enjoyable.

It is not only important to be respectful in one's mind but show it through gesture. Showing of respect helps in building mutual bonds and creates goodwill. How to show respect? Active listening, listening with patience, respectful body posture, showing interest, having eye contact, etc., generally indicate respect. However, gestures showing respect differ culturally across the world and it is important to consider such cultural gestures. Each culture has its own way of showing respect and it is important to appreciate them and be at home with such gestures. The point is that in any situation of learning any act of disrespect disturbs the process and limits the amount of learning that is taking place.

2.3 Imbibing Positive Body Language

This is a crucial part of PLA. For any interactive session/process, the significance of body language is immense. It can make or mar a PLA exercise. There is no known substitute for a positive and supportive body language. It is a source of researcher's bias. The way one presents oneself, the body posture, the language spoken, the voice and intonation, self-introduction, the way the questions are put, the references used, the honesty of purpose as presented, the dress, the level of involvement are all important considerations in a PLA exercise. They are important determinants and source of researcher's bias and one needs to be aware of them.

2.4 Reflections and Embracing Errors

Reflecting on one's own experience, personal behaviour and quality of participatory interactions are important aspects to consider in PLA. Such a reflection can be on a day-to-day basis or over time, of which the former is more effective. After a day's work some time spent on reflection helps in assessing one's performance in the light of the objectives at hand, helps in redefining objectives and prepare for future. Such reflection can be with reference to different facets of inquiry, the level of progress achieved and what remains to be done. It can also dwell on both quality and magnitude of interactive sessions carried out, the mistakes made, the level of progress achieved, the gaps to be filled and future work plans. Embracing errors is considered an important part of the value system of PLA. "To err is human" and the errors committed need to be accounted for and improved upon. Reflection is a kind of self-assessment to improve upon one's performance and to overcome weaknesses and strengthen one's personal qualities. Often reflection and embracing errors help in identifying issues important for achieving the objectives at hand and also helps in cumulative build-up of confidence and better practice.

Daily reflection and embracing errors when done honestly and objectively help in imbibing positive attitude and behaviour in the person concerned. Efforts at reflecting on a day-to-day basis on one's performance helps in learning from one's own mistakes and guards against repetition of similar mistakes. It helps in organising one's own activities more systematically as enriched by learning from one's own experience.

2.5 Code of Conduct for Field

Some field rules are basic to the principles of PRA.

- Respecting local communities and building rapport;
- Asking community for time and respecting community time;
- Clarifying objectives to the community and not raising their expectations;
- Having a flexible approach;
- Avoiding roadside bias;
- Using checklist of issues to be probed and taking notes;
- Sequencing participatory methods and cross-checking results;
- Reporting field results back to the community;
- Reflecting on lessons learnt and embracing errors.

2.6 Sharing Field Lessons

In PRA/PLA feedback to the community based on field findings are provided and also cross checked through application of different participatory methods, interacting with different groups at different places and time and also through peer group discussions.

2.7 Learning by Direct Observation

As development workers we need to sharpen our eyes and ears and learn how to use our power of observation in a range of situations. Such observation can vary in intensity and complexity from more formal observation to informal "looking" or "glancing" (Tilstone). Observation is not an end in itself but a process, which leads to critical investigation. However, there is a tendency to regard it as marginal. Some points which need to be considered for any process of observation are given below:

— While observing it is important to be objective and reduce subjectivity and also offset biases to the extent possible.
— It is useful to train one's eyes to clearly observe human activities and patterns and unfolding of events.
— In observation, the level of precision is generally determined by needs, interests and experience of the observer. However, it is important to inculcate a certain precision in observation by recording it and cross-checking it.
— Some experts are of the opinion that in order to make sense of observation, whether structured or unstructured, they must be carried out systematically. Structured observation yields more meaningful results than casual observation. Semi-structured observation has its own advantage and helps in flexible data generation and helps to cater for events, processes and activities which are outliers.
— Subjective impressions through observation can be a starting point for objective data gathering leading to better information and further observation in the process. Systematic observation, both structured and unstructured, helps in data analysis, re-looking at ideas and better ways of understanding and learning. The focus of observation can be product or process or both.

Two strengths of direct observation method are as follows:

— Observation helps to complement other methods.
— It is a means of obtaining information and a process which leads

to deeper inquiry. An outsider visiting a locality for soliciting participation can directly observe a range of activities in an area and also observe the effort, skill or knowledge involved in such activities. Such an outsider can have a first-hand appreciation of the activity in question. This helps in forming preliminary ideas about activities or processes observed from close quarters. It is better than guesswork or forming such ideas from a distance or from a remote official headquarters. However, such direct observation by itself is generally not enough. It needs to be supplemented by other participatory methods to make it participatory and in the process to enrich the information gathered.

2.8 Learning by Walking

Often, walking and talking to people on the way helps in learning more about an area. It helps in introducing oneself to the insiders and also taking a look at the area to see the social patterns, the habitat, the infrastructure of a place and the resources, which are ordinarily visible to the eye. Such a cursory glance at the area increases the knowledge of the outsider to begin with. For semi-structured interviews, questions can also be framed based on that knowledge. For a new area, it is generally useful to glance through the area by walking and talking to people around.

2.9 Taking Notes

It is important to make *in situ* field notes on what is experienced by the development worker. A development worker enters the setting with a range of questions, interests and orientations. A description of the setting is developed through the successive compilation and analysis of field notes. Field notes are unstructured as compared to filling forms and schedules or questionnaires. All of them suffer from personal bias of the development worker/researcher and hence it is essential to explicitly mention the basis on which selections and interpretations are made. However, there is an important difference between a field note and other structured formats to be filled during field visits. Brown and Dowling (1998) write that with the use of field notes as compared to use of schedules/formats, the empirical setting can be analysed across the period of fieldwork with successive sets of notes and the field worker/researcher can fine-tune the focus of his/her observations accordingly. Field notes allow a more open exploration of a setting.

Brown and Dowling (1998) write that there are important methodological and technical issues to be addressed when working with field notes. In making field notes it is useful to distinguish between the different kinds of information and the way to record them in order to facilitate comparison over time and across fields. An illustration of field noting from Brown and Dowling is provided below. While making field notes, the contextual details were recorded at the head of the first page such as number of villagers attending the session, the sitting location, the infrastructure, the number of women and men, the arrangements, etc. Underneath the opening sections, the field notes were divided into two sections. On the left-hand side, a chronicle of event was written in which each field worker kept a running record of what he observed including actions, interactions, extracts of spoken and written materials, etc. Use of abbreviations was handy. In the right-hand column, the field workers made notes of their own ideas, links with other data and thoughts about preliminary analysis. At the foot of the footnote for each session, a note was made of any additional information collected including information gathered from conversations at the end of the session. After each day's sessions the field notes were read and additions were made of those points which had been overlooked and not included. The analysis was also getting developed.

While making field notes it is important to devise a system to distinguish between notes that constitute the raw data and the analysis of such data. It is also important to have a cross-referencing system that allows information to be easily recalled and for links to be made with other materials collected. Such a system as described above helps in keeping different forms of information separate. This is a record of what happened from the perspective of the field worker and can be used as an empirical basis for subsequent analysis and action. In this way the field notes can be compared and common lessons derived. Being able to compare notes helps to guard against errors, omissions, faulty recording and memory lapses. The field notes provide greater flexibility than predetermined schedules/formats. They remind us of key events and provide us with information for analysis. They provide us with both qualitative and quantitative information and how we move from our observation to the analysis.

Sometimes, in some fieldwork, writing may not be an appropriate activity. In such cases notes need to be written down based on mental notes. It is also important to have a glance at earlier field notes and also reflect on the lessons learnt.

REFERENCES

Brown Andrew and Paul Dowling, (1998), *Doing Research/Reading Research, A Mode of Interrogation for Education*, The Falmer Press, London.

Epstein T. Scarlett, Suryanarayana A.P. and Thimmegowda T., (1998), *Village Voices, Forty Years of Rural Transformation in South India*, Sage Publications, New Delhi.

3

DOING SPADEWORK, FOSTERING TEAM SPIRIT AND ANALYTICAL SKILLS

PRA/PLA type activities involve teamwork and analysis by both insiders and outsiders. For PRA/PLA type activities some spadework is essential so as to enable adequate background preparation and follow-up exercises. There are tools/techniques and methods fostering better understanding of the topics to be probed, better preparation and analysis, garnering team spirit and teamwork so as to improve the quality of PRA/PLA. There are diverse ways to do the spadework, prepare for the field and improve analytical power of the team for conducting participatory inquiry. Without adequate understanding and appreciation of the background of PRA/PLA fieldwork, the quality of such work generally suffers. Again, the learning process does not stop once the field activities are done. There are ways for following up field activities thereby enriching the learning process through reiteration and its continuation. To start with fostering team spirit, doing groundwork, appreciating background of the field work, planning for activities, organising them, getting in touch with local communities/groups and requesting for their time are important ways for preparing for PRA/PLA-type exercises. For field work there are ways to improve the team's analytical power, improve facilitation skills and probing skills. Follow-up activities after fieldwork such as peer reviews are equally important ways of improving the quality of PRA/PLA exercises and cross-checking.

The following are some of the tools/techniques and methods for doing spadework, improving analytical power and fostering team spirit. They have been described below:

— Team building
— Organising activities
— Primary and secondary data review

— Social literature review
— Preparing mental/written checklist
— Selection of sites/focused groups
— Narrowing/broadening of field inquiry
— Gaining bird's eye-view
— Gaining worm's eye-view
— Exploratory probing
— Topical probing
— Using 8 helpers
— Evolving indicators/criteria
— Sequencing of Issues/Processes
— Sequencing of Participatory Methods
— Managing Expectations
— Peer Group Sharing
— Peer Group Review
— Peer Group Audit
— Cross-checking and Validation
— Participatory Management Information System

3.1 Team Building

For PRA/PLA-type activities, building the outside team is a crucial way to go ahead for undertaking participatory exercises. Such team-building when done with care can help in initiating the participatory process within the outside team itself. When team members spontaneously come together, start thinking as a team and establish strong communication linkages within the team, it helps in resolving team issues amicably in a spirit of "give-and-take". The team, which has team spirit and positive interactions amongst its members, is in a better position to initiate and sustain participation with local groups/community. When there are problems within the outside team, the cohesiveness of the team is reduced and its performance in the field is affected thereby. The team spirit of the outside team, its group contract and the understanding amongst the team members are important variables affecting PLA/PRA.

3.2 Organising Activities

Any participatory field inquiry will involve considerable preparation and decision making. Once the objectives of such participatory inquiry are clear, the groundwork includes setting up of investigating team/s, collecting background materials, discussing the broad contours of such inquiry—the budget, the time frame, the issues and tools, approaching localities, informing local communities, arranging logistics, trips, material, food, etc. Participatory interactions at each point help in better decision-making and active involvement of those concerned.

3.3 Primary and Secondary Data Review

Before conducting a PRA exercise it is often possible to get some background information on the area to be covered. Review of such information helps in describing the broad features and trends of the area concerned, covering different aspects at different points of time. Sources of such data can be both—primary and secondary. The primary source constitutes materials gathered first-hand and have a direct relationship with people, situations or events that are being studied such as court records, letters, minutes, memoranda, notes and diaries. They cannot be viewed uncritically which means one has to combine other materials and sources along with the primary sources (Burgess:1990).

Secondary sources of data can be found in published materials which may include transcript or summaries of primary source materials. Some secondary sources are surveys, books, reports, plans, official records, census records, project reports, maps, aerial photographs, journalistic articles, newspaper cuttings, research papers and data files from computers. The organisations and individuals who are usually associated with collecting such data are government, researchers, statistical agencies, local-level educational and technical institutions, non-government organisations, donor agencies, remote-sensing agencies, etc. These are generally data collected through the conventional methods and one needs to keep in mind the limitations of such sources, ways in which materials have been selected, analysed and presented. For use of all kinds of documentary evidence it is important to guard against problems concerning authenticity, availability, sampling, interpretation and presentation. Documentary evidence also provides data link-up with other data obtained through field research (Burgess:1990).

One of the important secondary sources is aerial photography, which can help to know more about the physical features of a certain area. They provide a visual medium to farmers to locate their land and other resources on the ground and explain them (Sandford:1989). They reduce spatial biases, which most field workers tend to encounter on the ground. Experience shows that farmers are quite comfortable with interpreting aerial photographs (Dewees:1989). Two main field uses of aerial photographs are as aids for mapping boundaries of land and as a focus point for discussion in interviews (Mearns:1989).

3.4 Social Literature Review

Not only data review is important but also relevant social/cultural literature can be scanned for undertaking participatory inquiry. Relevant literature review helps in flagging issues and results/outputs explored in earlier studies. A historical perspective about a locality/region/culture/practices can be acquired from literature. Literature review of reports/texts/documents also helps in pointing out the results of earlier studies though one need to minimize the bias of earlier results. Keeping such results at the back of one's mind one should be open and flexible enough for learning and exploring at the field level. One can also crosscheck such results when undertaking first-hand field inquiry.

Review of historical sources and secondary/primary data support PRA-type activities and also help in critical assessment of PRA/PLA-type activities. In Epstein *et al.* (1998), the principal researcher notes the importance of scanning secondary sources. For learning about the impact of irrigation in a historical perspective she collected all available primary and secondary data related to it. Past data clearly showed that canal irrigation had made the village prosperous and had raised their levels of living in the past. When approaching local community it is always better to do the groundwork by learning more about the community and the locality. An outside team undertaking PLA/PRA-type activities can be at a disadvantage in the absence of such knowledge about local cultural settings, practices and developmental aspects. Such knowledge helps in developing tact and in handling of unforeseen situations, though such information need not always be at hand.

3.5 Preparing Mental/Written Checklist

For any topic under investigation, it is useful to prepare a list of issues to be probed during a field inquiry. Such a list of issues touching upon all aspects of the topic helps in clarity of thought, ensuring coverage of important aspects and in better probing. It also helps in having a mental checklist at the back of the mind (or a written checklist for those who wish to carry it to the field).

A checklist of issues prepared away from field can at best be a starting point, which can then be improved upon from field experience. A checklist can be a generic list or one, which is comprehensive with minute details. A checklist is more realistic when it is field-based. A checklist for PRA/PLA field inquiry is not a questionnaire but only a list of issues to be probed. The questions to be raised on each issue would depend on the local situation, the context, the flow of participatory process, and the individual/group/community's perspective.

Two illustrations of checklists are given below. One is a short checklist for need assessment on animal health while the other is a detailed checklist on agriculture in urban and peri-urban areas.

Checklist 1—Animal Health: Priority Need Assessment

- Animal types—household-specific, group-specific
- Utility and purpose
- Status of animal health
- Disease/illness of animals—periodicity, seasonality and other details
- Indigenous methods/practices for overcoming disease/illness
- Source for treating animals and coping strategies
- Priority issues and activities possible/proposed
- Kinds of extension activities feasible and planning

Checklist 2—Agriculture and Livelihood in Urban and Peri-urban Areas

A preliminary generic checklist used by PA researchers, for field inquiry, had 4 broad parts.

1. Household livelihood strategies and role of urban/peri-urban agriculture
2. Constraints and problems of agriculture production
3. Ways in which such constraints and problems were being addressed
4. Impact of industrial area on agriculture

The items within the generic checklist are as follows:

(i) Household livelihood strategies and role of urban/peri-urban agriculture

- — households, socio-economic groups, livelihood pursued
- — livelihood in agriculture, description, nature, options, seasonality, etc.
- — description of seasonality and its impact on living and quality of life
- — role of agriculture to local economy
- — role of other livelihood to local economy
- — farming system practices, crops grown, land-related issues, quality of land-related issues
- — land ownership, labour involved, wages, agriculture inputs
- — loans, indebtedness—patterns/sources—influencing factors
- — crop rotation, yield trends, transport, markets
- — return from agriculture/other livelihood
- — income, savings, expenditure, food patterns
- — institutional structure

(ii) Constraints and problems of agriculture production

- — list of constraints/problems
- — inter-relationship amongst them, if any
- — prioritising constraints/problems
- — description of nature of constraints/problems
- — factors influencing constraints/problems
- — impact/damage of constraints/problems
- — estimates

(iii) Ways in which such constraints and problems are being addressed—coping strategies, support system, institutional support and networks, local initiatives and impact, measures undertaken/to be undertaken, role of local government/other organisations like panchayats/block office/CBOs/farmers' organisation/NGOs/others—farming system research/experiment, if any

(iv) Impact of industrial area on household livelihood and agriculture—benefits and costs—impact on agriculture including impacts on health or other aspects of life.

3.6 Selection of Sites/Focused Groups

Any participatory inquiry based on its objectives will need to select areas/

communities for participatory interactions. A pre-selection of area/ focused groups can be based on primary and secondary data. For selection of the actual location/groups, the outside team can involve local communities/groups/key informants. An illustration from the field experience of involving poor women and men for site selection is given below:

> "On arrival in the pre-selected thanas, they (team of facilitators) talked to key informants and villagers/slum dwellers in order to make the final selection of villages or "*bastis*". The basis of selection was always those areas, which were considered to be particularly deprived and where there was a high incidence of poverty. The information from key informants was always cross-checked to limit the chance of vested interest biasing the final choice of site." (UNDP:1996)

3.7 Narrowing/Broadening of Field Inquiry

For better appreciation of people's "worldview", we as outsiders require the flexibility in the use of tools and techniques. In participatory processes, one needs to be aware that there is an enormous flexibility in conducting field inquiry and subsequent analysis. Depending on objectives and situation at hand there is enough scope to move from general to particular issues and *vice versa*. For example, one can start by conducting participatory inquiry at a general level and then narrow down the focus on the selected topic. Or alternatively, one can start by probing into selected items/issues before probing for broad overviews.

Much depends on the situation at hand at the community level. Sometimes we as outsiders would like to have broad overviews on any topic before discussing selected aspects of that topic. Or, it is possible that a local group interacted with has limited knowledge on the topic under discussion and hence scope for focusing on issues becomes limited. For participatory inquiry we often require broad overviews before we concentrate on specific issues. For example, for a session on participatory appraisal of drinking water with local community members, the outsiders' team found it convenient to seek overview of water sources in that community before getting into specific topics/issues. This helped in understanding the context of such inquiry starting with an overview of such local resources and then focusing on drinking water in particular. In this case one other way would have been to start discussion about drinking water and then move on to more general discussions for learning about local water resources and the relevant context. While passing from general to particular and *vice versa* there are different layers of information sought under participatory inquiry and approaching it both ways is iterative.

3.8 Gaining Bird's Eye-view

For any issue to be inquired and for any local community/group to be interacted with understanding of the context and surroundings are crucial for it helps in fully appreciating the learning process and the lessons learnt. Gaining an overview of the area/topic/issue concerned like a bird from the sky helps in seeing the "whole" and its different parts, which constitute such "whole".

3.9 Gaining Worm's Eye-view

It is important to look at any community like a worm from the grass "below" on the ground in order to get a close look and increase situational understanding of the people and the area under consideration. It is important to look through their lens the characteristic features of people and resources by focusing on selected aspects and gaining focused understanding as if from the ground like a worm. Both "overview" like that of a bird and "underview" like that of a worm or insect are important for better appreciation and understanding of any community with which PRA-type interactive activities are taking place.

3.10 Exploratory Probing

Related to the flexibility of field inquiry there are two kinds of probing, one is to do with exploratory probing and the other is to do with topical probing. An exploratory probing helps in understanding broad patterns and trends in local communities. It helps in learning about different aspects of local life and also suggests the relevant issues to be pursued for participatory inquiry and action. It can form a basis for further probing into selected topics, which appear important and useful. A theme for further analysis can emerge out of such exploration which can help in undertaking either a PRA/PLA-type exercise or help in framing a questionnaire-survey based on ground realities. Exploratory probing helps in placing the topic in the relevant context and for general probing.

3.11 Topical Probing

Topical probing has to do with a particular topic, which either constitutes the area of investigation by the outsiders or has been suggested by the local people as a key area. For instance, in a topic such as 'seasonality' of poverty topical probing helps to reach the depth of related issues. A topic can be probed across different groups in a locality, across gender, caste, age, etc., as a community and over time. Its objective is to generate focused information on a selected topic. It is intensive in its approach and can help in analysing a particular topic at great length.

3.12 Using 8 Helpers

Use of 8 helpers—"why", "what", "which/who", "how" and "how much", "what", "where", "when" —assist in analytical rigour in field inquiry. These 8 helpers when stored at the back of our minds assist in conducting interviews, exploring "worldviews" on issues from different perspectives They help in bridging gaps in analysis and also in cross-checking of responses. In the list of 8 helpers soliciting answers to all of them may or may not be possible depending on the depth of knowledge, which a participant has. Nevertheless, the 8 helpers provide scope for both brief analysis and in-depth treatment of a topic as required. The same set of 8 helpers can assist in having discussions at length for seeking greater details.

3.13 Evolving Indicators/Criteria

Sometimes in participatory inquiry it is important to evolve a set of indicators for different purposes such as monitoring or impact assessment. Such indicators help in bench-marking and comparisons over different variables including time. To start with some generic indicators stimulate the thought process and help in clarity of thinking and better analytical framework. For evolving indicators through participatory sessions it is often useful to have some kind of an open-ended framework to support facilitation of PRA/PLA-type sessions for evolving indicators/criteria for any topic under consideration. Facilitation sessions of good quality imply good preparation and groundwork by the facilitator and clarity of one's role and topic under consideration. It has been found in many cases that a facilitator is good in facilitation skills but poor in grasping points and raising issues while learning from local communities.

3.14 Sequencing of Issues/Processes

In PRA/PLA-type of exercises, there are objectives to be achieved, topics to be probed, process to be adopted and methods to be used from a whole menu of participatory methods. In PRA/PLA-type activities, we can combine methods and processes to enrich field inquiry and attain objectives. We do this by means of sequencing. Sequencing helps us to probe through a chain of processes depending on the topic or the checklist under consideration.

3.15 Sequencing of Participatory Methods

Sequencing is a stepwise approach for inquiring into a particular topic. For sequencing the initial questions relate to the topic and the objective/s of inquiry. The next questions relate to the kind of check list suitable for the topic and what participatory methods to be applied and how can they be combined. The vast range of participatory methods can be sequenced one after another for in-depth probing into themes/issues. Selection of one particular method or combination of methods needs to relate to the problem being addressed within the framework of inquiry and context. Sequencing of methods provides the synergistic impact of such methods. One method leads to another depending on the topic being probed, the results achieved and the various aspects of a topic under inquiry.

Sequencing of methods generally depends on the theme, nature of probing, ways of expression, level of analysis, spatial location, local informant's knowledge base, etc. For instance, while exploring relationship of local community with local forests the method of 'problem scoring' can help to prioritise problems faced by local community with regard to localised forests, followed by semi-structured interview and mapping which can be used to explore further into the topic. Participatory mapping can provide a spatial view of the issue at hand which can be elaborated through resource mapping showing the different natural resources such as trees, bushes, shrubs, soil, wild life, degraded area, etc., in the concerned forest and other related areas. Selected locations can be identified on that basis for joint walks to be undertaken to such locations with local people who can then explain further about them. Probing can be intensified and refined by seeing such locations and asking relevant questions to understand issues from the perspective of local people.

Such probing can be followed by generation of solutions to

alleviate/reduce the problems raised through the method of "problem scoring", which can then be tied up with appropriate actions of local people and local organisations/agencies and others. Such sequencing can take time and it is important to have a relaxed space for such sequencing of methods so as to solicit participation of different groups by gender, age, class, etc. In terms of opportunities created by sequencing of methods it helps in leading into action by local people either by themselves or with supportive organisation/s.

3.16 Managing Expectations

Often objectives are stated by the outside team in a manner in which expectations of the local people are raised. It implies that the outside team is able to state its objectives in a manner without raising local expectations. One has to think clearly about such an impact and ways of handling such expectations. If expectations are raised without any realistic basis then there are inherent ethical implications. Here we have two views about raising expectations. One view is that expectations need to be minimized since one is not sure about the possibilities, both positive and negative, which a participatory process can lead to. Still another view is that expectations of local communities necessarily have to be raised for exploring possibilities of appropriate action/s at the local level. In general, many of us need to guard against expectations getting raised for all of us are not equipped to handle community expectations and manage them in the best possible manner. Sometimes such raising of expectations can lead to explosive situations difficult to handle. The message is that one must handle with care as far as community expectations are concerned.

3.17 Peer Group Sharing

Sharing and reflection in a peer learning group is a way to develop one's own capacity and team's capacity and thus improving upon mutual learning skills. Individual reflection happens during group-sharing and peer group reflection also takes place in peer-group sharing. In peer-group sharing, the members consult together and plan their actions towards attaining specified objectives, agree on a way of reaching such objectives. Such objectives may relate to areas of change, resources for bringing about that change, methods for change, time allocated, etc. Such a group may have an initial facilitator who becomes an influential peer at a later stage. The group keeps adapting its programme and objectives as a function of action and experience. It engages in self and peer-group assessment to assess the objectives and the programme in the light of their own experience.

3.18 Peer Group Review

From time to time outsiders meet insiders for holding discussions and reviewing progress. This helps in joint assessments and identifying areas of strength and weaknesses and adopting mid-way corrections. Such participatory reviews are quite handy when done with the honesty of purpose in an objective manner under transparent conditions. When participatory review becomes a regular feature, it helps in augmenting the quality of participation.

3.19 Peer Group Audit

Members of a peer group of professionals meet to co-research their capacity to monitor and improve their standards and performance of professional practice. In the process of group audit they do the following:

- They identify current standards and actual practice;
- They agree to apply more desirable standards and practice;
- They devise some form of self-assessment based on desirable standards;
- They go back to work and apply self-assessment schedule;
- They meet again for self- and peer-assessment session, where each person shares findings open to feedback, questions and confrontations from the peers;
- This may lead to revision of standards and practice;
- The group meets after some time to evaluate the whole experience and also validate its standard and performance of professional practice.

3.20 Cross-Checking and Validation

Cross-checking data generated constitutes an integral part of any PRA/ PLA-type exercise. Validation is important because any data is likely to have some errors and it is important to reduce the size of errors. It is useful to check the data for errors since any analysis, estimate, conclusion, finding, documentation and recommendation based on such data would be affected by such errors. Validation of data in PRA/PLA-type exercises can be undertaken in different ways, some of which are described below (Mukherjee:1995):

— Composition of outside team facilitating PRA/PLA-type exercises can be such that information generated is viewed and explored from different perspectives. It would help outside teams to have persons from different disciplines, experience, gender groups, age, etc.
— Information can be cross-checked by outside team members by approaching different groups/individuals either separately or in combination.
— Different participatory methods can be used to test and verify data. For example, after a semi-structured interview, a 'visual' method such as mapping can be applied followed by a seasonal calendar or some other appropriate method to check the validity of data generated.
— Parallel investigations changing the location and time of a participatory session can also help in validation of data.
— Comparing data from participatory methods with data from other primary and secondary sources can help in raising issues and reveal discrepancies and gaps.
— Multiple teams can also help in validation.
— Participant checking is another way to cross-check data, where participants who generate the original information re-look at their interpretation and conclusions.
— Peer-group checking is a way to validate data by having periodical meetings with peers not directly involved in the inquiry process. Such meetings help to raise issues and identify gaps in data set (Pretty:1993).
— Inquiry audit can be conducted to establish fairness of representations by examining the process of inquiry and end-results (Pretty:1993).

3.21 Participatory Management Information System

Shared learning from PLA can be enhanced, especially for a project, if an appropriate management information system (MIS) is designed at different levels, which can integrate and enhance the value of such information. Such system needs to be designed at the community level, which will prove effective only if it is fully participatory and owned by the community. Then the community will feel motivated to play its role and utilise the system and update it as well. There is need to store the information at the community level for easy retrieval as and when required. Much depends on what kind of information the community would find useful, which they themselves would like to maintain. The community generates such information and should be able to access, exchange and share such information.

The community perspective on the design and utilisation of such a system can be undertaken by means of PRA/PLA-type exercises. The MIS is also important for generating an integrated and holistic picture of the status of community empowerment emerging at different levels and at other levels like sub-national and national levels. Such MIS would help in providing regular feedback on the progress of community participation and mutual sharing of related issues at different levels and at different points of time. As far as PRA/PLA data storage and retrieval is concerned community-made plans and other primary data can be stored at the community level at some common place so as to be accessible to all. Progress charts can be maintained at local community places for the local community members to see, alter and validate such charts. It is not only important to display such information at public places but also to overcome the literacy bias to the extent possible. This is especially important for those community members which are illiterate or semi-literate and hence require enabling conditions to participate in the sharing of information that all of them together have created.

The innovative nature of PRA/PLA-type activities has helped in adding a large number of methods to its inventory. Such methods have provided local communities/groups with opportunities to express themselves and have been instrumental in exposing different dimensions of their living which normally remain unperceived or under-perceived. There are different aspects of community life not all of which can be expressed in quantitative magnitudes. Some of them can be quantified while others are better described qualitatively while some others remain hidden and elusive. Many aspects of community life can be expressed through mapping, ranking, scoring and relative comparisons, for example, wealth and well-being analysis. Some aspects of community life can also be sensitive areas and a direct approach to such issues can be a frustrating experience. These and other methods are discussed in the following chapters.

REFERENCES

Burgess Robert G., 1990, *In the Field; An Introduction to Field Research*, Contemporary Social Research Series, General Editor: Martin Bulmer, Routledge, London.

Deweees, Peter, 1989, "Aerial Photography and Household Studies in Kenya". *RRA Notes*, No. 7, September, I.I.E.D., London.

Epstein T. Scarlett, Suryanarayana A.P. and Thimmegowda T., 1998, *Village Voices, Forty Years of Rural Transformation in South India*, Sage Publications, New Delhi

IIED, *RRA Notes*, various issues, Sustainable Agriculture Programme, International Institute for Environment and Development.

Mearns Robin, 1989. Aerial Photographs in Rapid Land Resource Appraisal. Papua New Guinea. *RRA Notes*, No. 7, September, I.I.E.D., London.

Mukherjee Neela, 1995, *Participatory Rural Appraisal and Questionnaire Survey* (Comparative Field Experience and Methodological Innovations), Concept Publishing Co., Delhi.

Mukherjee Neela, 1994, *Participatory Rural Appraisal, Methodology and Applications*. Concept Publishing Co., Delhi, second edition.

Kloos, Peter, 1998, 'Restudies in Anthropology, Modalities. Limitations and Alternatives', in Breman Jan *et al.* (ed.) *The Village in Asia Revisited*, Oxford University Press, Delhi.

Pretty Jules, 1993, 'Alternative Systems of Inquiry for a Sustainable Agriculture', Sustainable Agriculture Programme, International Institute for Environment and Development, London.

Sandford Dick, 1989, "A Note on the Use of Aerial Photographs for Land Use Planning on a Settlement Site in Ethiopia", *RRA Notes*, No. 6, I.I.E.D., June.

UNDP, 1996, *UNDP' 1996 Report on Human Development in Bangladesh : A Pro-Poor Agenda, Poor People's Perspectives*, UNDP, Dhaka, Bangladesh.

4

BUILDING RAPPORT, HOLDING CONVERSATIONS

There lie many windows of opportunity in PRA/PLA-type inquiry and there is no end to discovery of participatory methods and practices. With each issue there can be many ways of expression, appropriate to explain that particular issue. It also depends on the person who applies a particular method/methods to express himself. As already discussed in the earlier chapters, participatory methods can be brcadly sub-divided into methods (indirectly or directly) supportive of PRA/PLA-type activities and methods which involve direct participation of local communities. In those methods involving direct participation, the local community members are involved right from the beginning and it is they who undertake to do their own analysis and generate information for further action. The use of different methods mainly depends on the ways of expression, ways of people's participation and expression of views, which local people find convenient.

In this chapter the focus is on rapport building and methods for holding conversations with local communities. The importance of conversation needs no emphasis and can be held in different ways. Hallowell (1999) writes about the importance of face-to-face conversation *per se* (in this age of internet revolution with e-mail and voice mail, which are considered quick and efficient), which is essential for true communication. He calls it "human moment", which has two prerequisites, people's physical presence and their emotional and intellectual attention. The focus on the person with whom one is and the response of that person in kind together create a force field of exceptional power, whose positive effects can last long though not indefinitely. So it is important to engage in human moments on a regular basis.

The following methods have been described in this chapter.

- Interacting with local group/community
- Greeting-meeting
- Establishing rapport
- Clarifying objective/s
- Learning-by-doing or do-it-yourself (DIY)
- Learning skills/knowledge
- Lend-a-helping-hand (LAHH)
- Time management
- Constructing indigenous knowledge inventory
- Practice of indigenous knowledge
- Sources of local knowledge
- Insights into local culture
- Dialogue
- Story-telling
- Interview
- Semi-structured interview
- Group discussion
- Brainstorming
- Narrative
- Case study method
- Historical profile
- Time line
- Oral trend
- Historical transect
- Time transect
- Daily routine/activity chart
- Livelihood analysis
- Group consensus building
- Presentation and sharing
- Conflict resolution
- Children's analysis
- Constructing word picture
- Logical framework analysis
- Problem-action analysis

4.1 Interacting with Local Group/Community

During any visit to a locality, it is important that interactions with members of the local community are held with utmost respect shown towards such group/community. Introduction about outsider's visit to local groups/communities and briefing them about the objectives of the visit need to be undertaken with clarity and honesty of purpose. It is important to strike a relationship with local community members and to solicit their co-operation for carrying out PRA/PLA-related activity. Rapport building is the first step towards interacting with local people and there are different ways of rapport building. Many obstacles in the field work are overcome when outsiders introduce themselves properly and establish gradual rapport with the community. Suspicions, doubts and curiosity in the minds of local community can be resolved with proper introduction and rapport building. It is important to repeat such clarification as and when required especially when new faces from the local community join in for having discussion with the outsiders.

Continuation of briefing sessions and introductions beyond preliminary visits are important especially during follow-up visits by outsiders for participatory activities. For each such visit it is important that outsiders properly brief the local community and explain their purpose and seek local people's cooperation and support. The role of the local groups/community needs to be clarified as much as the role of the outsiders and the steps involved in participatory approaches also need to be explained. The local groups/community generally take time to appreciate the role of the outsiders and it is important to provide such opportunity to them.

4.2 Greeting-Meeting

When a participatory session with the local people is being planned, it is important to inform them about such a session and also decide on a mutually convenient time. When approaching members of a local community it is useful to adopt a culture of greeting them spontaneously with an open mind, positive approach and positive body language. Often it is important to be conscious of what is culturally acceptable in that locality and greet the local people in their own style and language. Well begun is half done and it is important to be proactive in greeting the local people and striking a positive chord of camaraderie with them. Any outsider, going for the first time to meet local community members, needs to work hard to establish rapport with the community and clarify objectives. Mistrust, speculation, raising of hopes, suspicion, etc., are all parts of the story of any stranger visiting local communities. It is important for the outside development worker to clarify doubts, dispel suspicion and establish strong linkages and working relationships with the community members. This does not happen in a day. It happens gradually over time. Greeting community members, answering their questions, dispelling doubts, clarifying objectives of visits, allaying their fears go a long way in establishing relationships and nurturing them. Repeat visits to the local community help in building up their trust and faith in development workers from outside. In the long run, this helps in strengthening relationships and building bonds of goodwill. Such pillars of bonding help in building bridges between outsiders and local communities.

4.3 Establishing Rapport

There are different ways of rapport building. Scarlett *et al.* (1998), while describing their experience, write that each researcher had a different way of developing close and emotionally charged links with many of their major informants. Such close ties undoubtedly influenced their views. They also enabled them to establish good rapport and mutual trust. They also helped them to generate information and also do its cross-checking, which they would not have got otherwise. The researchers are convinced that personal involvement in field studies promotes reliability of a researcher's data, though the subjective part involved in such data also needs to be recognised.

4.4 Clarifying Objectives

Clarifying objectives constitutes an important part of the whole learning process. In the case of external objectives, they need to be clarified at an initial stage of any interactive session and also need to be re-stated and re-clarified as and when necessary. This is because people take time to understand and appreciate other people's objectives. External objectives need to be stated in a simple language, which others can appreciate and understand. As long as the objectives are not well understood and appreciated fully, the perspective of the session may not be clearly understood by those whose participation is solicited. Complicated objectives only make matters complicated and can adversely affect participation. Such objectives need to be de-mystified and explained in simple terms. Clarifying objectives and goals need proper preparatory work by any team of outsiders. Misleading statement regarding the objectives can lead to complications not easy to resolve. The best course is to build objectives from the grassroots, sitting and interacting with people and evolving people's objectives.

4.5 Learning-by-Doing or Do-It-Yourself (DIY)

The activities of local folks can be appreciated better if an outsider who wishes to understand local realities does them himself or herself. Generally, it appears that such activities involve simple skills of local people but can be difficult in actual practice. Do-it-yourself gives practical ideas of the complexities involved in the local activities. This can also help in rapport building with the local people. For instance, one can learn to plough a farm and have a first-hand experience of the activities of a farmer or walk with a poor woman for learning about the sources where fuel wood or fodder can be accessed and appreciate the difficulties involved in such jobs. Such participation of outsiders in local activities can often constitute a first step in rapport building.

4.6 Learning Skills/Knowledge

There are a number of skills and a whole inventory of knowledge that lies with the local communities. One way to establish a better relationship with the local community is to appreciate and learn some skills that they have. In one PRA/PLA exercise in Sylhet, Bangladesh, the project team during a field visit introduced themselves and interacted with the women members of the community and learnt some of the skills that they were willing to teach. The team broke up into small groups and had at least one of the local teachers to teach them the preliminaries of any one skill, which they practised and supervised by the teacher. Such skills included sewing, embroidering, making leaf plates, sowing papaya plants, transplanting, preparing manure, etc.

4.7 Lend-a-helping-hand (LAHH)

There are a number of ways in which rapport can be built with local people. One of them is lending one's hand in the daily work that they need to do. For building rapport with household members in a village in Bangladesh one woman from the outside team offered to peel and cut vegetables that were to be cooked. Such help for peeling and cutting vegetables was appreciated by the local people concerned and the ice was thus broken. This gradually helped in carrying on further dialogue with the members of that household and others in the locality.

4.8 Time Management

Time is precious, the time of both the local group/community and the project team. Hence, ways can be discovered to use time effectively. In this regard, some ways are suggested below:

— One way is to have proper group discussion amongst the project team, clarification of objectives, preparation of preliminary checklist (more points for checklist would arise from discussion with local group/community) for component/s before any visit to a local community. This helps in better understanding and clarification of roles/doubts within the team and for better usage of time.

— One step in this direction is that the project team does a preliminary brainstorming on way of sequencing participatory methods and processes, prior to their visit to a local community. However, the way of sequencing to be actually adopted would depend on the field situation.

— Another way for the project team is to meet the village group/ community as a team and after mutual introductions have discussions about the objectives and strategy of approaching the subject under consideration. The local groups/community can provide many ideas of making the best use of time.

— Still another way is to get divided into smaller teams. Such small teams can then divide the work amongst them and continue with the process of facilitation of local people.

— Another way is to give the local community/group enough time to think and discuss amongst them and prepare their own points, which can be discussed at a later stage with the outside team.

4.9 Constructing Indigenous Knowledge Inventory

For approaching local communities it is important to appreciate the indigenous knowledge sources which are available in local areas. These sources are a rich repertoire of culture, practices, beliefs and approaches for understanding and appreciating the local people. Learning about local knowledge from different sources can be an important aspect of any PRA/ PLA exercise. It can help to set the context of views expressed by the local people. Much of it is embodied in art, history and culture of the place concerned. There may or may not exist books to read on the local culture and practices but they can be better appreciated through other medium of expression such as local art, culture, dance, drama, etc. Some of the knowledge and practices of local knowledge are described in Box 4.1.

Box 4.1 : Knowledge and Practice of Indigenous Medicines at Village Arjuni

The local women and men of villages Krishna Rakshit Chak and Bhururchati of District Midnapore have their own medicinal knowledge and practice. They use trees, leaves, herbs, roots, plants, bushes, creepers, etc., as primary treatment for their diseases/illnesses. This is their primary health care. Only if this fails then they approach a doctor or the primary health centre (PHC).

Some of their local medicines/treatment are indicated below:

— **Dysentery** - They take a few guava leaves and grind them into a paste with which they mix the barks of "Babla" tree and "Arjun" tree and "gur" from sugarcane and eat it to treat blood dysentery. In case the dysentery has mucous then they use a different herbal medicine like the leaves of "Piplas" made into a paste with "misri" and eat it.

— **Diarrhoea** - They take roots of "Ishamul" plus 5 "bel" leaves plus sugar, grind them together and this controls diarrhoea. They can avoid diarrhoea if they boil the water and drink it. Sometimes they also buy "ghee" and fry "chura" with it and eat for cleaning their digestive system.

— **Common cold, cough, fever and headache** - For this they mix "Chandro" roots with one small chilly, eat it and overcome the illness. For bad cough they take "Kalo Jeera" plus dried ginger and pepper. They also gargle with warm water. When they have common cough and cold they have a mixture of "tulsi" leaves with honey, for asthma, they have juice of "basak" leaves. In case of fever they take "chappatis" instead of rice, which helps them to overcome fever.

— **Fever in elders** - For treatment of fever in elders they grind 6/7 pieces of "biri kalai dal" in mustard oil, cool it and apply it to their chest.

— **Cold and cough in small children** — For small children of 6 months for cold and cough they try to bake leaves of

(Contd.)

"Mansa" plant and give the juice to the child after mixing it with 5 drops of honey. The phlegm gets relieved in 3 days and the lungs become clear.

— **Post-natal problems** - Especially in those cases where women start having fits after childbirth, they treat them with the following. They take three spoons of the following mixture—one fruit of "Hijal" tree with 5 small chillies mixed with hot water.

— **Itching and boils** -They apply powder of "Neem" leaves plus green turmeric. They also boil "Neem" leaves and apply them to the boils.

— **Women-related diseases** - Some women often have fever, headache and stomach ailments. They have watery excretion and occasional fits. This is a female disease for which they catch and kill a female rabbit from the forest, which is pregnant and dry its foetus. The dried foetus is mixed with a kind of potato called "sutko" and is taken by those women for treatment.

— **Chicken-pox and measles** - They pray to God and touch the boils with "Neem" leaves.

— **Dogbite** - When a person has a dogbite then they boil milk, remove the cream and mix it with the powder of the buds of "Akunda" plant boiled in milk and apply it. Or alternatively, they call the local "ojha" who performs some magic, places a plate on the bite and sucks the poison out.

Village Analysts: Narayan Nayek (Lodha), Jharna Basu Mallik, Paban Dandapath, Basudeb Dandapath of village Krishna Rakshit Chak and Bhururchati, Midnapore, West Bengal, India.

Source: Field Notes of Neela Mukherjee from villages in Midnapore, West Bengal (India).

4.10 Practice of Indigenous Knowledge

The poor women and men are dependent on the forests/trees/common property resources (CPR's)/micro environments for the medicinal trees, plants, herbs, roots, leaves, animals and other produce. These provide them with their traditional medicines and lend support to overcome their health-related problems. Such items accessed by the villagers of villages Krishna Rakshit Chak and Bhururchati in Midnapore, West Bengal

(India) from local forest/trees/CPR's/micro environments are listed in Box 4.2.

Box 4.2 : Selected Items Accessed from the Forest/Trees/CPR's/ Micro Environments

There are many medicinal items accessed by the local communities from the forest close to village Arjuni. Some of them are as follows:

- Leaves of guava
- Bark of Babla tree
- Bark of Arjun tree
- Leaves of Piplas
- Roots of Ishamul
- Buds of Akunda plants
- Leaves of bel
- Roots of Chandro
- Fruits of Hijal tree
- Leaves of Tulsi
- Leaves of Basak
- Leaves of Neem
- Honey
- Chilly plant
- Ginger
- Black cumin seed
- Sugarcane
- Female rabbit
- Sutko – a kind of potato
- Green turmeric

4.11 Sources of Local Knowledge

The following are the varied sources of local knowledge.

Local History: Local history, whether found in research reports and books or narrated by local people can provide background materials and insights for cultural perceptions. These can highlight the socio-economic basis and the evolution of legal basis of land ownership and common property resources to explain the local people's way of life. Oral history as narrated by the local people is generally rich in content and serves various purposes for a development worker. It can constitute the basis for dating and imputing ages to people as required by different studies for instance, nutritional studies. It can also be used in trying to put a time scale on a local vegetation change and can form an excellent way of breaking the ice with the local people in order to initiate discussion on different topics (Mearns:1988).

Stories, Profiles, Case Studies and Portraits: These are anecdotal evidence and other real-life experiences narrated by the local people describing different incidents and happenings in the area concerned. They are generally oral when recounted by a local person and help in depicting the conditions of livelihood, the major historical events and the coping strategies of the local people. A study conducted in a village in North-West Pakistan describes how portraits and stories provided colourful descriptions recounted by the local people. These portraits and stories helped to bring to life the conditions of the local people which were otherwise difficult to express through other modes (Pretty:1988) such as visual representation.

4.12 Insights into Local Culture

Sometimes informal chatting with the local people provides good insights into the local culture. Epstein *et al.* (1998) writes that besides more systematic information they gained a lot of insight into the local culture by listening to their gossip, especially in the evenings. The talks with the villagers lasted till late nights and the outsiders wrote their notes about what they learnt. They attended all the functions and ceremonies that took place in the villages. All information learnt was cross-checked with the informants. Though this way of life was quite demanding it was an excellent way of learning about different cultures and ways of life and at a personal level an opportunity for shared joys and shared sorrows. With no privacy around and continuous presence of villagers sometimes the researchers had difficulty in adjusting with negative feelings creeping in. But such negative feelings were far outweighed by the joy of belonging to the local community.

Folk-lore, Folk tales, Proverbs and Poetry

Each locality, tribe or community can have its literary and artistic materials, which can contain a considerable amount of information depicting its local culture, the legends, the rituals, the legendary characters and practices. One can learn about them from the local people and have them explained. These can depict the conditions, the beliefs, the problems, the perceptions, and the traditions of the local community/ group concerned. They can also form a basis for learning and help in interpreting the current conditions in the light of a community's culture and tradition.

Sharing Practices and Beliefs

Sharing of practices and beliefs of villagers with outsiders can improve the level of interaction and can help in de-mystifying village practices and beliefs to the outsiders. The history of beliefs and practices of a community and their rationale, if any, can also be unravelled through group interactions.

Traditional Management Systems and Farming Practices

The traditional management system of a village and its local resource inventory can act as sources generating information about the local people, their conditions, their knowledge-systems, their perceptions of local resources and their way of resolving problems through their knowledge and capabilities.

Local Analysts or Key Informants

Local analysts or key informants can be found amongst the more knowledgeable persons in the locality who can help in analysis of information and in raising issues for further probing. The current issues and problem areas can be summarised by a local analyst and his or her views can be sought from time to time. However, the reliability and validity of such views can be cross-checked with those of others. There can also exist local organisations, which can be approached for gaining further insights into the issues concerned.

4.13 Dialogue

Carrying out one-to-one dialogue is often an important tool for building rapport and strengthening relationships. An interactive process of conversation between two or more persons helps them in warming up and establishing mutual rapport. It can be general dialogue sharing thoughts and experience or a focused dialogue on selected themes. An illustration of a simple dialogue is given in Box 4.3 between a villager and an official from the Water Department.

Box 4.3 : Illustration of a Dialogue between a Villager and an Official

Outsider –	"Good day! Today, we have come to visit your place and learn more about your group work. Do you have some time to talk to us?"
Villager -	" Take your seat, I am relatively free now to talk to you".
Outsider -	"Thank you. Did you receive the message that we were coming?"
Villager -	"I did receive the message and that is why I was waiting for you."
Outsider -	" I am from the Water Department and have come to know that your local water group is doing good work in this area on water harvesting".
Villager -	"Yes, we have formed our own group and are trying to solve our problem of water scarcity."
Outsider -	"I have visited nearby villages which are facing similar problem. Your experience can be of use to those villages."
Villager -	"Which are these villages that you have visited? What water problem are they facing?"
Outsider -	"These are your nearby villages like Durganhari and Gerashuli, which are facing acute water scarcity and the water level is falling and rainfall is low."
Villager -	"I have heard of those villages and their problem and I think our experience can be of some use to them."
Outsider -	"This is a good idea. Will you find some time so that we can visit those villages together and talk to the villagers?"
Villager -	"Yes, I think we can find some time to help our neighbouring villages. It will be good to have some more members of our water group to accompany us."
Outsider -	"That will be really useful. So will you talk to your group and decide the date and time of your visit?"
Villager -	"Yes, I will do that tomorrow and you can come on the following day to know about our decision."
Outsider -	"I will do accordingly. Thank you."

4.14 Story-telling

This method involves telling stories on different themes for making any point. Often short stories, incidents and events, appropriate to the occasion, can be interesting and absorbing and can illustrate and simplify issues and sustain the interest of the person listening. Such stories can be real or imaginary. Both outsiders as facilitators and local communities as insiders can make use of story as a method to get across difficult points, to flag them, to raise and discuss issues, to draw lessons, to exchange views, etc. Story is a powerful medium for expressing ideas and focusing on issues for further discussion.

Given in Box 4.4 is a story told by Kulmoni Rout (blind of one eye), an elderly woman of village Durganhari in Midnapore about how their lush green forest in the locality had turned into a barren land. She described the good old days of the local Rajah when the forest had many fruit trees and women and children could derive many benefits.

4.15 Interview

Based on Richardson *et al.* (1965) and Massarik (1981) we find that there is a whole range of interviewing procedure. There are at least 6 types of interviews.

1. The hostile interview: It is characterised by mutual hostility of interviewer and interviewee in an atmosphere of mutual distrust and absence of goodwill. The kind of circumstances and limited information sought necessitates the interview in the first place. Such interviews are brief with minimum objectives.

2. Limited survey interview: There is relative indifference or minimum trust in conducting the interview. The focus is on predetermined, structured question-asking procedure, e.g. market research done by telephone or brief personal contact.

3. Rapport interview: This opens the door for establishing human relationship between interviewer and interviewee. With establishment of rapport, positive interpersonal vibrations are in evidence. There is mutual trust, open-ended questioning and information seeking based on mutual cooperation.

4. Asymmetrical trust interview: This is characterised by a substantial imbalance in trust relationship between interviewer and interviewee. The interviewee is more trustful of the interviewer, while the latter is not much concerned about mutual rapport building, e.g. relationship between

Box 4.4: Story of their Local Forest

As told by Kulmoni Rout, aged 80 years, a poor woman from Village Durganhari, Midnapore, West Bengal (India)

"The forest belonged to the local Rajah and it grew local fruits like jamun, wild kundri, mahua, borums, kendu and women were free to gather and sell many fruits. Their children also ate fruits. Life was much easier for women. They had full access to the forest. They gathered fuelwood, fodder, medicinal plants, wild food in plenty and were able to cope with their bad days with the support provided by the forest. Their men could gather timber for making plough and beds.

Once the government took over the forest, their access to forest declined and suddenly there was scarcity all around. During seasonal scarcity, the people could not get enough to fill their stomachs, not much work was available and neither did they have access to the forest as much as in the good old days. With increased poverty, some were forced to cut trees and adopt it as a means of livelihood especially in the month of "Aswin", "Kartick" and "Bhadra", which were deficit months. The poor women with children to feed were forced to fell trees in the forest and some were caught by the foresters and fined. The forest slowly started disappearing. Whatever patches of trees were left were felled by the Forest Department, which got the money from the sale of such trees. Nobody was able to save the earlier forest. The poor women felt its adverse impact and were forced to walk far to make a living. Now that the forest is young and growing, women's access is still limited. The local forester has explained the utility of the forest but they are at a loss. They are not able to have any means of livelihood, wild food and timber for making their beds, plough etc."

(*Source:* Field Notes from Kalaikunda Forest Range - Neela Mukherjee).

physician and patient.

5. Depth interview : This involves an intensive process on the part of the interviewer to thoroughly explore the topic with the interviewee as compared to the typical rapport interview. It goes beyond rapport building in its search for depth of information. The time for such open-ended interview is relatively flexible and the interviewee also seeks clarifications, asks questions and participates actively.

6. Phenomenal interview: This is characterised by maximum trust building on a mutual basis and a caring two-way relationship between interviewer and interviewee. Both interviewer and interviewee actively participate and share information, ideas, experience, views and imageries. Such relationship is equitable where both are committed in a flexible time frame. Interviewer and interviewee have free access to one another and iterative opportunities for review and clarification.

Learning from the interview types we find that the semi-structured interview, which is a major method of PRA/PLA, draws from both rapport interview and depth interview and in the long run also from the phenomenal interview. Interviews enable an interviewer to explore complex issues in detail and allow to provide clarification, to probe and to prompt.

Some limitations of interview have been listed below (Brown:1998):

— Interviews are time-consuming and thus place practical restrictions on sample size.
— Answers to open-ended questions can be difficult to analyse.
— There is scope for interviewer/interviewee bias.
— In its most structured form, an interview can resemble a personally administered questionnaire with the interviewer following a standard format. It simplifies the gathering of information from a large sample.
— No interview can be without any structure, there has got to be at least some agenda or purpose at the back of the interview. This makes it semi-structured, which more closely resembles a conversation based on some topic and a checklist. The interview is also recorded in some way depending on the intensity of the interaction. Such unstructured or semi-structured interview is based on the constructivist approach, which generates an open form of interview.
— Each step in the construction of the interview is important. First is the location of the interview, which can affect the proceedings and make it biased. So the impact of the setting need to be minimised to the extent possible. The manner is important in which the interviewer presents one's self with regard to his present position and the purpose of the interview. The "power" and "authority" relations may not be conducive to frank discussion. The positioning strategy brought into play in the interview setting is also important to consider. Gender and social class relations also affect the form an interview takes. Hence the management of the interview itself requires equally

close attention (Brown:1998) for questions such as "how the interview begins?", "how the objectives of the interview are clarified?", "what to introduce for context?", Do you ask consent for tape-recording?". In the initial stages, the interviewee should feel at ease through a "warm up" period and at the end a "cool down" period to close the interview and present feedback by the interviewer.

— As a rule, it helps to move from the particular to general as interviewee often finds abstract questions difficult to handle. Questions of sensitive or personal nature can be avoided or asked towards the end of the interview.

— The form that questions take will vary according to the type of interview. The 4 kinds of questions are those which are close-ended, leading (the question is suggestive of the answer), open-ended and probing (analytical questions). Open-ended and probing questions help in flexibility, analysis and ease with which an interviewee faces the interview.

— It is also important to decide as to how far probing is required and in what form. Sufficient thoughts need to go into the design and realisation of the interview. Carrying out some pilot interviews and refining the approach on that basis is useful. It is important to practice interviewing skills.

4.16 Semi-Structured Interview

A semi-structured interview is different from a structured interview based on a set of pre-determined questions. While structured interview has its own merit in terms of uniformity of questions and responses which are easy to process, a semi-structured interview is a participatory method, based more on open-ended and probing questions and, hence, has a great deal of flexibility. In a semi-structured interview, open-ended questions lead to different kinds of responses based on which further questions are designed and asked. A sequence of open-ended questions help in conducting in-depth probing of issues and their cause-effect relationship (Mukherjee: 1995). Open-ended questions render the respondent considerably flexible in giving appropriate answers in terms of content, manner and length. Such flexibility is relatively low in cases where the questions are a fixed set.

Semi-structured interviews are partly structured and mostly unstructured depending on the responses of the person or group with whom the interview takes place. For the local communities, it is conducted in an informal manner in a relaxed setting where queries emerge according to the responses received. It is a combination of the outsiders initiating the interview followed by discussion by the local people on the topic concerned. The local people bring in different aspects related to a topic of interview. The interviewer being free to probe into different aspects asks subsequent questions according to the response received. The questions are required to be open-ended. Hence the interview can start with a few pre-set questions and further questioning would depend on the answers received. The interviewer generally has a mental checklist. This helps in maintaining a broad framework for the inquiry and for the flow of queries to be an orderly exercise, as the semi-structured interview progresses. Semi-structured interviews can be repeated as and when required. After presentation of visual diagrams verbal interactions become necessary for explaining the diagrams. Sequencing of semi-structured interviews with other participatory methods (discussed later in this book) help in filling gaps, refreshing memories and communicating one's point of view.

Semi-structured interviews can be conducted with local community members/groups. This is one of the forms of group interviews. Apart from meeting casual groups in localities there are permanent groups based on common interests and activities. In a village permanent groups can be community groups such as those of small farmers or landless labourers, groups of specialist individuals such as rural artisans or silk weavers; and structured groups, with a mix of age, wealth, caste and religion (McCracken, Pretty and Conway:1988). Outsider teams can meet different groups separately or together to know of their problems and opportunities through semi-structured interviews and other methods. There can be key probes through semi-structured interviews. Probing is continuing to investigate areas perceived as key issues in a participatory exercise. Probing into areas, which the local people perceive as important, can be a combination of semi-structured interview and other participatory methods.

Semi-structured interviews conducted for an evaluation exercise of a poverty alleviation programme brought to the fore a critical point in loan repayment by the beneficiaries. This evaluation was conducted in a few villages in the State of West Bengal for households owning income-generating assets through an official credit-subsidy programme. Many of these households had a poor track record on loan repayment, amongst other problems. Many of the beneficiaries while responding to questions expressed their views on problems of loan repayment. They pointed out that most of their assets were such that they generated daily income such as bullock/camel-carts, rickshaws, selling vegetables, eggs and other commodities whereas there was no official provision for repayment of loans on a daily/weekly basis in "bits and pieces". Hence, even when they were willing to repay their loans in small instalments at the end of the day, they were unable to do so due to lack of arrangements for daily repayments. They were unable to save money for future repayments. The beneficiaries' preferred arrangements for loan repayments, which suited their repaying ability and time. This was an "eye-opener" for outsiders who were under the impression that either beneficiaries' loan repaying ability was poor or they were defaulters out of choice. The semi-structured interviews brought to the fore individual problems of loan repayments which the beneficiaries, like petty traders and rickshaw-pullers, were facing. The concurrent evaluation questionnaire-survey of such a programme indicated the number of loan defaulters, the average period after which they defaulted and the different reasons for default (such as loss of income-generating asset, sale of assets and others). The survey results, however, did not reflect the mismatch between the beneficiaries' convenience and ability to repay the loans as indicated above and the official payment arrangements of the local banks, which had offered such loans. This is an illustration of the depth of probing, which a semi-structured interview can help attain.

In the case of a semi-structured interview, it helps in having a checklist of issues on which questions need to be asked. Once the interview starts, other issues can be added to such a checklist which appear relevant to the theme under consideration. Open-ended questions help in evolving such checklist as compared to close-ended questions. This helps in broadening the theme under consideration and discussion of relevant facets of such a theme. It is better to approach local communities as a multi-disciplinary team so as to conduct probing of issues from different angles. While interviewing, recourse to at least six helpers, namely, "why", "how", "when", "where", "who" and "what", can be of great help in eliciting responses. Noting of the interview in a small notebook is another important aid for recording and recollection of questions and answers. Generally, as a point of good behaviour, it is courteous to ask the local community members for their permission before such noting begins. From the side of the interviewer, impatience and causes for interruption need to be minimised so as not to block/hinder/disturb the flow of thought of the respondent/s.

4.17 Group Discussion

In this method, a group is facilitated around a topic for discussing the issues and aspects, which are relevant and important. Each member of the group is encouraged to participate and think about the topic or theme at hand. The facilitator's role is to encourage others especially those who are weak and shy and generally do not speak. The facilitator tries to create space for those whose voices are generally overlooked and not heard. When the group discussion starts it is good for the facilitators to withdraw from the group and watch the proceedings from a distance and let the group do its own talking. It is important for the facilitator to explain to the group the utility of group discussion and how to conduct an effective group discussion.

4.18 Brainstorming

In this method, the brains are racked or stormed for generating ideas and discussing issues as a group. Such brainstorming sessions can be held amongst local community members for listing problems and opportunities, prioritising them, evolving strategies and work plans, resolving issues and arriving at decision. A facilitator's role is to oversee that all concerned have a chance to participate in such brainstorming sessions, get a chance to express their views and thoughts, especially the weak, the disadvantaged and the marginalised members of a local community. Such brainstorming can be both exploratory and topical. In topical brainstorming, it is important to have those persons who are more knowledgeable about the topic. Brainstorming is a quick method for ideas/views expressed by different persons. Facilitation skills are important for eliciting such views and responses and arriving at group consensus, if necessary.

4.19 Narrative

In this method, a person or a group narrates an incident, evidence, and the past and present experiences. The person who facilitates such a session does it in such a manner that the objective of narration is clear and focused and the narrator is able to see the utility of such a session. Hence, the objective/s and the method are to be explained well in advance. It is important to "warm up" for the session and provide adequate time for the narrator to think about the topic to be narrated. At the beginning of a narrative session, providing some clues to the topic helps in organising thoughts and experience. Once the narration starts it is better not to interrupt flow of thoughts. Hence, a facilitator's role is to create congenial conditions for such thoughts to be narrated without much interruption. Active listening, comfortable sitting posture, positive body language, respectful attitude and polite behaviour are important factors, which help a narrator to feel comfortable and narrate without inhibition. Narration can be both continuous and/or discontinuous depending on the individual trying to recollect her/his thoughts and also the outside disturbances affecting such narration. Narration can be short and/or long depending on the narrator, topic of narration, listening skill of a facilitator, etc. Two illustrations are provided below, one is that of a solo narration by an individual woman (Box 4.5) and the other is that of narration by a group of women (Box 4.6), one taking up lead from the other.

Box 4.5: Narrative

"I am a wage labourer. We as wage labourers get paid for agricultural work only after a year. There have been changes in the village. Earlier, we filled water from the well. We had mud houses. Wage labourer prefers to work in factories rather than agriculture. There are not many opportunities for the poor people. Nobody has regard for them or feeling of oneness. The rich people do not like the poor people. They are just interested in the labour provided by poor people. They come for the labour. They do not help or contribute during marriage. The sarpanch is also partisan, he favours developmental work in his own area not in the poor hamlets. If there is some work problem created by the poor labourers, it is immediately reported to the village leaders, police and litigation follows. Wage employment is not available on a daily basis. It is for 20-25 days.

We do harvesting in others' field and get 5 kg of wheat after harvesting. This lasts for 3 days. It also takes time to fetch water from water pipes. Nowadays the wells are not cleaned and not disinfected. There are insects in the well and the water has got polluted. We need to spend Rs. 50 daily on food and soap for 6 family members. We put potato salad/chutney between 2 chapatis and eat that to fill our stomach. In 2 to 3 months we get a herb to eat from the field known as "Bathua" (similar to the herb called "Pudina"), we collect around 1 or 2 kg of that. The forest near the village has "kikar" and "neem". Around

(Contd.)

"Aghan" and "Pus" months we get "sarson ka sag" (mustard leaves) from the field. From the forest near the dirty canal we get fuel wood. We also steal them from others' fields and forest. We survive by any means.

Our weddings are expensive. For weddings we need to spend on food and invite 40 houses in the locality (Rs. 3000/Rs.4000) plus arrange for new clothes and jewellery. If a loan is taken then Rs. 5 a month needs to be paid on Rs. 100.

Source: From the field notes of Neela Mukherjee on survival strategies by Ram Kaur, age 70 years, woman from Jatav Muhalla, Harijan Basti, Village Khandavali, Faridabad, Haryana (India).

Box 4.6: Group Narrative

Many of us were engaged in spinning threads in our homes for cotton sarees. We are landless, were allocated tiny "khas" lands by the government and do not have many skills. Our saree spinning as means of livelihood has almost closed down since hand-spun sarees have been replaced by sarees spun by machine. When our skills became irrelevant with closing of the hand-spinning units we tried to cope by eating less, skipping meals and borrowing from different sources. We desperately looked for other sources of income earning activities without much success. Sometimes some of our family members could get jobs for 10 to 15 days while at other times there was a lot of uncertainty. No options were available. This reached a crisis point and we decided to follow the example of one or two migrant families. When they visited home we requested them to take us along to Delhi where we had heard that finding jobs was easy. We were mentally prepared to undergo a lot of discomfort and difficulties but we wanted to live and make our lives better.

Before migrating, we had to make some arrangement for someone to take over our household work and also look after our family members. Such job was to be entrusted to our daughter-in-law. This also meant getting our sons married. We learnt that our husbands and other men of our families cannot accompany us since no jobs were available for them. Jobs available are more for women like jobs of maid, cook, looking after children, etc., but not for men. Our husbands and other men in our families cannot undergo much

(Contd.)

discomfort and would find it difficult to undertake so much of stress. Our husbands are aged and some of them are sick and are not that mobile. Hence we women had to migrate away from our homes. Our migration to Delhi and getting jobs was a major way in which our families coped with the difficult time. Our mutual networking helped us to get jobs in Delhi. We support each other and also help each other to get jobs. If some of us are not able to find jobs immediately we provide shelter and food and mutual support. There are many work opportunities in Delhi and the wage is also relatively high. For instance, for the same job as domestic help one gets Rs. 50 in Calcutta and Rs. 200 in Delhi. We live as a group in rented accommodation.

Our concept of ill-being/well-being

To us both ill-being and well-being are same and equal. We work and we live from day-to-day. We are able to eat and are able to provide food to our families. We do not think we can ever be free and happy. It is only in death that we can be in peace.

The "do-ables"

The Government must consider the problems of the migrant women from poor families especially the train fare and improving the public distribution system. We are prepared to work hard but the government can take measures to reduce the rent, make water available and provide us with security regarding our stay in urban slums.

Source: From the field notes of Neela Mukherjee on narration by a women migrant group (elderly women) from West Bengal/Madhya Pradesh (including widows and those deserted by their husbands) of Alaknanda Slum Cluster, New Delhi (India).

4.20 Case Study Method

A case study is a focused study undertaken either for an individual/household/group/community in relation to one or more events or phenomena or, alternatively, a study of some socio-economic or political change in relation to an individual, household, group or a community. The difference between the traditional case study method and the participatory case study method is that in the latter case it is essentially based on a participatory mode based on the principles of PRA as discussed earlier. A case study on gender issues and social forestry is described in Box 4.7. The case study was done in interactive sessions with tribal women and men groups of village Avale in Thane district of Maharashtra (India).

Box 4.7 : Case Study – Gender Issues and Social Forestry

The following is a case study on gender issues and social forestry in village Avale in Tehsil Murbad of Thane district in Maharashtra (India). While interacting with women it was revealed that the poor tribal women spent a large part of their energy, long hours of hard toil under inconvenient circumstances in collecting fuel wood, fodder and other materials from the nearby forest. As stated by the local medical attendant, most of the women in that village were anaemic and weak and yet they were forced to put in considerable hard work for procuring requirements for their households and livelihood. In this context the issue was regarding the social forestry scheme in the village in which, the pressing needs and priorities of poor tribal women were overlooked.

While probing into the workload of women a map drawn by the women group showed the sources of water from which water is collected and the forest from which the women gathered fodder, fuel wood and leaves. The sources of water were Kalu Nala and Durgawol, a natural spring. Durgawol (Durganala) and its adjacent well were 2½ kms away from the village. The "nala" had water from June to November after which the women used the well near the "nala" as an alternative source of water. This was supplemented by water from tankers supplied by the local administration.

While describing their daily activities the women group pointed out that during off periods of cultivation they weeded out "roots" from the fields. They were also involved in bamboo work for which they spent three hours every day except during the cultivation period when they had no spare time. The women spent around an hour in cooking while the men looked after the grazing of the cattle. Based on a discussion with women, some aspects of women's role in collection of water, fuel and fodder are listed below:

— Collection of fuel and fodder was quite time-consuming. The women spent 4 hours daily for such an exercise for at least 5 days a week.

— Apart from their daily requirements of fuel and fodder they were also required to collect additional quantities to take care of the rainy season.
— The women collected water from the Durga Nala which provided water for 6 months from June to November after which there was acute water scarcity. In lean periods the demand for water was partly met through the well and partly through the water supplied officially from outside through tankers.
— The women were required to walk around 5 kms at one stretch to fetch water and a little less distance for collecting fuel and fodder. Most of their time was spent in collecting water, fuel and fodder.
— They spent an hour or so in cooking and other household work. The women also spent around 3 hours in field work for weeding out roots and/or bamboo work.

While talking about social forestry with the men group, it was found that the gram panchayat of village Avale had planted trees under the Jawahar Rozgar Yojana in 1989. They had planted some 350 saplings of "Khair" (*Accacia catechu*) in an area of 0.5 hectares. A local person donated the site for plantation while the plants were procured from the local forest nursery at Re. 1 per plant. The local men group associated with the social forestry discussed the utility of Khair in terms of generating both short- and long-term benefits as indicated below.

— Wood from Khair tree was used as poles for construction of huts.
— Leaves of Khair trees were burnt and the ash was used as fertiliser for paddy cultivation.
— Wood from each Khair tree fetched around Rs. 250 after a period of 8 to 10 years after which they were required to be re-planted.
— Planting of Khair was convenient, since such plantation did not require supervision as compared to fruit trees like mango or teak trees.
— Planting of Khair for social forestry had a low cost where less labour was required and the plants did not require much water or fertiliser.

One major disadvantage of Khair as pointed out by the villagers was that it could not be used as fodder nor was it good as fuel wood

(Contd.)

since it was not very "leafy". Hence, though the type of plantation for social forestry had both short-run and long-run implications in terms of benefits to the villagers, it was not of much practical consequence to the poor women in the village in terms of their priorities and problems. The plantation under the social forestry scheme could have been of greater relevance to the village women, if they had a chance to contribute to such decision-making at the local level. The village men were not adequately sensitised to the problems of women and their decision reflected different priorities altogether. As far as women's activities of collecting fuel and fodder were concerned, Accacia plants did not produce any fodder but merely some leaves for fuel. Hence such plants could not meet their requirement for fodder. Neither could they meet their need for fuel. In this context, the social forestry scheme in village Avale was a missed opportunity in terms of providing respite from the hardship experienced by village women. Considering women's priorities would have helped the women group to reduce their workload and provide rest to the poor women. This would have directly benefited the households concerned and added to their quality of life.

Source: Field Notes of Neela Mukherjee on Village Avale in Tehsil Murbad of Thane district in Maharashtra (India).

4.21 Historical Profile

Both past and future profiles of village, communities, self-help groups are possible through participatory "verbal" methods. In a historical profile, the villagers provide a historical account of how different aspects of village life have changed over the years. It can then be used for probing various aspects of quality of life of local people and the different changes, which have taken place over a span of years. A historical profile is described in Chart 4.1. It is a historical account of the community development process from 1961-98 in village Tien Phong in Bo Trach District of Quang Binh (Vietnam). The profile drawn by the villagers describes the number of beneficiary households, ways of managing activity, provision of fund and the opportunities and problems associated with the community development process.

4.22 Time Line

Time line is a participatory method for tracing local changes in different

CHART 4.1: Community Development Process of Con Ruong Reservoir, Tien Phong Village, Bo Trach District, Quang Binh, Vietnam

Year	No. of Beneficiary Households (HH)	Activity Management	Fund Provision	Experience and Opportunities/ Difficulties
1961-65	All 200 HH involved; fields belonged to cooperative	Done by cooperative	Fund provided by cooperative labour provided by households	Cooperative was newly formed, people willing to try, performance was quite good
1965-72	All 250 HH involved; field belonged to cooperative	Done by cooperative	Fund provided by cooperative, labour provided by households	American war damaged field, dam and disrupted life; not effective performance
1973-82	All 270 HH involved; field belonged to cooperative	Done by cooperative	Fund provided by cooperative, labour provided by households	American war ended; restoration of war damage started; cooperative proved in ieffective due to large size.
1983-87	All 280 HH involved; field belonged to cooperative and later to HH	Irrigation management unit formed by cooperative production groups managed by cooperative	Irrigation fee paid by HH; land given to HH; labour provided by HH	Dikes/dams rehabilitated; effective use of irrigation water with fields belonging to HH; sense of responsibility increased and farmers became proactive
1987-98	All 320 HH involved; land assigned to each HH	Irrigation management units formed of 8 persons each	Irrigation fee paid by HH; land given to HH; labour provided by HH	Farmers were proactive and hence performance was better with small groups of 8 each, doing irrigation management

Village Analysts : Men group Tien Phong Village, Bo Trach District, Quang Binh, Vietnam.
Source : From the field notes of Neela Mukherjee.

variables over time such as food patterns, wages, days of work, kind of work, survival strategies, changes in vegetation, farming practices, livelihoods, quality of life, etc. Events/changes of recent and not-so-recent origin, having an important bearing on the local community, can be discussed with a group of elderly community members and their time periods can be identified by the members in that process. This helps in contextualising any relevant issue through a chain of events and provides a historical perspective to the same. This helps in analysis of the issue/s concerned and also highlights past experience and efforts undertaken in that direction, if any. Any analysis of an event is more meaningful with proper understanding of its past context.

In order to construct a time line, one sits with elderly women and men in a community who slowly try to reconstruct the historical pattern of changes in different variables that have taken place in their locality/community. They may or may not be able to state the precise time/year of such changes but they are generally able to connect such changes with major historical events, whether political, economic or social. With a group of elderly people, such time lines are constructed naturally through discussing major changes relating to different time-periods and cross-checking them during subsequent discussions. A time line constructed by an elderly person can also be cross-checked with other elders in a locality.

Selected Remarks on Time Line

— Historical narration of events, their impact and changes can differ across participants depending on their perceptions, and it is useful to keep track of the broad time-period to which they refer to rather than specific dates.

— Time line provides indications of changes in land-use, in community preferences, in community problems, in socio-economic changes, changes in bio-diversity, land-use, water and other developmental activities.

— Important changes/events in the not-so-recent past can be selected and taken up for further probing. These can then be presented to groups for cross-checking, addition and alteration.

In the method of time line, elderly villagers narrate their life histories. Since it is often difficult to remember the exact dates of important changes, a villager can be facilitated to broadly connect such changes with major events, political/social/economic/cultural.

It was through the method of time line, as shown in Chart 4.2, that an elderly villager described wages, quality of food and environmental degradation in a village over a period of 70 years. As indicated in Chart 4.2, the wage rate of the poor villager named Sri Achaiah of village Madhapur (Andhra Pradesh) went up from 6 paise (Indian currency) per day in 1920 to Rs.15.00 per day in 1990 but the value of money had fallen drastically. Hence, even with a considerable rise in the wage rate his purchasing power had eroded over time forcing him to purchase lower quantity of food. His quality of food had also deteriorated and he no longer enjoyed the option of having good and nutritious food. On the basis of the time line, he explained his years of hardship, which started in the decade of the 1980s and continued in the 1990s. In these years he had access to the public distribution system to avail of subsidised food prices but he was forced to compromise on the quality of rice and pulses procured from the public distribution system. He was unable to afford meat and also ate lesser quantity as compared to the earlier periods. In the time line, he also described ecological degradation of his locality over time as witnessed by him. The village and its nearby areas had a rich forest cover with wildlife of different kinds, which gradually started eroding over the years. The village has many boulders with almost no trees in sight. One direct impact of the disappearance of forest cover, amongst others, as explained by him, was an acute water shortage in the village.

4.23 Oral Trend

Sometimes it becomes important to learn about historical trends orally. Such oral trends are more of broad overviews of selected issues comparing two periods, an old period and the current period. Such trend can be eco-trend, social trend, cultural trend, etc. The local people describe trends in local conditions from a historical perspective. The method helps in providing a historical background to any issue. An illustration of the oral trend is given in Box 4.8 as provided by a group of landless labourers, a minority group in village Khandavali at Faridabad (Haryana).

4.24 Historical Transect

A historical transect can be done with a group of elderly villagers or with a single elderly person who has knowledge of the village for a long

CHART 4.2: **Time Line**

APPROXI-MATE YEAR	WAGE RATE PER DAY	KIND OF FOOD	TREES
1920	Re 0·06	CHAPPATI, GOOD QUALITY RICE	
940–45	Re 0·15	CHAPPATI, GOOD QUALITY RICE, MEAT OCCASIONALLY	
1980	Rs 1·20	INFERIOR RICE, PULSES, POTATOES	
1985	Rs 10·00	INFERIOR RICE, DILUTED PULSES, POTATOES	
1990	Rs 15·00	RATION RICE, POTATOES, DILUTED* PULSES (*PREPARED WITH MORE WATER, LESS PULSES)	

Analyst : Sri Achaiah, Village Madhapur, Hyderabad, Andhra Pradesh, India.

Box 4.8 : Oral Trends by a Group of Landless Labourers

At first the chapatis made of wheat used to be soft. We also had "Jou" and "chana" to eat. In those fields, which had rainfall, the crop used to be 15 maunds per acre. There were no tubewells. The yield of wheat was low. Bullocks ploughed the field. We used to work as agricultural labourers. Now in 1999, wheat is 40 maunds per acre in 5 bighas. Now there is problem of water and electricity. We do not get opportunities for employment. The harvesting has got mechanised. We cannot get jobs. Whatever jobs are there, they are taken up by cheap labour from other regions. The agricultural and other work are done by outside labour for half the rate at Rs. 40/Rs. 50. The outside labour lives in "Jhuggis" and have low cost of living. Now there is also the problem of health. Earlier, there used to be fever, small-pox, etc. Now cough, cold, fever, etc., keep occurring. Almost 90 per cent have these 3 to 4 times in a year. There is cough due to pollution from the factories as per the younger generation. Older generation thinks it is due to weather fluctuations. Agricultural activities have increased, the means of agriculture have improved. Many have tractors in the village.

Earlier both women and men used to work hard in the field, now less people are required to work because of mechanisation. Only 2 people are needed and the rest can enjoy leisure. Now people have time to raise livestock. There are 3 crops grown—paddy, wheat and jowar/bajra—and because of this the workload has increased.

The workload of women has also increased. Now they have cash to buy soap and wash clothes, which takes more time. The women do weeding/cleaning of fields. Their workload at home has also increased. Earlier they had mud houses and now they have pucca houses which they need to clean (mud houses required less time for cleaning). Earlier 10 per cent used to drink alcohol and now 60 per cent do it. Dowry payment has also increased to Rs. 70,000. Earlier there was no dowry.

Participants: Group of landless labourers (Dalit), village Khandavali, Harijan Basti, Faridabad, Haryana (India).

Source: From the field notes of Neela Mukherjee on peri-urban villages in Faridabad.

CHART 4.3: **Historical Transect**

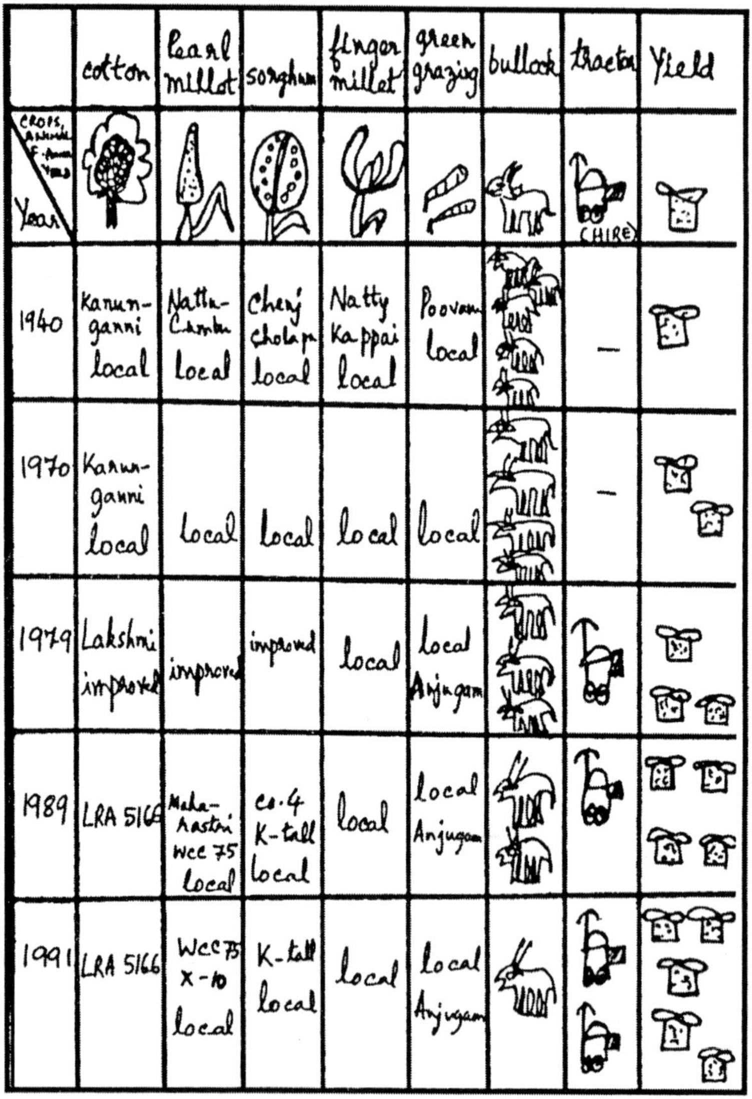

Note : Farmer Group from village Meenakhsi Puram, Tamil Nadu, India.

Source : Vijay Raghavan R., Subramanian S.R., Pretty Jules N. & John K.C. (ed.) (1992), Participatory Rural Appraisal for Agricultural Research at Aruppukotal, Tamil Nadu, Department of Agricultural Economics, Centre for Agricultural and Rural Development Studies, Tamil Nadu, Agricultural University, Coimbatore & IIED, London.

number of years and is able to provide a historical account of physical changes in the locality. It can be done separately with women and men groups to bring out the difference in gender perspectives. Such historical transect can account for the changes in the cropping patterns of resource-poor farmers, changes in the kind and number of trees, changes in natural resources, degree of environmental degradation, etc. Chart 4.3 depicts a historical transect for crops, animals, farm power and yields in an Indian village for the period 1940 to 1991.

4.25 Time-Transect

This method is a combination of time line and physical transect of a cross-section of a locality. It is more focused than a general time line since it is on a narrow segment of the locality under consideration. Chart 4.4 depicts such time-transect in village Binh An in commune Gia Ninh in Quang Ninh, Vietnam. It shows specific changes over the years 1954 to 1997 in the farm activities, housing conditions, surrounding environment and population in one part of village Binh An.

4.26 Daily Routine/Activity Chart

Daily routine charts reflect the kind of activities which one does on a daily basis. The different activities throughout the day are listed in a sequence. It can show the time spent in different activities and also the size of the work involved. For instance, women spend different hours of the day in activities like feeding children, cooking, fetching water, grazing livestock and collecting firewood and fuel wood. It is possible to identify general patterns from the daily patterns. The general patterns of different groups can then be compared. Such daily routines can also be depicted on a seasonal basis in order to identify constraints and workloads of different groups related to different activities.

Throughout the world women spend more time than men working, including both paid and unpaid work. So are the rural women in poor households, who are generally busy throughout the day mostly in their households. A large number of them also work outside on their own or share outside work with the men members of their household besides having tremendous responsibilities for running of households. In coping with their day-to-day responsibilities, rural women seldom find much time either for relaxing or doing something different. In an interactive session in village Banstaol, district Tangail, Bangladesh, a group of

CHART 4.4: **Time-Transect, Vietnam**

Year	Farm Activities	Housing Conditions	Surrounding Environment	Population
1954	Rice—old variety, low yield large areas sown, low income, low living standard, no co-operative	Roofs made of leaves for 60%, low living standard, updated techniques, war going on	Good environment, serious protection of forests, few sand covers, many animals; War time, forest destroyed by bombs.	No crowded population
1967	Rice—40% new varieties, 60% old yield, government management through communes, updated techniques, better living standards	Roofs made of leaves for 40%, better techniques	Deforestation, increasing sand which covered land	Increase in population, increase in family members, cultivable land was extended
1975	Rice—new variety by 30% only, better yield, better techniques, larger area	More brick houses, better techniques, furniture purchased	Forest was destroyed, new plantation, no protection and maintenance, forest destroyed by bombs	Growth of population, more labour force, fall in living standard, more land required
1988	Rice—Most of the varieties new, many changes in rural areas, cultivated lands, better techniques, provision of agriculture services, better living standards	Most houses with brick roofs, better techniques, more furniture, more better off households	Investment by forest department, more effective plantation, better protection of environment	Crowded population, more labour force, land exploited more, increase in livestock and plantation
1997	Rice—New variety, yield, good plantation protection, better techniques, improved living standards, many families have changed ways of doing business.	90% having brick houses, better living standards, expensive furniture	More investment, serious protection, land allocation, better environment	Demand for land increasing, crowded population, extending land towards the sea, more investment loans needed

Village Analysis: Men group, village Binh An, Commune Gia Binh in Quang Ninh, Vietnam.
Facilitator : Officials, ARCD Project, Quang Binh (Vietnam).

women were approached in order to learn about their daily routine of activities. They described their daily work profile in a sequence starting from early in the morning to late in the night as described in Box 4.9. A daily routine profile of women from Banstaol, Bangladesh, was prepared in the process.

Box 4.9: Daily Routine of Household and Farm Activities of Rural Women

Routine of Household Activities

- — Early morning waking up and reciting prayers;
- — Sweeping the front portion of the hut;
- — Taking the cattle out from its shed and giving it fodder;
- — Taking out goats and tying them in places where they can eat on their own;
- — Sweeping the back portion of the hut;
- — Cleaning utensils;
- — Cleaning the children and their teeth;
- — Fetching water for cooking;
- — Preparing food for household members and serving them;
- — Getting the children ready and sending them to school;
- — Fetching water for bathing;
- — Cooking for lunch and serving;
- — Giving fodder to cattle and goats;
- — Tying them at places where they can find more food;
- — Sweeping and cleaning the house;
- — Fetching water for cooking;
- — Cooking food for evening and serving;
- — Reciting prayers before sleeping in the night and going to bed.

Routine of Off-farm Activities

- — To weave mats from local grasses and sell them;
- — To weave fences from the bamboo sticks cut by them and to sell them;
- — At the time of ripening of fruits like "bel", mango, jackfruit, tamarind, borums and "jalpai", the women help in collecting them while the men pluck them from the trees.

(Contd.)

Routine of Farm Activities

- — Women weed the field once ploughing is over;
- — For orchards growing bananas, the women arrange the soil to heap them together near the roots of banana trees;
- — It is the women who carry water in earthen pots to water the fields at least 10 to 20 times a day as required;
- — They carry food, water and "hukka" pipe to the field for their household male members;
- — They carry fertilisers of different varieties to the field;
- — They pick the grass growing in the field and decompose it for making fertilisers;
- — In orchards growing bananas they prepare the soil, plant the seedlings, water them and pick weeds.

Village Analysts: Women named Kadarjan, Mayjan, Kamla Khatun, Sonacham, Hasina and Baleka of Shaplakuree Mahila Samiti of village Banstaol, Mirzapur, Tangail district of Bangladesh; Facilitated by Neela Mukherjee.

Source: Field Notes of Neela Mukherjee on Mirzapur, Tangail district, Bangladesh.

After completion of household work the rural women generally perform other activities depending on their spare time and season. The role of women in farm activities was also probed into. On this aspect, the women replied that they were actively involved in growing of brinjals and bananas as well as other food crops. Preliminary activities in the paddy fields were also done by them. However, they did not practise cultivation. They were basically engaged in supplementary activities in the fields.

4.27 Livelihood Analysis

This method helps in listing and analysing livelihoods for further probing. Generally poor women and men have diverse livelihoods and coping strategies. Such livelihoods pursued vary in terms of labour intensity, preferences, returns, opportunities, location and time. For learning about their livelihoods it is important to meet both women and men at different places and ask them about their livelihoods. Once the livelihoods and the groups pursuing them have been tracked, it becomes easier to have more interactions with those key performants who are actually pursuing such livelihoods. There exists livelihood-specific groups amongst local communities. This method helps in tracking such groups once a list of livelihood emerges from general discussions with members of local communities.

Box 4.10 lists sources of livelihoods as described by a group of poor women in the villages of Kalaikunda, Midnapore, West Bengal, India.

Box 4.10: Diversity of Livelihoods of Rural Poor Women

- Collecting forest/agricultural produce and selling them—mushrooms, fruits etc.
- Catching/collecting fish, crabs and snails from local water bodies and selling them
- Collecting water plants/vegetables from water bodies and selling them
- Raising plants in homestead/home gardens and selling vegetables
- Doing weeding in agricultural fields
- Carrying head-loads of earth, paddy and different other materials
- Sweeping leaves, twigs, stems, fruits droppings from trees and local plantations and selling them
- Sowing paddy, etc., in farmers' fields
- Harvesting paddy, etc., in farmers' fields
- Making paddy stacks for farmers
- Collecting paddy droppings and strewn paddy from paddy fields
- Winnowing for other farmers
- Catching fish from agricultural fields and selling them
- Making puffed rice/"chura" from paddy and selling it
- Rearing animals like goats/calf as a source of livelihood
- Stitching plates, etc., from "Sal" leaves
- Collecting fuel wood/dried branches, making stacks and selling them
- Collecting green leaves, etc., from trees and selling them
- Migrating to other areas with household members.

(Contd.)

Village Analysts : Different women groups from villages of Kalaikunda, Midnapore. *Source* : Field Notes of Neela Mukherjee on Kalaikunda villages, Midnapore, West Bengal (India).

4.28 Group Consensus Building

The method of group consensus building comes handy where there are multiple views and opinions prevailing within a group thereby affecting the process of arriving at a decision. In any group meeting, when views, opinions and options are more than one then all of them need to be listed and discussed for self-selection by the group/s involved. Each of the view needs to be separately looked into for judging its strengths and weaknesses in practical terms. This is also a process of elimination for narrowing down the list of options and gradually focusing on one or two for further group discussion. The process of consensus-building helps in bringing to the fore different views/alternatives/options; scanning them for their strengths and weaknesses through group discussion, eliminating those that the group decides, thus focusing on the best options and deciding on their feasibility and course of action.

However, on certain occasions it has been observed that consensus building can be an arduous task and may be time-consuming due to the nature of issues at hand and also the personality types or past experience. Acceptance through raising of hands can also be adopted for assessing group views on issues concerned. Much depends on the facilitator who plays a key role in mobilising groups for consensus building. It is important for the facilitator to ensure that views of the minority, downtrodden and marginalised groups get considered during group meetings.

An illustration of group consensus building is provided below. In a group meeting at village Chowki in Uttar Pradesh, problems listed earlier in small groups were brought in for prioritisation and action. Many opinions on prioritisation emerged during group meetings. All such opinions were flagged and the larger group was asked to form smaller groups and discuss feasibility aspects of such problems and their prioritisation. On placing the views of the smaller groups in the plenary the larger group was able to sort out views on the problems and prioritise them for action through self-help groups and project-supported activities. There may also arise occasions when such group discussions may not be feasible owing to the nature of the issues involved.

4.29 Presentation and Sharing

One method for dissemination of findings of PRA/PLA-type activities is holding group presentations and sharing such findings with local people. Such group presentations are interactive processes where local community members are invited to participate in such presentation sessions and discuss and debate the findings presented and also raise related issues. If the local people feel free to raise issues that they consider important then further discussions can take place for the field findings get validated in the process. This is an important method. Such presentation sessions are held at common places where local people generally meet and interact. Many field findings may need revision during the presentation sessions because of cross-checking by other community members who were earlier not available for interaction.

4.30 Conflict Resolution

It is natural for conflicts to arise within groups/communities and ways to resolve them are important. Some ways are listed below:

- Doing participatory problem analysis separately with the interest groups/individuals and then holding joint sessions.
- Doing participatory problem analysis with all the interest groups/individuals together and resolving conflicts.
- If it is a disputed area then a joint walk with interest groups to the area helps in flagging issues and sorting them out.
- Influencing opinion of interest groups through neutral personalities at the local level who are acceptable to the interest groups/individuals.

4.31 Children's Analysis

Children are different from adults and approaching them for their views requires an intensive process of rapport building. Their problems are different from those of adults and often they need enough trust in the facilitators for expressing such problems. Children of disadvantaged groups are often scared to speak out their minds. Hence, it is important to have them in separate groups, build mutual trust and goodwill, have enough patience and listen to them for appreciating their "worldview". Many of them do not open up at once and need encouragement and support to talk about their issues. Many of their ideas/views may appear naive and not worth pursuing but more probing into such ideas/views can help in contextualising such views and appreciating their true worth.

Experience shows that children are keen observers and quick learners and learning from them about their experience, ideas and issues can open a whole window to children's world of ideas, experience, problems, constraints and dreams fulfilled and unfulfilled. An illustration is provided in Box 4.11 from a PLA exercise with street children from Dhaka for learning about their problems, coping strategies and suggested actions.

Box 4.11: Prioritised Problems of Street Children

(i) Difficulties of shelter, basic "security" and amenities
(ii) Difficulties in accessing food
(iii) Attitude and behaviour of people who call them by names and misbehave
(iv) Ill treatment, exploitation and violence by employers
(v) Difficult conditions of work and accompanying hazards
(vi) Teased/abused by boys/men/women/touts
(vii) Lack of affection
(viii) Difficulties in accessing clothes, keeping cash, attending school
(ix) Health problems due to work
(x) Troubled by musclemen/thieves and child-lifters

Coping Strategies of Street Children

— sleep wherever space is available
— stay without bathing for 2-3 days together
— use open space for toileting
— stay without food by fasting and skipping meals
— try to collect waste food from roads
— sometimes take food by begging
— take low-grade food
— tolerate beatings and ill behaviour of adults
— always feel scared and unwanted

(Contd.)

Suggestions for Actions by Street Children

— government can provide shelter to them
— government must take action to punish those adults who trouble them
— they must be able to access a place for finding cheap food

Source: UNDP, Bangladesh (1997) PRRA field output/matrices for Community Empowerment Programme Formulation Mission and gender-specific Problem Prioritization Charts of selected communities/areas, typescript.

4.32 Constructing Word Picture

The word picture is yet another "verbal" method for creating verbal descriptions of any phenomenon for consideration. Examples of such word pictures can be "vulnerable households", "socio-economic categories in a community", "subsistence living", "categories of well-being" etc. Such word pictures help in painting of a scenario with words chosen by the groups interacted with. It is their description of any item, a condition of existence or a phenomenon, in their way and in their words. Such word pictures evolving from the group/community members in a participatory manner are practical and realistic and also help in involvement of group/community and their feeling of "ownership" for such word pictures. Word pictures evolved separately by women and men groups' help in focusing on gender issues and revealing gender perspectives. One illustration of word picture is given in Chart 4.5 from Pratapgarh, Rajasthan (India), where tribal groups evolved their own word pictures for "worst" household and "best" household in terms of access and ownership of natural resources.

4.33 Logical Framework Analysis

The logical framework, a standard method used for project design of core activities, project outcomes and key indicators for monitoring can be applied as a field method with local groups and communities. In the process, the verifiable indicators can become more realistic and field-oriented. For revising project log frame and making it more realistic participatory log frame analysis can be useful especially for identifying verifiable indicators for monitoring. With small group discussions and

Chart 4.5 : Word Picture of Household's Access/Ownership of Natural Resources

Worst Picture	Best Picture
Little or no land; one or two month's food available from own land; quality of land is poor, having red soil with low fertility; land is located on a slope in such a position that rain water washes away the seeds sown and the top soil and hence reduce its fertility; traditional seeds are used; some have given away land as collateral; no source of irrigation; no land for growing fodder for livestock; owns one or two livestock; no milk produced; low access to forest produce.	More of black fertile soil; more land; grows one's own fodder on one's own land; fertile land with more moisture retention power; more produce from land; grows and sells cash crops; grows vegetables; grows high yielding variety seeds; lends seeds to others; irrigation facilities available round the year; land is near the forest; access to forest produce; some have government permit to grow opium; has many fruit trees; availability of home grown food throughout the year; many livestock, high returns from livestock.

Note: The word pictures run across different categories of households from the 'worst' to the 'best' in terms of degrees. There are 5 word pictures within the range of 'worst' and the 'best' for household access/ownership of natural resources. Only 2 word pictures have been described here.

Source: Field notes of Neela Mukherjee on Output Monitoring Workshop with village key informants and project team of IFFDC, Pratapgarh, Rajasthan (India).

Chart 4.6: Log Frame on Self-help Groups for Output Monitoring

Output	Activities	**Verifiable Indicators**
Sustainable self-managed common interest groups in 75 core villages	Self-help groups, both women and men, organised: training, exposure visit, meetings, regular savings, credit, other productive activities, bank and other input providing linkages	Criteria for monitoring group participation — Punctuality of group members in attending meetings — Participation of group members in discussions — Productiveness of meetings — Following rules and regulations of the group — Regular meetings and savings

Note: The above is adapted from the output monitoring workshop results of IFFDC, Pratapgarh Project. The final result has a different set of verifiable indicators for each cluster criteria for sustainable groups, which are not included here. For the sake of illustration one set of criteria for group participation has been considered as above. Key village informants, both women and men, participated in the output-monitoring workshop along with project team members.

Source: Based on workshop notes of Neela Mukherjee on IFFDC, WIRFP, Pratapgarh, Rajasthan (India).

plenary presentation such workshop can help in improving log frames. Such a method was applied by the project team of IFFDC, Pratapgarh, to build community-based monitoring system on "group sustainability". Key village informants, both women and men, from project villages were invited. Selected results are indicated in Chart 4.6.

4.34 Problem-Action Analysis

In this method local people list and describe a set of problems and the associated opportunities. Chart 4.7 provides an illustration of a PRA/PLA session with a local group in village Chowki near Dehradun in Uttar Pradesh (India) revealing their local problems and the existing opportunities.

Chart 4.7: Problem-Action Analysis

Problems	Opportunities
Lack of income generating opportunity	Can be done by Watershed Department and some by District Rural Development Agency
Absence of a bridge on the local river	Can be done by Public Works Department, Planning Department and local political representative
Absence of proper road	Can be done by Public Works Department
Lack of electricity	Can be done by Rural Electrification Unit
Damaged irrigation channels	Can be done by Watershed Department and local community members
Thick growth of "Lantenna" (a kind of weed growing in the field and elsewhere, difficult to uproot)	Can be done by community members

Note: Based on preliminary discussion sessions with Chowki village group where each problem has been described.

Source: From the field notes of Neela Mukherjee on village Chowki, Dehradun, Uttar Pradesh (India).

Though methods for holding conversations with local people are important there are other participatory methods, which involve walking with local people, their mapping of ideas/areas, ranking, diagramming and depiction of the "seasonality" factor in their lives and livelihoods. These methods have been discussed in the subsequent chapters.

REFERENCES

Brown Andrew and Paul Dowling (1998), *Doing Research/Reading Research, A Mode of Interrogation for Education*, The Falmer Press, London.

Burgess Robert G., (1990), *In the Field, An Introduction to Field Research*, Contemporary Social Research Series, General Editor: Martin Bulmer, Routeledge, London.

Dewees Peter, (1989), "Aerial Photography and Household Studies in Kenya". *RRA Notes*, Number 7, September, IIED. London.

Epstein T. Scarlett, Suryanarayana A.P. and Thimmegowda T., (1998), *Village Voices, Forty Years of Rural Transformation in South India*, Sage Publications, New Delhi.

Grandin Barbara, (1988), *Wealth Ranking in Smallholder Communities: A Field Manual*, Intermediate Technology Publications, London.

Guijt Irene & Pretty Jules (1992), Participatory Rural Appraisal for Farmer Participatory Research in Punjab, Pakistan, IIED, London.

Hallowell, Edward, M. (1999), "The Human Moment at Work", Harvard Business Review, January-February, pp. 58-66.

Jayakaran Ravi, (1991), "PRA Camp at Mahilong, Bihar, 27-30, November. 1990: Krishi Gram Vikas Kendra", *RRA Notes*. Number 13. August, IIED. London.

Kanji Gopal K. & Mike Asher, (1996). *100 Methods for Total Quality Management*, Response Books. New Delhi.

Mascarenhas Jimmy & Prem Kumar P.D., (1991), "Participatory Mapping and Modelling: Users' Notes. RRA Notes. Number 12. July, IIED. London.

Massarik, Fred (1981). "The interviewing process re-examined", in Reason Peter *et al.* (ed.) *Human Inquiry, A Sourcebook of New Paradigm Research*. John Wiley & Sons, Chichester.

McCracken Jennifer A., Pretty Jules N. & Conway Gordon R., (1988), An Introduction to Rapid Rural Appraisal for Agricultural Development, Sustainable Agriculture Programme, IIED. London.

McCracken Jennifer, (1989), "Diagrams for Participatory RRA", *RRA Notes*, September, IIED, London.

Mearns Robin, (1988), "On Oral History and Local Calendars: Experiences in the Field in Papua New Guinea", *RRA Notes*, Number 3, IIED, London.

Mearns Robin, (1989), "Aerial Photographs in Rapid Land Resource Appraisal, Papua New Guinea", *RRA Notes*, Number 7, September. IIED, London.

Mukherjee Neela (1992), "Villagers' Perceptions of Rural Poverty Through the Mapping Method of PRA", *RRA Notes*, No. 15. IIED. London.

Mukherjee. Neela (1993), *Participatory Rural Appraisal: Methodology and*

Applications, Concept Publishing Company, New Delhi.

Mukherjee, Neela (1997), *Participatory Appraisal of Natural Resources*, Concept Publishing Company, New Delhi.

Pretty Jules, Irene Guijt, Ian Scoones and John Thompson, (1995), A Trainer's Guide, International Institute for Environment and Development, London.

Pretty Jules, (1988), "Portraits and Stories", *RRA Notes*, Number 3, IIED, London.

Reason, Peter and John Rowan (ed.) (1981), *Human Inquiry, A Sourcebook of New Paradigm Research*, John Wiley & Sons, Chichester.

Richardson S.A., Dohrenwend B.A. and Klein D. (1965), *Interviewing Its Forms and Functions*, Basic Book, New York.

RRA Notes, (1991), Number 13, August, IIED, London.

Sandford Dick, (1989), "A Note on the Use of Aerial Photographs for Land Use Planning on a Settlement Site in Ethiopia", *RRA Notes*, Number 6, IIED, June.

Scoones Ian, (1988), "Learning About Wealth: An Example From Zimbabwe", *RRA Notes*, Number 2, October, IIED, London.

Scoones Ian, (1992), "Wealth ranking: Insights into Patterns of Rural Differentiation in Southern Zimbabwe", typescript, Sustainable Agriculture Programme, IIED, London.

Shah Parmesh, Bharadwaj Girish & Ambastha Ranjit, (1991), "Farmers as Analysts and Facilitators in Participatory Rural Appraisal and Planning", *RRA Notes*, Number 13, IIED, London.

Theis Joachim & Grady Heather M., (1991) Participatory Rapid Appraisal for Community Development, A Training Manual Based on Experiences in the Middle East and North Africa, IIED & Save the Children Federation.

UNDP, "Who are the Question Makers? A Participatory Evaluation Handbook", United Nations Development Programme, New York.

5

WALKING TOGETHER

In PRA/PLA, those methods involving walking with others (such as local community members) provide important opportunities for first-hand learning-by-observing and discussing related aspects. Such methods associated with "walking" are important both for gathering overviews and for focused learning. Such walking exercises of outsiders with others can be undertaken with the objective of gathering some general idea about the locality or a specific area or location within an area. Or, alternatively, such a walk can be systematic and broadly structured with a specific purpose in view, for example, studying a local utilisation pattern of a localised natural resource, for example, a forest or studying the social aspects of a locality such as the type of housing conditions in an area. Such a "walk" can precede or follow "verbal" and/or "visual" interactions. For example, a focused walk can be undertaken to a site based on a participatory mapping exercise of a locality. In this Chapter, four methods relating to participatory walking have been explained as follows:

— Joint walk;
— Physical transect;
— Social transect;
— Walk to the demonstration site.

5.1 Joint Walk

The method of joint walk based on "seeing-is-believing" relates to learning from local communities through undertaking joint walks with them. Such walking with communities helps in observing different aspects of a selected area/s in a locality, which require on-site observation and detailed discussions with the community members. For example, a degraded forest area identified through a map can be jointly surveyed by the community members and outside agencies for discussion in terms of the causes, nature and action in terms of regenerating such forest area. Such walks can be either casual, random or systematic based on a checklist of items to be probed. Such walks undertaken with local groups, women and/or men groups help in having a better knowledge about the locality or selected cross-sections of the locality. The observations and findings from such joint walks can be noted, shared/ presented in a tabular form.

Joint walks with local communities can help in directly observing and probing on different issues. In such a method, the external team walks with local groups/community members from one selected point in an area to another selected point. While walking the local people explain and discuss the issue/s related to that area, whether of natural and/or social resources, the problems, priorities and opportunities. For an external team such joint walks provide quick "overviews" or help in detailed understanding of issue/s related to that area. A sequence of such joint walks can be organised depending on locations in question.

The method of a joint walk comes handy as follows:

— It helps in providing quick "overviews".
— It helps in in-depth physical probing of an area.
— It also helps in observing micro-environments which tend to get overlooked in maps.
— It helps in direct observation, discussion and cross-checking the intricacies of the issues involved.
— It helps in concretising discussions and make things tangible in the sense that the local people can also show the physical locations/items while describing them verbally. It helps the local people to establish their points through site visits.
— It also helps interventionist agencies to have first-hand knowledge about any location/item/situation/condition.

Some areas for application of the method of joint walks are as follows:

— It can be applied for understanding an area, generally within walking distance. The area can be selected in consultation with the local community on the basis of participatory mapping in order to focus on it. Some areas for joint walks are given below as an illustration:

- — Water bodies, for example, canals, ponds, etc.
- — Drinking water sources
- — Field and fallow lands
- — Kinds/levels of forest cover
- — Types of housing and patterns of habitat
- — Grazing areas
- — Location of institutions/facilities such as school, bus stand, etc.
- — Micro environment

5.1.1 Micro Environment

A micro environment is a "distinct small-scale environment which differs from its surroundings, presenting sharp gradients or contrasts in physical conditions, internally and/or externally. Micro environments can be isolated, or contiguous and repetitive, and natural or made by people or domestic animals" (Chambers:1990). Some illustrations of micro environments are as follows (Chambers:1990):

- — Home garden/homestead
- — Vegetable and horticultural patches
- — River banks and riverine strips
- — Levees and natural terraces
- — Valley bottoms
- — Wet and dry watercourses, for example, nullahs
- — Silt trap fields
- — Ponds including fishponds
- — Forms of water harvesting
- — Hedges and windbreaks
- — Clumps, groves or lines of trees or bushes
- — Pockets of fertile soil

A generic checklist for a joint walk on a selected "resource" is outlined below:

- — Types of resources in the village
- — Description of resource
- — How is the resource utilised
- — Diagnosis of resource and its use

- Local knowledge and practices related to resources
- Opportunities for better utilisation of resources and constraints

5.1.2 Lessons from Field Experience on Joint Walk

- The area for joint walk with local people is required to be within manageable limits of walking so that in-depth observation and discussion can take place without the walk becoming tiresome.
- Such walks can involve joint walking to selected spots and covering areas, which constitute focal points of discussion.
- For large areas involved, more than one joint walk is required. Sometimes joint walks covering large areas can be tiring and time-consuming.
- Joint walks with men and women, young and old, rich and poor tend to give widely differing perspectives.
- Joint walks with different key informants from a locality can help in having in-depth discussions from different angles.
- Joint walks to areas/sites, which are conflict-ridden, can help in resolving issues with different parties to the conflict. They can enable a mediator to directly observe and discuss different aspects of such conflicts and their spatial basis.
- Having an overview of the area concerned whether by mapping or otherwise helps in identifying sites for joint walks for direct observation and better probing. Joint walks can be repeated as and when required.

5.2 Physical/Social Transect

Participatory transect walks involve *systematic walking* with local people across a cross-section of that locality and discussing about different aspects of landuse and ecological areas observed during such walks. A transect walk is a useful method for knowing local ecological conditions and the accompanying social dimensions. A transect walk from one point of the locality to another in a rural area setting enables an external team to observe different aspects of local agro-ecological conditions and to discuss with local people about different soil conditions, landuse patterns, crops, livestock, micro environments, habitat patterns, social issues, etc. The importance of transect walks lies not only in knowing the ecological zones and social aspects in a locality but also in getting an in-depth account from the accompanying local persons about their uses, problems and opportunities. Earlier, transect walks were more focused on physical resources. However, transect walks can be of different kinds, for probing into social aspects, health, sanitation and infrastructure. One transect walk can be supplemented by other similar walks so as to enable the outsider to learn more about a locality and clarify doubts. Transect walks become more meaningful when based on local gender perspectives.

Some steps in transect walks are suggested below:

- — Deciding on the focus issue;
- — Identifying the area to be visited;
- — Having an overview of the area to be visited — how the area stands in relation to others;
- — Selecting a set of criteria related to the issue at hand;
- — Selecting the basis for division of zones, for example, distance/ landuse/soil conditions;
- — Taking care of not missing the micro environments located in that area;
- — Taking care of not missing the social implications of local resources.

As far as the local agro-ecosystems in rural areas and their physical variations are concerned, they can be appreciated better through transect walks which provide a visual exposition of the physical features of rural areas along with the local people's interpretation. This helps in overcoming the "roadside" bias associated with field visits (McCracken, Pretty and Conway:1988). Transect walks help in carrying out a detailed participatory appraisal of the ecosystem and socio-physical profile of an area under consideration. It can reveal local perspectives about localized natural resources, whether resource-rich or resource-poor, the inter- and intra-variations in physical resources and ecological conditions existing in an area. However, if the area under consideration is large and has considerable variations then it may be difficult to have a full grasp of that area through a single or multiple transect walk/walks. Transect walks across selected agro-ecological zones in an area prove effective in conjunction with participatory resource mapping of that area. For urban and semi-urban areas the focus of transect walks tends to be more on

Chart 5.1: Physical Transect

Criteria						
Landuse	Forest and Fallow land	Homestead land	Agriculture land	Mid-land	Low land	Canal
Soil	Laterite stones, boulders, sandy loam	Sandy loam	Sandy loam, clay loam	Clay loam	Clay	Clay
Tree	"Sal", cashewnut, eucalyptus, accacia, date, "mahua", "piyal", "kendu", mango, "jamun", wild berry, "bel", borrom, bamboo	"Neem", "sirish" "challa", "arjun", "krishna ber", custard apple, mango, "jamun", date-palm, eucalyptus, bamboo	"Kusum", palm, "babul", tamarind	"Babul", date-palm	Omri, ipomia, shrubs	—
Crop	Paddy, "kakri", "kalam", "bhutmari" "sarkari HYV"	Brinjal, sweet potato, gourd, bottle gourd, "kundri", raddish, ground nut	Paddy: "bhutmari", "jangujata", "jhingasal", "sarkari HYV", vegetables	Paddy: "jhingasal", "patnal"	Paddy : "Champa kala" "sarkari boro" in winter	—

(Contd.)

Chart 5.1 *(Contd.)*

Criteria						
Animal/ Bird	Hare, rat, jackal, snake, frog, squirel	Domestic animals —goat, sheep, pig, duck, hen, dog, buffalo, cat, fish	Fish (during monsoon fish grows in rice fields)	—	Fish— seasonal— "bele", "tangra", "bagal", "basi", "bhulsi", cat fish, predator "punti", etc.	Fish— in season
Soil erosion	Slight	More	Medium	High	High	—
Water source	Nil	Tanks-12 Wells-20	Pond-2 Seepage tank-1	—	—	Canal
Fodder	"Burru", "shone", "khara" grass, "ber" leaves	"Ber" leaves, "sahara", "sabai" grass	Grasses grow during monsoon and on the field after paddy harvest	—	—	—
Problem	Lack of irrigation	Lack of fodder in	Lack of irrigation	—	Road	—

(Contd.)

Chart 5.1 *(Contd.)*

Criteria						
	for paddy, soil erosion, low fertility	rainy season, cattle menace and irrigation	in summer, low fertility		communication	
Opportunities	Digging wells and ponds, making ridges, tree plantation, etc.	Fencing well, digging, tree plantation	Digging ponds, irrigation, fish cultivation	Installing shallow tube-wells	Making bridge and renovating canal	—

Note : Based on transect walk with a village group in Chandabila, Midnapore, West Bengal (India).
Facilitators: Kamal Kar and Sumit N. Datta.

problems and opportunities related to habitat patterns, sanitation standards, trees and plants, water sources, infrastructure, facilities and other social aspects.

Findings of one transect walk are summarised in Chart 5.1 of village Chandabila in West Bengal (India). It describes different features of the area covered such as the soil conditions, the landuse patterns, the trees, the crops and vegetation grown, the water sources, the problems and the opportunities. A set of problems have been stated for each agro-ecological zone as described in the transect table. The opportunities identified at the micro level are also in accordance with the zones.

Box 5.1: The Vietnamese Pictorial Time-Transect

In Thon Tien village, Vo Ninh Commune, Quang Ninh District, Vietnam, a group of men villagers went for a transect walk with an external team in the afternoon of 19th December, 1997. Upon completion of such transect walk the villagers drew a cross-section of the village starting from the sea-shore to the extensive sand dune cover at the back of the village. It was a coloured portrayal on a huge chart paper of a cross-section of socio-agro-ecological zones of the village covering sea, beach, field, water bodies, households, forest and sand dunes. Underneath the cross-section, the village group described the historical profile of each zone including a time line of the years 1954, 1964, 1975, 1988 and 1997 where the changes over time were illustrated. The pictorial time-transect mentioned the number of households over time and described changes in the living standards, type of houses, demographic changes, changes in assets, investment, labour force, credit, livestock, etc. The Vietnamese time-transect also included historical transect of different crops, yields, agricultural practices, techniques, sand dune cover, landuse, tree plantation, surrounding environmental conditions, etc. It was a mega-transect prepared by the local people. It was amazing to see the visual breadth and depth of information, which emerged in the process of constructing the pictorial time-transect.

Source: From the field notes of Neela Mukherjee on PRA planning exercise, ARDC Project, Quang Binh, Vietnam.

5.3 Walking to Demonstration Site/Plot

Demonstration sites are important locations to be visited during joint

Box 5.2: Demonstration Site Visit: Maldives

In Maldives, in Noonu Atoll, a site visit by an external evaluation team to an island was undertaken where a local women group was collaborating with each other for growing vegetables on patches of community land. They were growing different kinds of vegetables and were eager to explain how they manage work, how they collaborate and consult and how they propose to distribute the earnings from such vegetables. They also showed the problems like pests that they faced in growing vegetables and the treatment they were giving. Visiting the site helped in physical observation and raising and clarifying issues through a process of dialogue. Such visits helped discussion to proceed *in situ*, where both external team and local participants could discuss issues based on physical observation, and demonstration by women groups and physical verification.

Source: From the field notes of Neela Mukherjee on Noonu Atoll, Maldives.

Demonstration Plot and Visual Extension Package: Maldives

A joint visit by an external team and local people of Thinadhoo island, Vaavu Atoll, Maldives, was undertaken to a demonstration plot located in the island. Given land of very poor quality, some local women and men with the help of an UNDP-funded Project had engaged themselves in a demonstration plot with two rounds of training-*cum*-demonstration arranged by the Project. While discussing with the participants it was observed that the local people were growing vegetables on that patch of land based on the training that they had received and a "visual" training manual provided during training, which the participants/community members were able to consult, as and when required. It was found that soil and plant treatment and protection against pest attack and diseases were also included as part of the extension module. Based on discussions, the point was made by local participants that participatory extension in agriculture is better suited for poor communities. It helps to combine local experience and knowledge with an appropriate quantum of modern technical practices.

Source: From the field notes of Neela Mukherjee on Thinadhoo island, Vaavu Atoll, Maldives.

walks. The effectiveness and significance of such site/s can be assessed by means of such walks. It helps in gathering first-hand view of the opportunities and constraints associated with such site/s. Two illustrations from the Maldives as given in Box 5.2 show that the best way to learn about community initiative is to visit such site/plot along with local community members. It is important to learn directly from those local people who are actually managing such site/plot. Walking together helps in having a first-hand knowledge of the *modus operandi* of such site/plot and seek clarifications *in situ.*

REFERENCES

Chambers, Robert (1990) *Microenvironments Unobserved*, Gatekeeper Series No.22, Sustainable Agriculture Programme, International Institute for Environment and Development, London.

6

VISUAL PORTRAYAL : MAPPING AND SKETCHING

In this chapter, a range of "visual" methods related to mapping and sketching has been described. There are different PRA methods involving direct participation, many of which are based on mapping and sketching as an integral part. Such methods include social mapping with topical focus such as resource mapping, facility mapping, literacy and health mapping, livestock mapping, watershed mapping, harvest mapping and others. Natural resource mapping includes both locality-specific resources and micro-resources through microenvironment mapping. Mapping on a temporal basis is illustrated through mapping, past, present and future, children's vision mapping and mapping "future's possible". Aspects of well-being/poverty/wealth are included in this chapter through methods involving mapping, grouping, ranking, construction of matrices and distance grouping. Participatory concept mapping, which helps in evolving local concepts from the grassroots, is also included together with the method involving model-building of areas, resources, assets, plans, etc.

METHODS FOR MAPPING/SKETCHING

The following methods have been described in this chapter:

— Use of symbols
— Sketch mapping
— Resource mapping
— Forest/Park mapping
— Social mapping
— Census mapping
— Facility/social infrastructure mapping

— Literacy mapping
— Health mapping
— Microenvironment mapping
— Children's vision mapping
— Mapping—past, present and future
— Mapping "before" and "after"
— Status mapping
— Mobility mapping
— Livelihood mapping
— SHG household mapping
— Livestock mapping
— Model-building
— Participatory risk mapping
— Body mapping
— Anonymous body spotting
— Mental well-being mapping
— Well-being/poverty/wealth mapping
— Well-being/poverty/wealth grouping
— Wealth ranking
— Social matrix
— Social distance grouping
— Participatory concept mapping

6.1 Use of Symbols

For mapping and model-building "visual" elements are important. They help in illustrating the different aspects/topics/items, which are under consideration. For making mapping and model-building as "visual" as possible there is a wide usage of symbols in application of these methods. A few of them are illustrated in Chart 6.1. Whether such mapping is prepared on the ground or paper or on other medium, diverse symbols are used for representing different items in maps and models. Usage of materials, such as stones, pebbles, seeds, sticks, leaves, twigs, stems, flowers, etc., helps to illustrate the different items showed on maps and models and also enables illiterate and semi-literate persons to participate in the preparation of such "visuals". Symbols help in visually portraying items and transferring mental pictures on to visual maps and models. Symbols help in construction of mental maps and enable the weak and the voiceless to place their mental pictures/views/symbols, which are often difficult to express otherwise.

CHART 6.1: **Use of Symbols**
From Ha Giang Vietnam

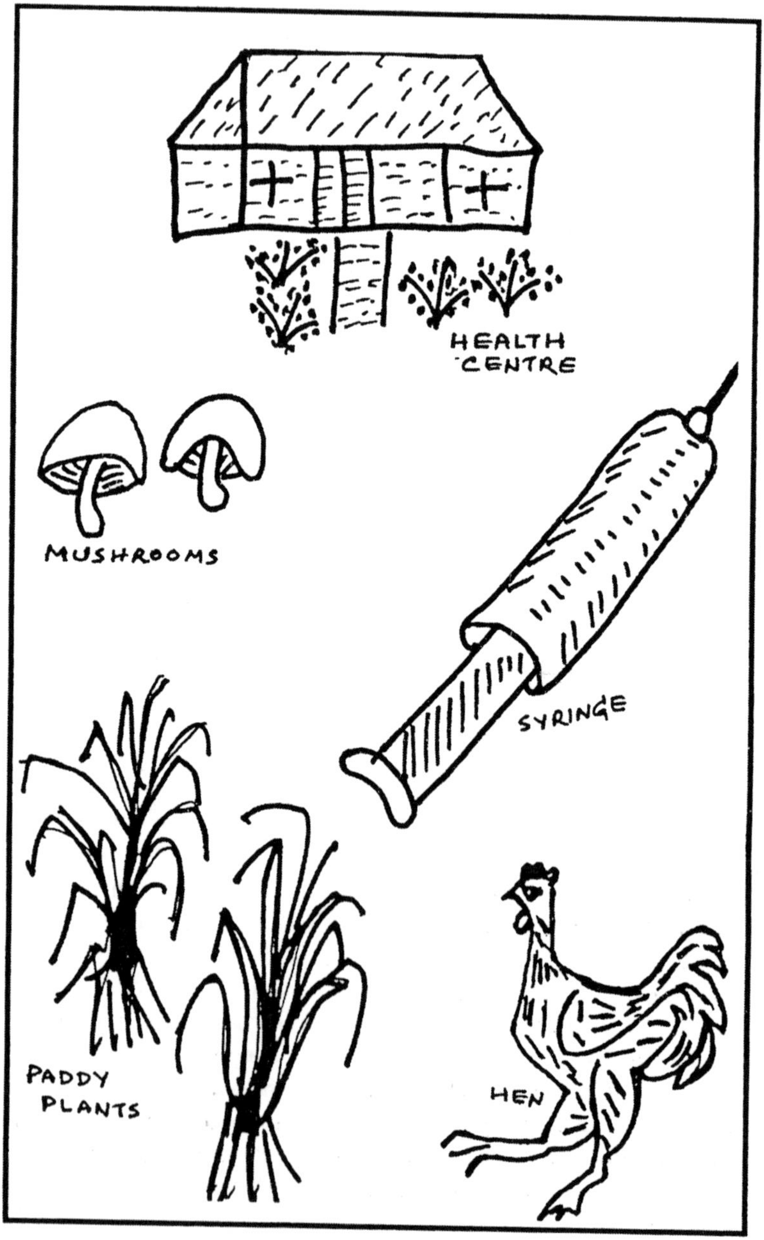

6.1.1 Participatory Mapping

Participatory mapping is an important method for PRA/PLA-type exercises and can help in highlighting different aspects of community life such as social aspects, resources, livelihood, health, wealth, literacy, census, livestock, harvest, economic activities, social stratification, etc. Such mapping can portray the image of dwellings in a community, of huts, houses, natural resources, open spaces, farms and fields, water collections, forests, soils and of many other aspects depending on the topic under consideration. In participatory mapping and model-building, local communities prepare the map/model of their locality with chalks, colour powders and other materials such as stones, leaves, flowers, etc., either on ground or on paper.

Participatory mapping involves spatial drawing of any area, drawn on ground, paper or on other medium by the local people to show and explain their locality and other related areas, such as residential areas, forests, fields, etc. Participatory mapping can include a range of items like households, school, office, infrastructure, crops, livestock, farm size, water bodies, fields, forest, trees, roads, facilities, common property resources, literacy, diseases, etc. depending on the theme/themes under discussion. Such mapping can be theme-specific such as a resource map indicating natural resources of the locality; social map showing households and other buildings in the area; health map showing health status; literacy map showing literate/illiterate/semi-literate, etc.

6.1.2. Who maps?

Such participatory mapping is done by the local people themselves, whether women, men or children. It can be done individually or in a group depending on the situation. Often one or two persons lead a participatory session (they do the drawing of the map) while others present there help them in doing so. Key performant/s are person/s who actually draw the map/diagram. Other local people, present during mapping sessions, generally extend active help to those who do the mapping; watch it getting done; remind the key performant/s of those items which they tend to leave out; and also cross-check the mapping for errors and omissions. Often, for focused topics some key informant/s (person/s with more information on the topic provide lead to the mapping process) of a locality lead/s a mapping process. Key informants are those persons from a community who provide key information on different aspects of the locality concerned.

6.1.3 Significance of Mapping

Participatory mapping is a rich tool and is commonly used in PRA/PLA-type exercises. It has an enormous potential. By drawing maps local community/group provides a basis for explaining different aspects of a locality, for instance, the location of dwellings and buildings and land-use pattern showing the position of households in a locality and their socio-economic characteristics. A local resource map can also show different kinds of natural resources and microenvironments. In a resource map, the participants draw locality-specific resource profiles depicting different kinds of fields, soils, rivers, ponds, trees, crops and microenvironments. The problems can be described and discussed on the basis of a resource map along with the opportunities and constraints. Participatory mapping can also form basis for joint walk with local community members to selected areas in the locality. A resource map combined with a social map is shown in Chart 6.1. With preparation of a social map by the local community members it becomes easy for them to describe locations in terms of roads and rivers, in terms of the characteristics and conditions of their households, the ownership of dwellings and buildings and land-use patterns. In terms of poor and non-poor households in a locality, social maps visually present the location of such households and their key features. In addition, there is also scope for presenting other kinds of information regarding households such as the heads of households whether a woman or a man, dependency ratios, ownership of assets, cattle, beneficiaries under State programmes, health/wealth/poverty characteristics and so on. In any locality, social maps form a useful basis for identifying opportunities and problems in different households, their conditions of living, livelihoods and other features. For example, a social map can form an excellent base for a health map indicating the health problems in different households. Maps can be followed by semi-structured interviews.

Selected utility of participatory mapping is listed below:

— It involves local people/groups and empowers them to map, illustrate and explain their own locality.
— It helps in ownership of data by the local communities/groups/individuals.
— On many occasions, it helps in rapport building with local

people.

- It helps in catalysing group participation especially when maps are drawn in open spaces and common meeting places.
- It helps in generating a wide variety of data in a relatively short period of time.
- It provides an overview and background material/data for probing into relevant themes.
- It helps in projecting spatial view with regard to a locality and related areas.
- It provides a basis for further probing, undertaking joint walks or other participatory methods.
- It helps in cross-checking by participants for errors and omissions.
- It helps in arriving at a group consensus.
- Resource maps help in clarifying the extent of accessibility of the local people to the local resources.

6.1.4 Mapping from Field Experience

A few remarks based on field-level experience on participatory mapping are listed below:

- Participatory maps are generally mental maps of individuals/ groups/communities. They reflect community perspectives and are different from professional maps, which are drawn from the professional point of view and have explicit reference to size and scale.
- Maps done on the ground can involve active participation of more people than maps done on paper, the latter, however, can be retained easily.
- Process of participatory mapping, once started, can continue on its own without much of outside facilitation.
- It is important to have participatory mapping, genderwise, so as not to lose track of perceptions of different gender groups. Similarly participatory mapping is influenced by caste, class, age, etc. Maps made by men and women, children, old and young, rich and poor can vary widely depending on their relative perceptions of the topics covered.
- Local communities can also do participatory mapping focusing on different localities. They can identify the households through

numbers or household names. Such information can be cross-checked by visiting each household in the map concerned.

- The type and magnitude of information generated through mapping by the local participants tend to vary across individuals, groups and communities, depending on their knowledge base, experience and "worldview".
- Illiterate and semi-literate persons can draw maps with ease and explain different items with the help of selected symbols.
- Participatory mapping can be presented to the local people in different sessions by the local participants themselves and cross-checked on that basis. It can also be checked on a household basis for the validation of data.
- Where there are many enthusiastic people to map they should actually enjoy the opportunity created by the mapping process. Hence a facilitator can initiate more than one small group to map on the ground rather than having concentrated mapping done by one or two individuals. Those not willing to actively do such mapping can be encouraged to provide information and cross-check such maps from time to time.
- Sometimes it is difficult to map big localities as a single entity due to insufficient knowledge of key informant/performant. It can also be difficult to handle such information on account of its size and hence may not be efficiently manageable. Such an activity can often be time-consuming. Hence few ways to overcome such a problem are:

    - Mapping (locality) in parts;
    - Mapping of localities by different individuals;
    - Maps carried from one part of locality to another for further additions and alterations;
    - Mapping in bits and pieces on different days/duration by different people.

Selected points for participatory mapping :

- For villages/slums with a large number of houses, poverty mapping may become difficult. In such cases it is best to go for identifying locations of hamlets/areas where poor households are situated. Key informants can be involved in such identification of pockets of poverty.

— The criteria for grouping of poor households are very important. They can differ across gender, caste, class, age, etc.

— Mapping method helps in direct identification of beneficiary households/groups for activities related to planning, implementation, monitoring, impact assessment and evaluation activities.

6.2 Sketch Mapping

A sketch map generally provides the outline of a locality and its neighbouring areas. It has quick and rough outlines indicating the relative location of a place with reference to nearby areas. It does not cover details of a location, rather indicates where a locality is situated within a broader area. It is mainly used for identifying localities, hamlets, slums, residential areas, etc. It comes handy for getting a first-hand idea of locating areas and their neighbourhood. It can provide a useful overview to start with. It helps in identifying a specific locality in an area, localities with similar and dissimilar features in nearby areas and other overall features for inquiry, for example, total number of households in a locality.

For preparation of the Human Development Report of Bangladesh (1996), Part 3 by UNDP, sketch mapping was utilised for sampling of poorer localities within a village. Whenever a selected area was visited for field inquiry, one first thing was to approach some individuals in that area for a sketch map of their locality and nearby localities. Groups of local people near a tea stall/other shops were approached for sketching local areas, which were relatively poor and hamlets within such areas considered to be poor. Such sketch maps were also cross-checked with other groups in the locality.

Chart 6.2 is a sketch map done by a villager showing a cluster of villages in Faridabad (Haryana) and their links with the main road to Delhi. This sketch map helps a development worker to understand the locational contours of areas under consideration, their relation to adjacent areas. It also provides some idea of distance and other information in terms of an overview of the socio-economic aspects like the number of households, kinds of social group, etc., including a local road map in terms of identifying localities in an area.

6.3 Resource Mapping

A resource map basically portrays a general picture of natural resources

CHART 6.2: **Sketch Map**
Location of Village Sagarpur, Faridabad, Haryana, India

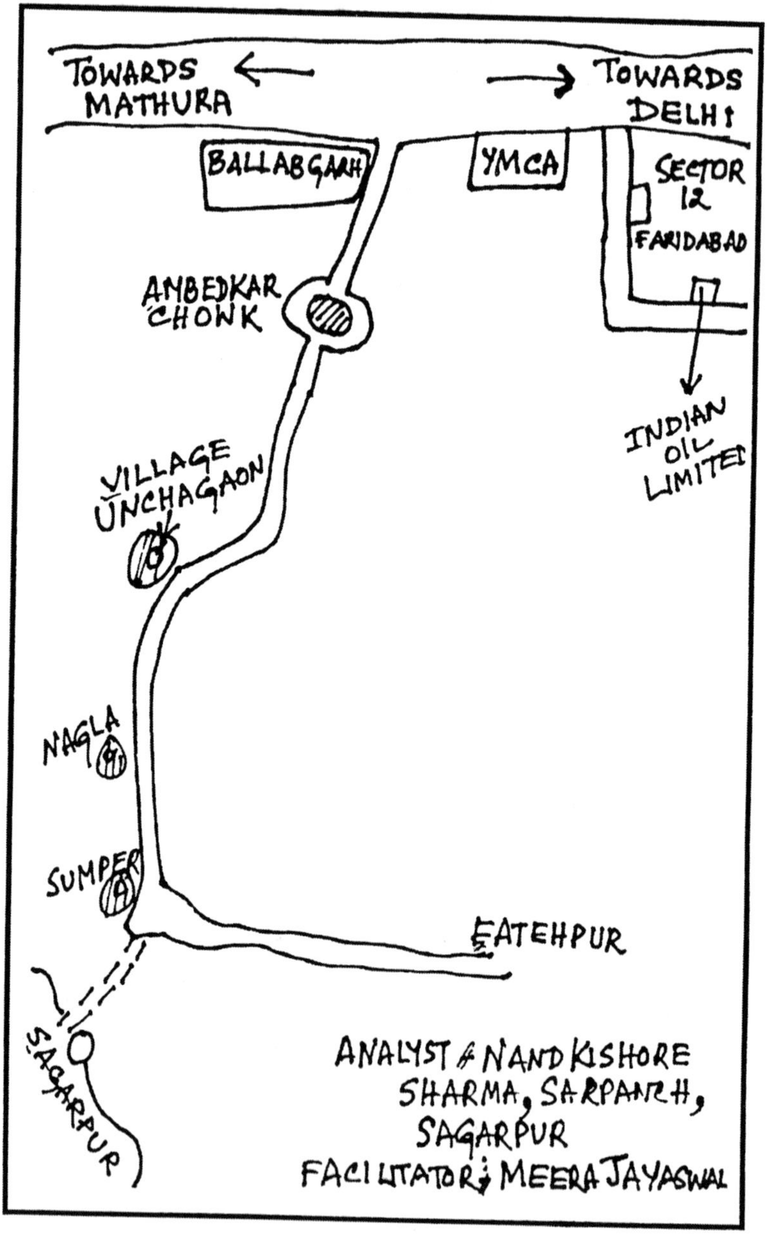

CHART 6.3: Resource Map

Village Bhagwanpur Jullon, Dehradun, India

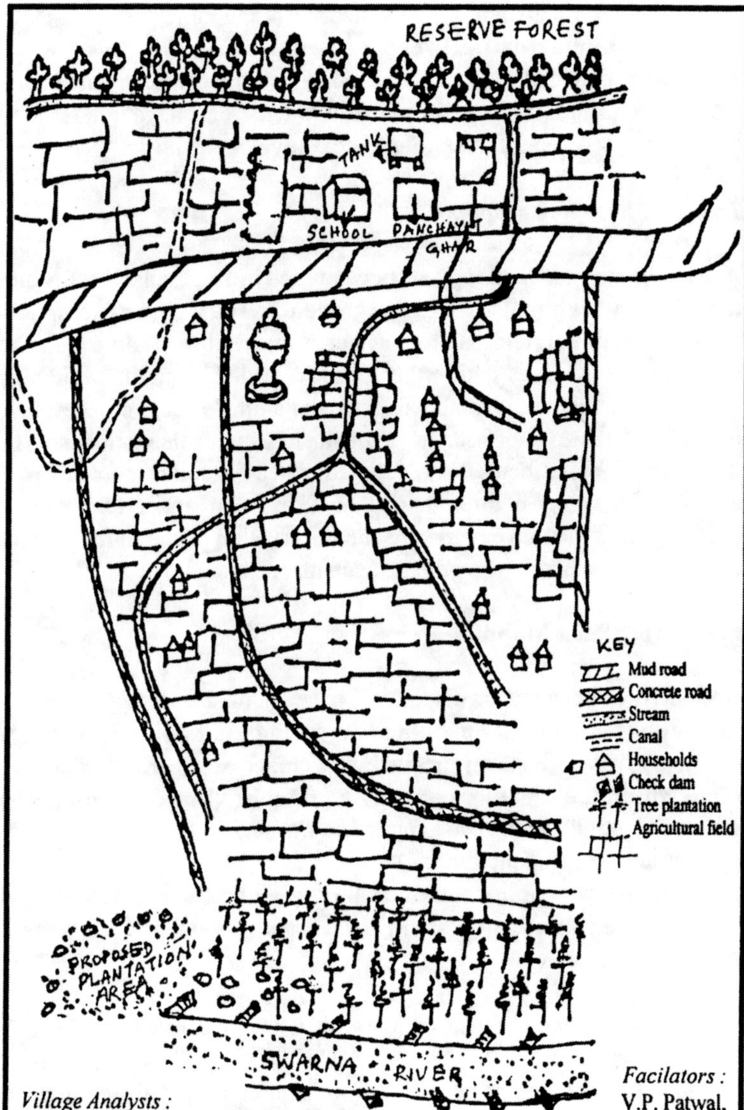

Village Analysts :
Gajendra Singh, Anil Kumaqr,
Kumari Cheti, Kasturi Devi,
Kumari Rekha, Bhagwati Dutt Saklani

Facilators :
V.P. Patwal,
B.S. Kahti,
V.P. Jakhmola
Date 25-1-1995

of a locality, like fields, water source, trees, forests, ponds, wells, rivers, canals, dams, etc. It shows the resource base of a locality and helps to assess the locality in terms of resources. Chart 6.3 is a resource map of village Bhagwanpur Jullon near Dehradun in Uttar Pradesh. In the resource map natural resources in terms of reserve forest, agricultural fields, plantation under social forestry, canal, stream, check dam, river, proposed place for plantation, tank, panchayat ghar, metal road, approach road, households, etc., have been shown.

Thematic Resource Mapping

A resource map can have topical concentration in a particular locality and thematically highlight a particular group of resources, for example,.a forest, agricultural fields, a protected area for wildlife. Chart 6.4 shows the natural resources inside the Kaimur wildlife sanctuary such as different tree species, animal dens, kinds of animals, areas of forest fire, location of trees, water sources, paths inside, etc. A thematic resource map is much more focused and detailed than a general resource map. It also shows the range of information which key informant/performant has. It also reflects the rich experience and observation power of those local community members who prepare such maps.

6.4 Forest/Park Mapping

In Chart 6.4, the outsiders discovered a wealth of knowledge within the indigenous community members regarding their adjacent wildlife sanctuary, which the latter mapped with great ease. Such mapping was done within the sanctuary area by a group of villagers, which was followed by walks with them to parts of the sanctuary to identify different species and describe their uses.

The local people knew the sanctuary and lived around it and interacted with it on a daily basis. They mapped (Chart 6.4) and discussed the following:

- Those parts of the sanctuary, which were degraded and which were not;
- The degrees of degradation of sanctuary in different areas;
- Kinds of land-use in the sanctuary;
- Habitat of the wild animals live, kinds of habitat and the rationale;

CHART 6.4: **Sanctuary Map**

Kaimur Wildlife Sanctuary, Mirzapur, Uttar Pradesh, India

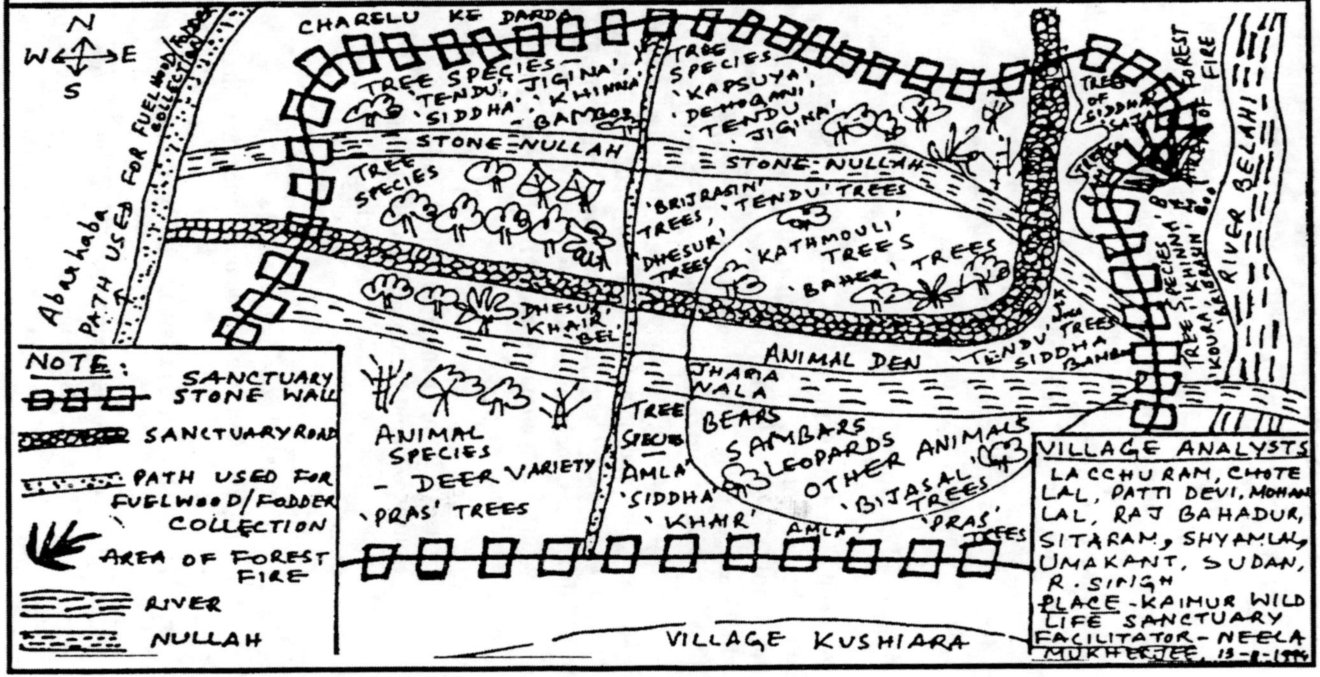

- The variety of existing tree species, their locations in the sanctuary and their location-specific density;
- The link roads in the sanctuary;
- The footpaths in the sanctuary used by the villagers for collecting fuel wood and fodder;
- Places of common occurrence of forest fire and the accompanying reasons;
- Water sources;
- Seasonal variations of flora and fauna;
- Usage of trees and plants;
- Myths and beliefs concerning the sanctuary; and
- Drought and forest food.

6.5 Social Mapping

A social map depicts the social aspects of a locality, for example, households, their social categories, literate households, illiterate households, women-headed households, schools, roads, hospitals, clinics, etc. A social map shows the social profile of a locality and provides insights into the social aspects and social life. It gives us an overview of the socio-economic status of the households in terms of advantaged and disadvantaged households, livelihood, livestock whether member of self-help group, levels of literacy, level of health, status of roads, disabilities, social infrastructure, etc.

In Chart 6.5, a social map of village Krishna Rakshit Chak highlights the following:

- Houses with mud/concrete walls and tin roofs;
- Houses with mud walls and thatched roofs;
- Houses made of bricks and concrete;
- Canal;
- Pond;
- Disadvantaged households –no. 24
- Those who have constructed huts under the Indira Awas Yojna – no. 4;
- Those households undergone family planning measures – no. 24;
- Those households having leprosy patients – no. 3;
- Those households having tuberculosis patients – no. 4;
- Those households which are literate – no. 6;

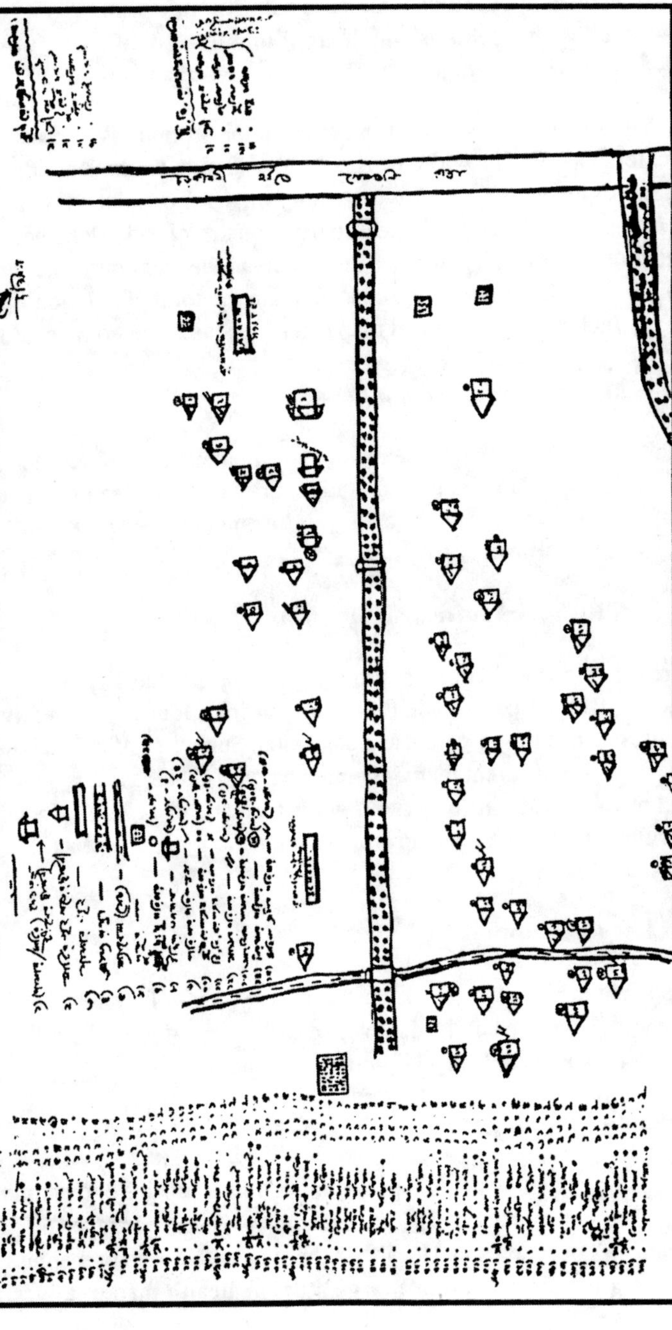

CHART 6.5: Social-cum-Census Map
Village Krishna Rakshit Chak, Midnapore, West Bengal, India

— Those households which are semi-literate – no. 41;
— Those households which are illiterate – no. 20;
— Those households which are women-headed – no. 6.

The social map as in Chart 6.5 has summary numbers for the social indicators and also provides census of households on the left side. All households are numbered so as to identify them for population statistics. The names of the households are also listed on the left side along with the number of males and females and their total number per household. From the listing on the left side one can calculate the total population of the village. Such a thematic social map can be a census map of a locality.

6.5.1 Thematic Social Mapping

Social mapping can also be thematic and can focus on different themes such as infrastructure facility, sanitation, drinking water sources, health facility, etc. For example, the status of infrastructure is an important part of the social profile of any facility.

6.6 Facility/Social Infrastructure Mapping

Chart 6.6 is a thematic map showing the health facility in village Dhakrani, Block Vikas Nagar, Dehradun. It shows four clinics of private doctors, one health sub-centre and a hospital. Such thematic social maps are focused on different themes connected with social aspects. General social maps provide an "overview" while thematic ones help to focus on particular topics. Literacy map is also a thematic social map focusing on the topic of literacy.

6.7 Literacy Mapping

The social map in Chart 6.5 also includes mapping of literacy where the households have been divided into three categories—literate households, semi-literate households and illiterate households.

6.8 Health Mapping

Participatory mapping helps in projecting different aspects of community health. The state of health in a local community is best portrayed through mapping of households in a locality either in a single map or mapping in parts for a locality covering a large area. A health map of a locality

CHART 6.6: **Health Facility Map**
Village Dhakrani, Vikas Nagar, Uttar Pradesh, India

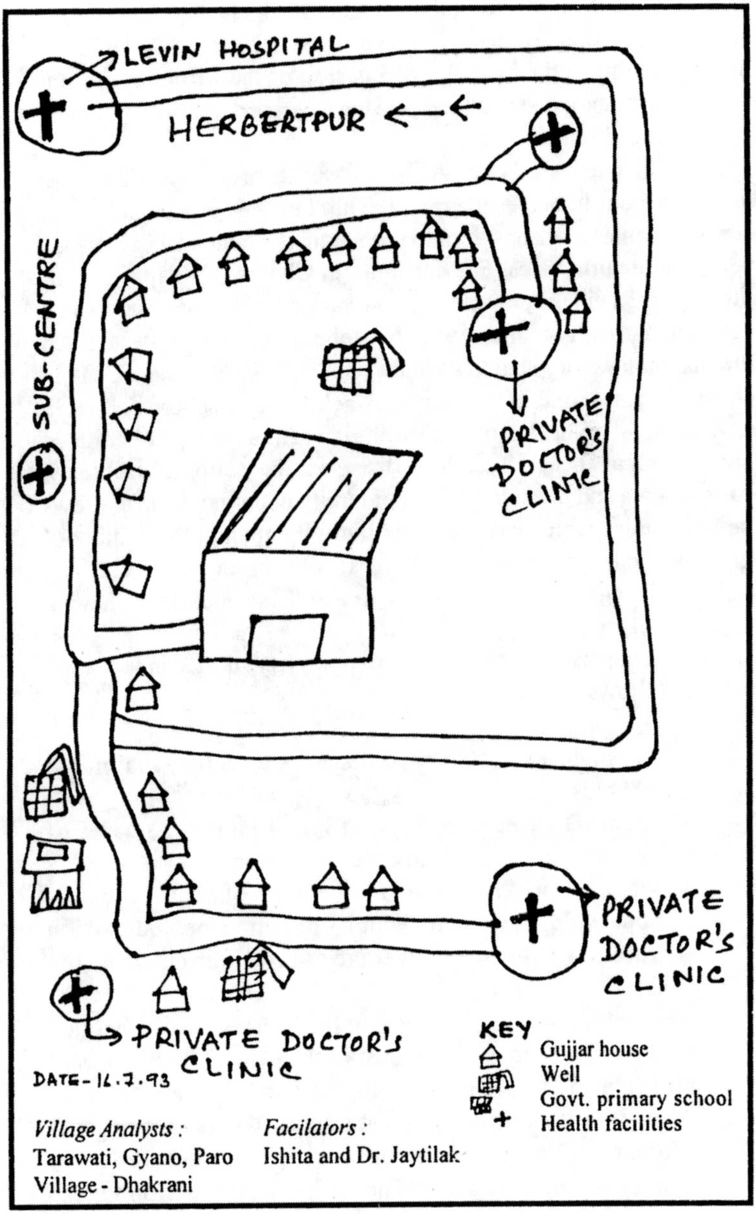

provides broad indications of the health status of that locality apart from indicating individual health status. It can illustrate the major illness affecting the locality, the age groups afflicted by such an illness, the frequency of such an illness and other details. Such maps can show a broad range of variables relating to health at a particular point of time. They can also form the basis for discussion of the nature of present illness, the symptoms, the treatment, the local perspectives on such illness and other related issues.

A health map inclusive of the social aspects of households such as poor or non-poor indicates the relationship between health and social issues. It becomes a "visual" tool to probe into the relationship between poverty and health status. For example, in Chart 6.7 the mapping of health status of a village projected on its social aspects clearly shows how ill health and poverty in many poor households go hand in hand. Such health mapping was applied to a village named Krishna Rakshit Chak in gram panchayat Arjuni in Kharagpur Block I of Midnapore district in West Bengal. The health map shows different aspects of health of villagers such as those affected by diseases like polio, tuberculosis, leprosy, asthma and piles. In the area of family planning the map shows those households which have adopted family planning, the number of pregnant women, lactating mothers and cases of abortion. The health map also shows old age as an aspect of health and those households having aged people in them.

Some of the features of village households as indicated in the health map are as follows:

— It gives a brief summary of diseases affecting individual households.
— There are 3 cases of piles, 4 cases of leprosy, 3 cases of tuberculosis of which one case was cured.
— 10 women were "lactating" mothers out of a total of 68.
— 22 households had adopted family planning methods, which was around 45 per cent coverage of total households in the village.
— The health map also shows that of the 13 households identified by the village group as "poorest of the poor" 7 households or more than 50 per cent have adopted family planning.
— All the 4 cases of leprosy are to be found in the "poorest of poor" households. The limited earning capacity of persons affected by leprosy is well understood. The social stigma confronting the

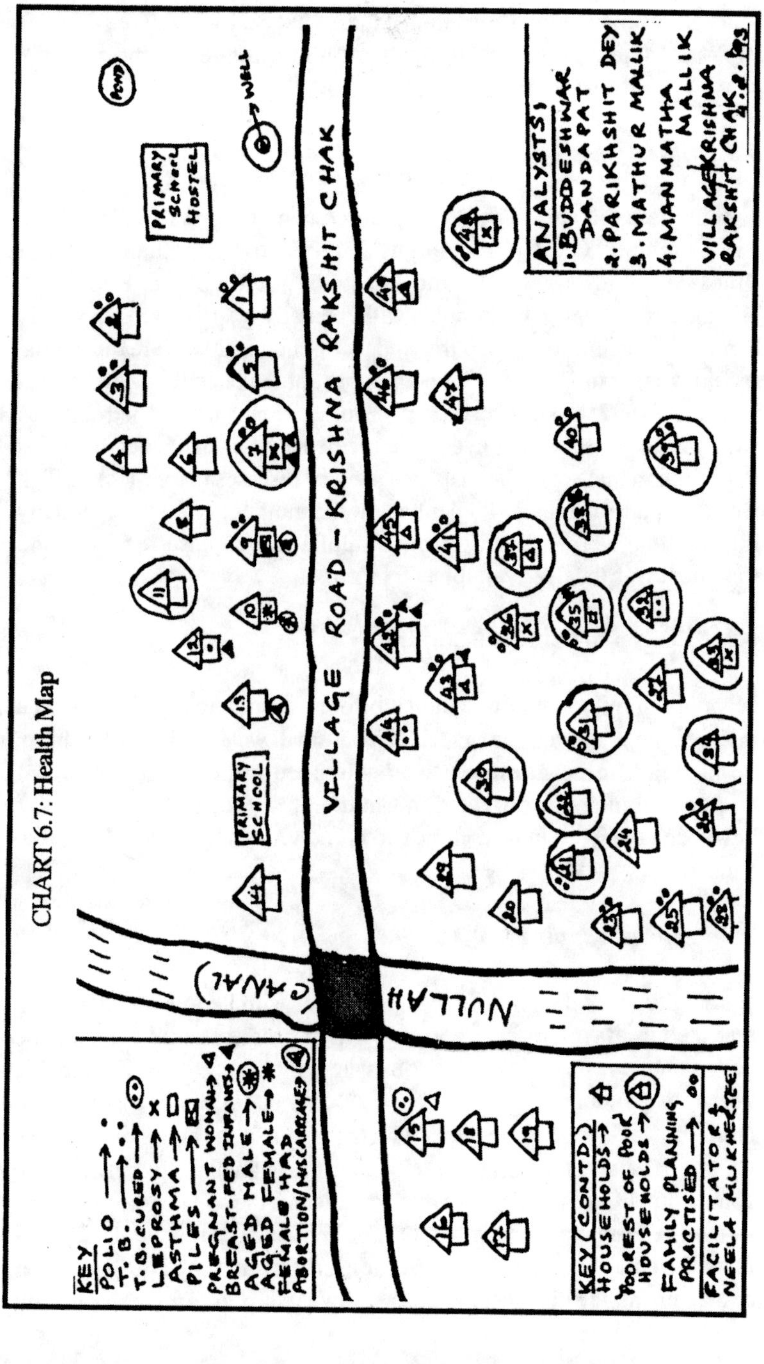

CHART 6.7: Health Map

leprosy-ridden households is also not easy to resolve.

— Incidence of TB and asthma and old age are more in the "poorest of the poor" households.

6.8.1 Illness Map of Women, Children and Livestock

A household map made by a group of women villagers of village Binh An, Commune Gia Ninh in Quang Ninh District, Vietnam, showed illness of children, women and livestock in the village. It showed, amongst others, those households with mentally retarded and physically handicapped children due to the impact of chemical warfare during the American war in Vietnam. Such an impact of the chemical warfare still persists in 1997 through the birth of deformed and handicapped children with yellow spots in their eyes. The incidence of birth of such babies is quite high in that area. The map also showed diseases in livestock, which were rampant and nearly 80 per cent of the mother pigs, covering many households, were suffering from an unknown disease for which no treatment was locally available.

6.9 Microenvironment Mapping

Mapping of microenvironment can be done in minute detail in which a microenvironment such as a patch of land, small water body, a small farm, homestead/home garden, etc., is focused upon. An example of microenvironment is provided in Chart 6.8, where small water bodies have been depicted in households in commune Phuong Do, Ha Giang, Vietnam.

6.9.1 Farm Mapping

Coming to individual households, a villager with her/his own farm can be asked to draw a map of her/his farm in order to show what she/he grows on the farm and the locations where they are grown. Chart 6.9 is a farm map of a farmer in a village in Botswana. It shows the different crops grown on the field together with the layout of the house on the farm. Chart 6.10 shows the farm profile of a farmer in a village in India, which apart from different crops grown also indicates the soil conditions of the farm. The farm map is an ideal tool for knowing the minute details of a farm, its soil conditions, the variations, different crops grown, water management, fertiliser use, yields and ownership. A farm map can help

CHART 6.8: **Microenvironment Map**
Commune Phuong Do, Ha Giang, Vietnam

CHART 6.9: **Farm Map**

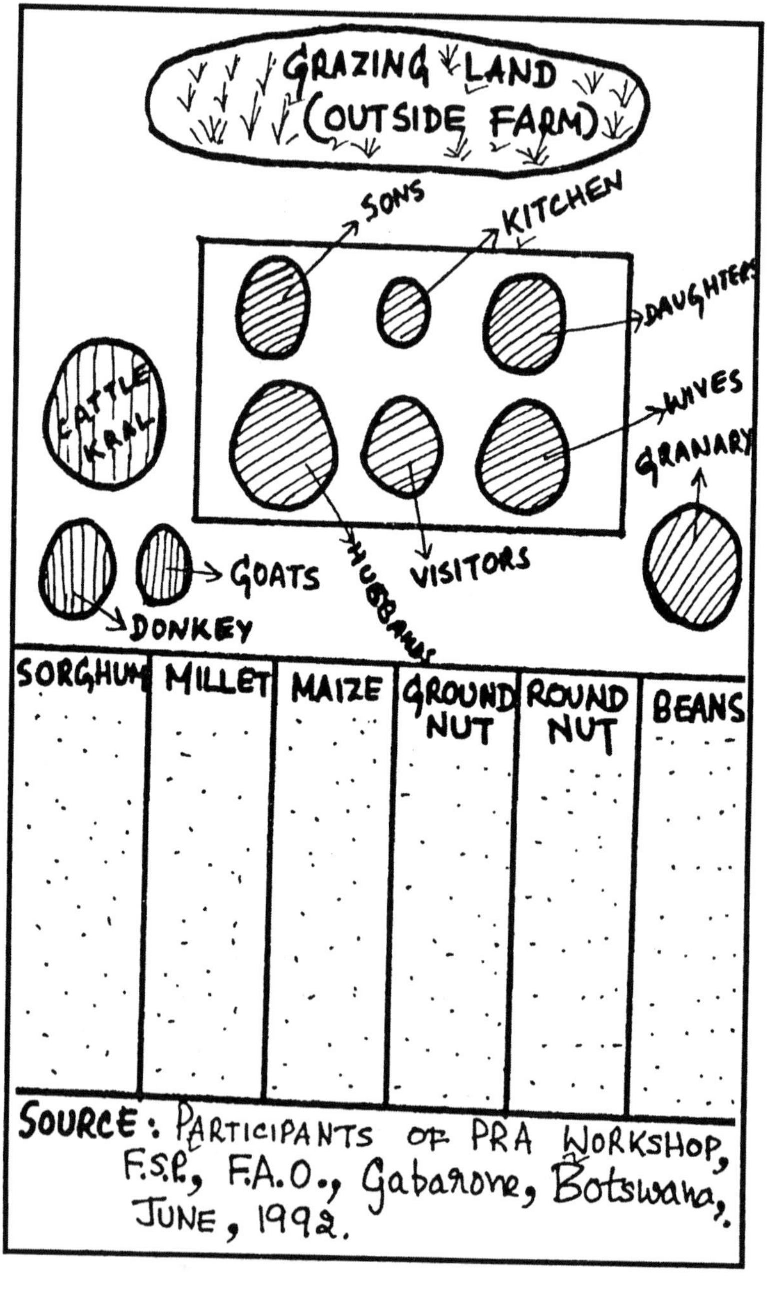

CHART 6.10: Farm Map

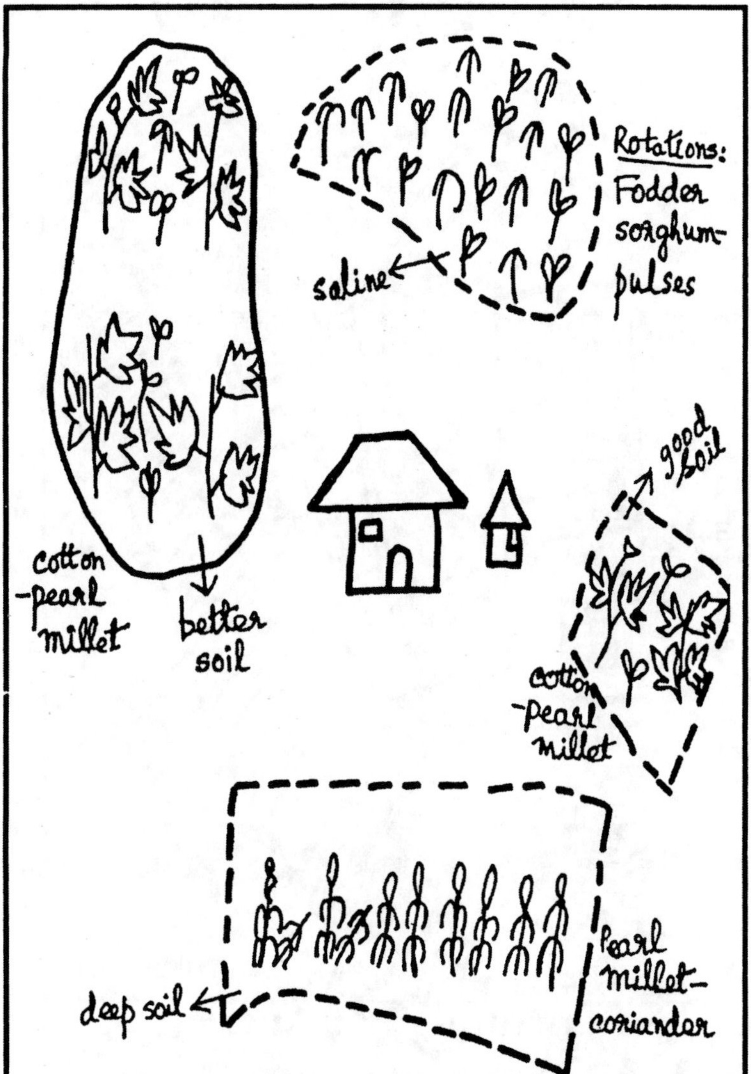

Source : Vijayraghavan R., Subramanian S.R., Pretty Jules N. & John K.C. (ed.) (1992), Participatory Rural Appraisal for Agricultural Research at Aruppukotal, Tamil Nadu, Department of Agricultural Economics, Centre for Agricultural and Rural Development Studies, Tamil Nadu, Agricultural University, Coimbatore & IIED, London.

CHART 6.11: Children's Vision Map
(Bangladesh)

in the discussion about livelihood patterns of resource-poor farmers and related aspects.

6.10 Childrens' Vision Mapping

Children are good at mapping the vision of their locality. They dream what their locality can look like in future and translate such a dream onto a map on ground/paper. On asking what their locality should look like in future years, children of a village in Bangladesh showed it through a map as in Chart 6.11. They mapped electric poles indicating electrification of their area, a gate at the level crossing near the railway track, a big mosque, two hand-pumps for drinking water, big trees in and around the locality and toilets.

6.11 Mapping—Past, Present and Future

This method helps in constructing comparative pictures of a locality over time. It helps in appreciating the past and present status of living and future dreams/hopes/fears/vision. it helps in comparing pictures of three periods in assessing them and often chalking out ways of improving conditions of the living. Such maps can depict changes in a wide variety of items/aspects in a locality over a broad spectrum of time. There are three maps/pictures drawn showing changes in resources, use of resources, changes in livelihood and levels of living, changes in infrastructure, men/women's workload, etc.

While mapping—past, present and future, a rural women group impoverished by urban expansion stated that they were losing their wealth like land, house and livestock due to rapid industrialisation and urbanisation. The women group doing agriculture in Chandawali village of Faridabad, Haryana felt powerless against the rapid pace of industrialisation. They emphasised that the social costs of urbanisation and industrialisation outweigh the benefits and visually illustrated their thoughts about the bleak future for themselves and their children. They drew three pictures (Charts 6.12, 6.13 and 6.14) to illustrate how their village Chandawali was 40 years back, how it is now and how it will look like after 40 years.

Chart 6.12 shows that 40 years back the local residents owned land, bullocks to plough, good crops, trees, water, well, school for children and their skills in artisanship. Today, as illustrated in Chart 6.13, the residents possess little or no land, their agricultural land being gradually taken up

CHART 6.12: **Mapping—Past, Present and Future**
Village Chandawali, Faridabad, Haryana, India

CHART 6.13: **Map—Present**

CHART 6.14: **Map—Future**

for industrial units, like cement factories, brick kilns, etc. The little agriculture that they do has become external input-oriented with tractors, pesticides and fertilisers. Those with little or no land work as labourers in nearby factories while outsiders/the local urban department of the government keeps acquiring land at low prices for construction of houses. After 40 years, as shown in Chart 6.14, the women expect to see multi-storey flats/buildings in the locality built by the urban department of the government and sold to outsiders. The original residents would lose all their land, their fields and their livestock and would be forced to work as household maids in the flats of those multi-storey buildings. There will be a nice big park and supermarkets to cater to the "well-to-do" residents living in the high-rise flats. But the erstwhile villagers would have nothing to look forward to. They and their children will lose their identity and will have to struggle hard for survival. They will live in nearby slums and work as maids/labourers in the multi-storey flats.

6.12 Mapping—"Before" and "After"

This is another method for portraying changes in a locality following an event/development intervention/natural disaster, etc. which trigger other changes in that locality. The time period between "before" and "after" depends on the situation/objective at hand. It is a useful method to capture changes, if any, whether positive or negative. In Charts 6.15 and 6.16 village Bohrakul of Bhimtal in Uttar Pradesh, has been sketched in two maps depicting the situation "before" and "after" the project activities. This was made in order to capture the changes brought about through activities initiated by the project.

In the "before" situation in village Bohrakul, as shown in Map 6.15, one can see the wild bushes, severe soil erosion, few trees, few fruit trees, hill erosion, bank erosion, degraded forests, etc. Whereas, Map 6.16 provides the "after" project scenario where the progress made in the village has been mapped. Such progress made through project-initiated activities is shown through a rise in the number of orchards; rise in the number of fruit trees; rise in the area sowing good quality seeds and crops; rise in the area under plantation; control in the level of soil erosion; control over the growth of wild bushes, etc.

6.13 Status Mapping

This method shows the present status of an area in terms of selected

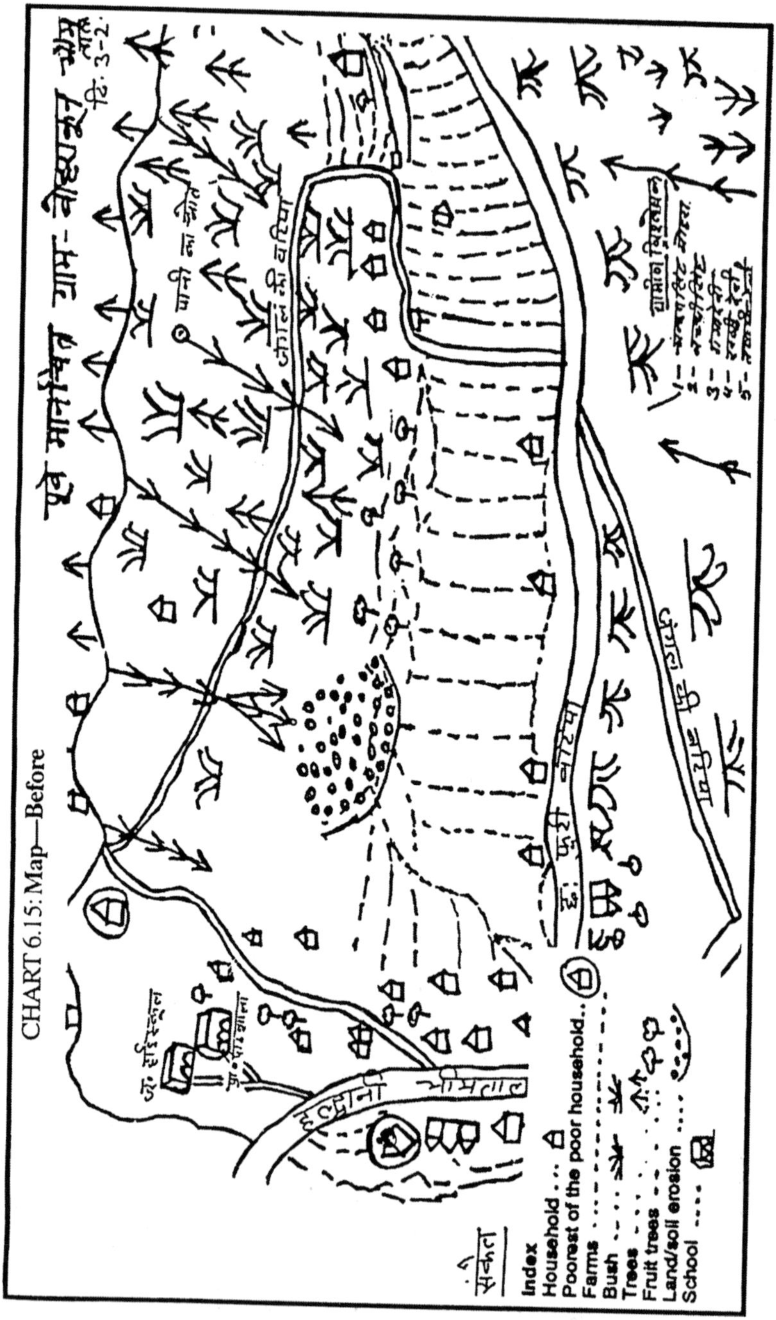

CHART 6.15: Map—Before

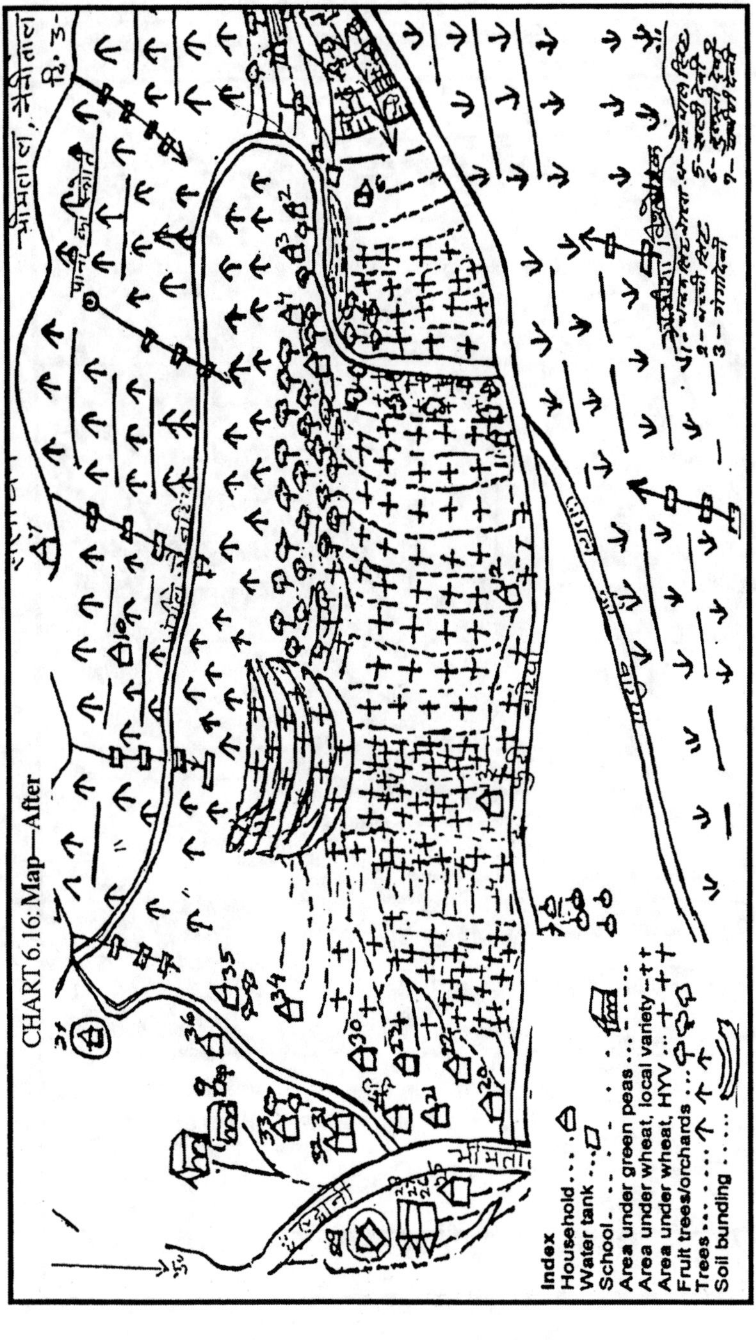

CHART 6.16: Map—After

CHART 6.17: **Status Map**

Status of Pastureland Development (2 Hectares)

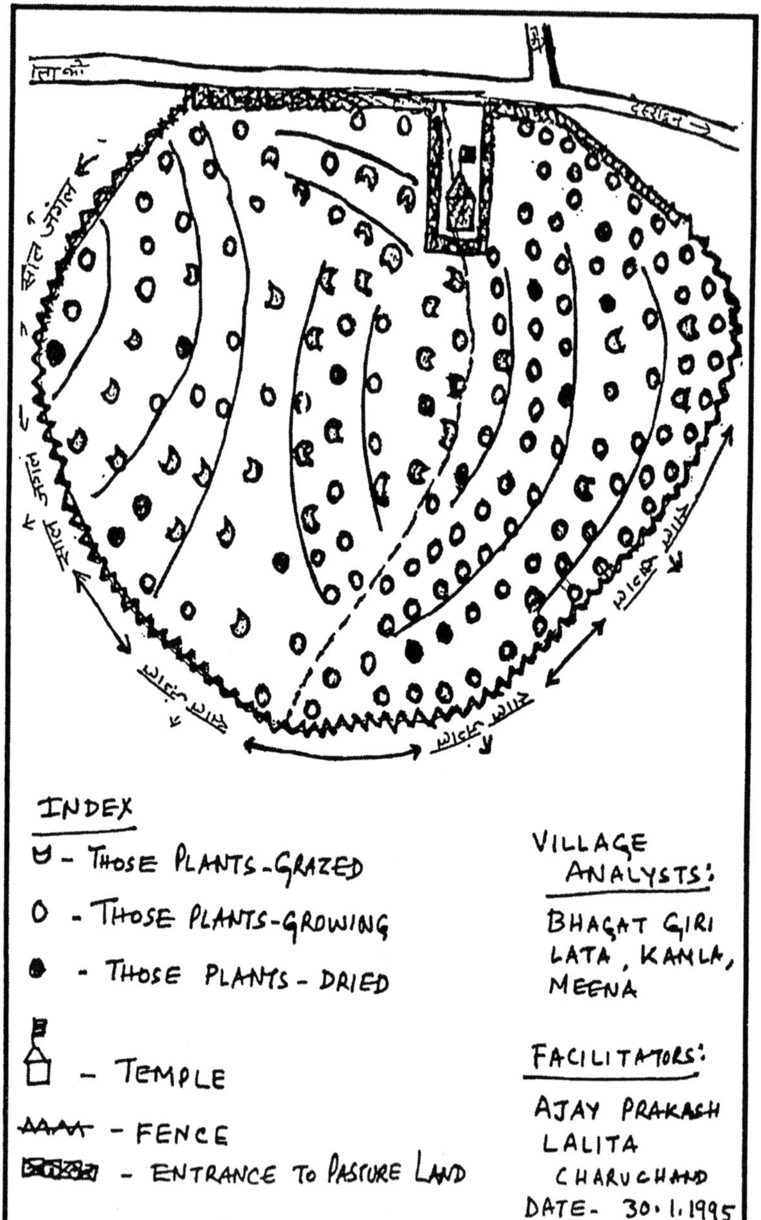

activities undertaken for development purposes. In Chart 6.17, the development status of a pastureland by a village group is shown. The village group planted different fodder trees and the area was fenced by fixing logs of dried wood and branches. The Chart shows that the local state forest surrounds the pastureland on three sides. Around 400 species were planted by the group in the pastureland. The status map in Chart 6.16 indicates what species were planted, how many still survive, how many dried up, how many were grazed by livestock, etc.

6.14 Mobility Mapping

This shows the pattern of spatial mobility for different sections of a community with respect to different activities. Patterns of mobility of the local people tend to emerge from mobility maps. Mobility maps of a locality, based on socio-economic aspects, gender, age groups and other criteria, indicate the nature of work, physical mobility and linkages with the outside world, within the locality and with other localities in a village. It shows the degree of mobility of rural groups and communities and the importance of different areas in terms of different activities and inter-linkages. It can also indicate location-specific activity profile.

Chart 6.18 depicts a mobility map of women from the Qarara area in the Gaza Strip. The map shows that the women move from their locality to other areas on account of different reasons such as work, health, visiting, shopping and education. The most important reason for mobility is work for which women travel from Qarara to at least four places, namely, Gaza city, Noseirat Camp, Derel Belah, Khan Yunis and Rafah. Women travel to Egypt exclusively for education. The map also shows inter-linkages between Qarara and Gaza city and Qarara and Khan Yunis whose links are the strongest in terms of mobility of women. The distance, however, between Qarara and Gaza city is far greater than that between Qarara and Khan Yunis.

6.15 Livelihood Mapping

Livelihood mapping is a kind of social mapping illustrating the different livelihoods pursued in a locality. It can be an exhaustive mapping of livelihoods of all households in a locality or it can be mapping of a group of households pursuing similar livelihoods. A livelihood map is useful for discussing livelihood-related issues. Livelihood mapping becomes meaningful when mapped together with the asset status of households,

CHART 6.18: **Mobility Map**

Mobility Map of Women in Qarara, Gaza

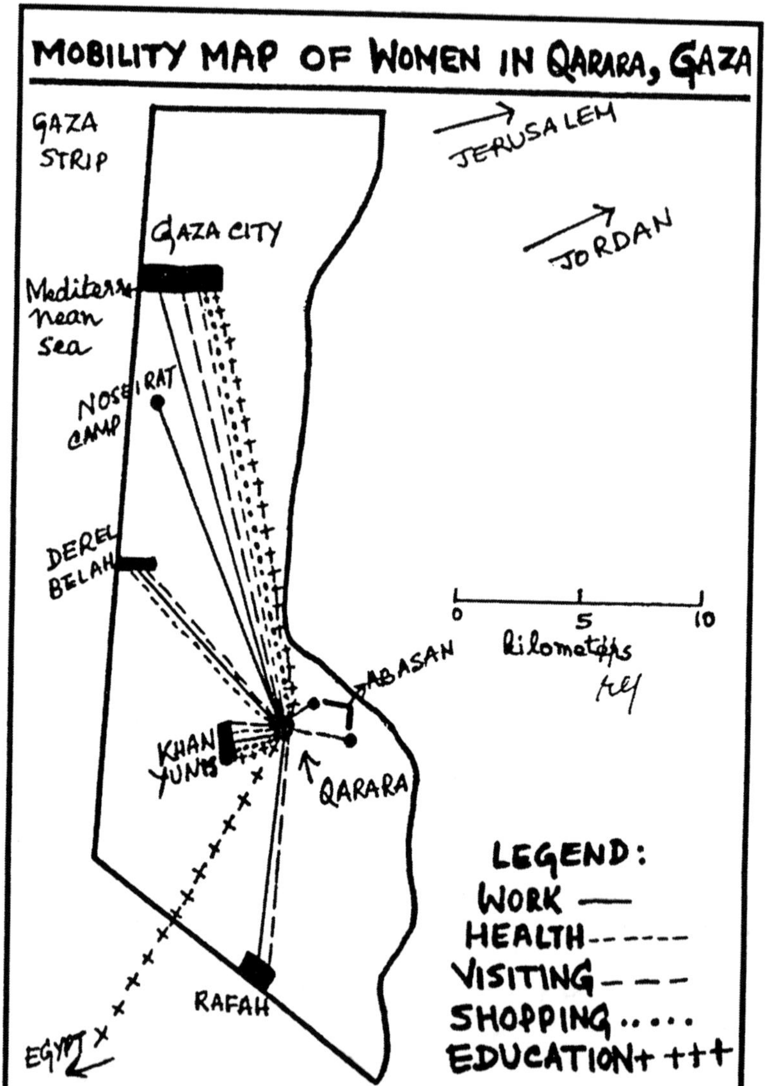

Source : Theis Joachim and Grady Heather, M., (1991), Participatory Rapid Appraisal for Community Development, A Training Manual, based on Experience in the Middle East and North Africa, IIED and Save the Children Federation, London.

access to resources, health, wealth, poverty and other social aspects.

6.16 SHG Household Mapping

In localities where self-help groups (SHG) exist a social map can indicate members of SHG amongst other households and also map their status at different points of time. Such a map can help in assessing the impacts of self-help group activities on the households, which are members as compared to others which are not members of SHG. Again, mapping of different social variables for different households will help in analysis of difference between SHG member households and other households.

6.17 Livestock Mapping

Possession of livestock by different households can be mapped for different reasons such as assessing livestock wealth in a locality or for doing local livestock planning or for ascertaining diseases of livestock, etc.

6.18 Model Building

Models are an advancement over mapping and represent three-dimensional figures, and therefore, adding height differences in the landscape. They can be made with local materials. Models are useful for land-use planning and watershed planning, for which the problems, treatment and opportunities can be shown on the model itself. A model or a map can also be historical (representing past shape or form), current or futuristic (showing future shape of a village or area) (Mascarenhas and Kumar:1991).

6.19 Participatory Risk Mapping

Smith *et al.* (2000) have applied participatory risk mapping (PRM) for mapping risks faced by East African pastoralists. They have defined "risk" as uncertain consequences and exposure to potentially unfavourable circumstances, or the possibility of incurring non-trivial loss. Risk is undesirable and may vary across individuals living in similar environments. Risk mapping technique is a two-stage system of ordinal rankings, wherein respondents first identify risks and then they rank such risks. Smith *et al.* (2000) applied an open-ended questionnaire approach to the first stage so that informants could list as many or as few risks. The informants were encouraged to discuss amongst themselves and decide whatever they thought were the major risks faced by their community. The second stage was asking informants to rank in order the risks they identified by assigning a value of one (1) to the risk identified as most severe, two (2) to the risk identified as second most severe and so on. After ranking of risks, informants were asked to detail each in turn making sure they discuss how they used to solve each of these or how they would like to solve them.

The method is quick, low-cost, letting informants speak for themselves. Risk maps can bring to the surface important issues underemphasized or overlooked by outsiders. However, inter-connected risks can make categorization of responses somewhat arbitrary. Again, one primary shortcoming of participatory risk mapping is that it is a static representation and can capture little seasonality. The value of participatory risk mapping lies in its ability to identify quickly what worries and where for future research and assistance. It helps in designing of long-term questionnaire surveys in order to identify which issues we should be concentrating on. The method's value to outsiders goes up as one becomes more aware of spatial and temporal variations in perceptions (Smith *et al.* 2000).

6.20 Body Mapping

Often an outline of a human body as in Chart 6.19 is mapped for health-related discussions. Sometimes human organs are also shown in that outline. During group discussions such body mapping helps in highlighting different parts of the human body which are causing problems. It can be an effective "visual" medium for carrying on conversations on health/body-related issues like skin disease/stomach-related problems/others. The common health problems can be listed and ways can be discussed for handling them.

6.20.1 Anonymous Body Spotting

Another method close to body mapping is anonymous body spotting. The method helps in focusing on disease/illness, which is private in nature and would not be revealed unless privacy is maintained and often only private discussion is possible. One application of this method is described below. One way is to draw the outline of human body on a big Chart and hang it in a separate room where different individuals can go in private and place coloured stickers on any part of the body to

CHART 6.19: **Body Map**

Village Khandavali, Faridabad, Haryana, India

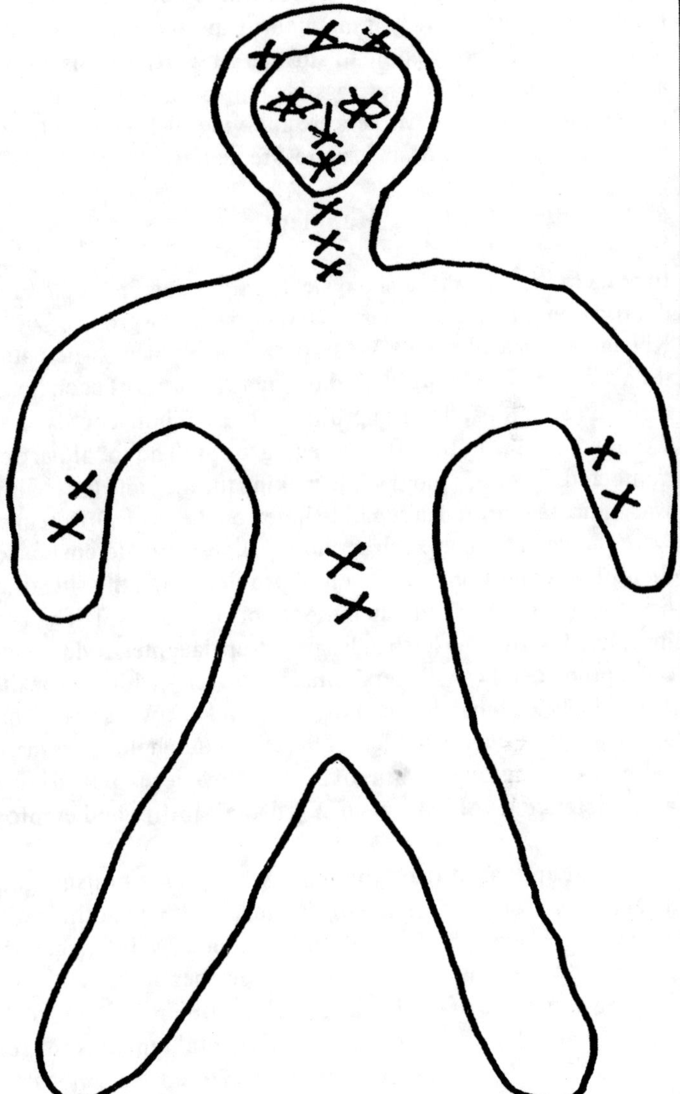

Village Khandavali, Faridabad, Haryana, India

highlight those parts in which they have a problem. The whole process is anonymous but there will emerge broad results as shown by the stickers, which can then be followed by means of group discussions for remedial action concerning preventive, promotive and curative health. In this way privacy is maintained and at the same time different problems of the body come to surface on which discussions follow about their cause, effect and possible remedies. Some medical doctors and community health workers are applying such a method to identify diseases of private parts and suggest remedies.

6.21 Mental Well-being Mapping

In order to show mental and physical health status and socio-economic deprivation, a map as in Chart 6.20 was made by a group of villagers in Kalsigeriya in Midnapore, West Bengal where men participated more than women. The map showed the health status of each household reflecting health and social problems of poor households relating to women belonging to different age groups. The local participants numbered each household while making the map and the health status was indicated through a separate index on the map. Different aspects were shown in the map such as chronic illness in different households, disabilities and sources of mental problems. On the side of mental health, the villagers indicated those households, which had cases of insanity, desertion by husbands, grown-up daughters, widowhood and other problems. The villagers combined poverty with their health map. They identified those households, which did not own any land or assets and hence were deprived. Most of the other households were marginally better than this group in terms of owning tiny pieces of land but were at a subsistence level in terms of food availability and employment opportunities.

As it appeared from the map, while some households were affected by problems related to physical health, the others were in a state of excessive stress in the absence of mental well-being. Economic problems were acute for some households beginning with those not owning any piece of land, while social problems related to women caused considerable difficulties and mental tensions for selected households. The village map as in Chart 6.20 showed, amongst others, those locally identified problems related to gender position and poverty and those emanating from the social position of women who were under stress and strain. The major problem categories and the numbers

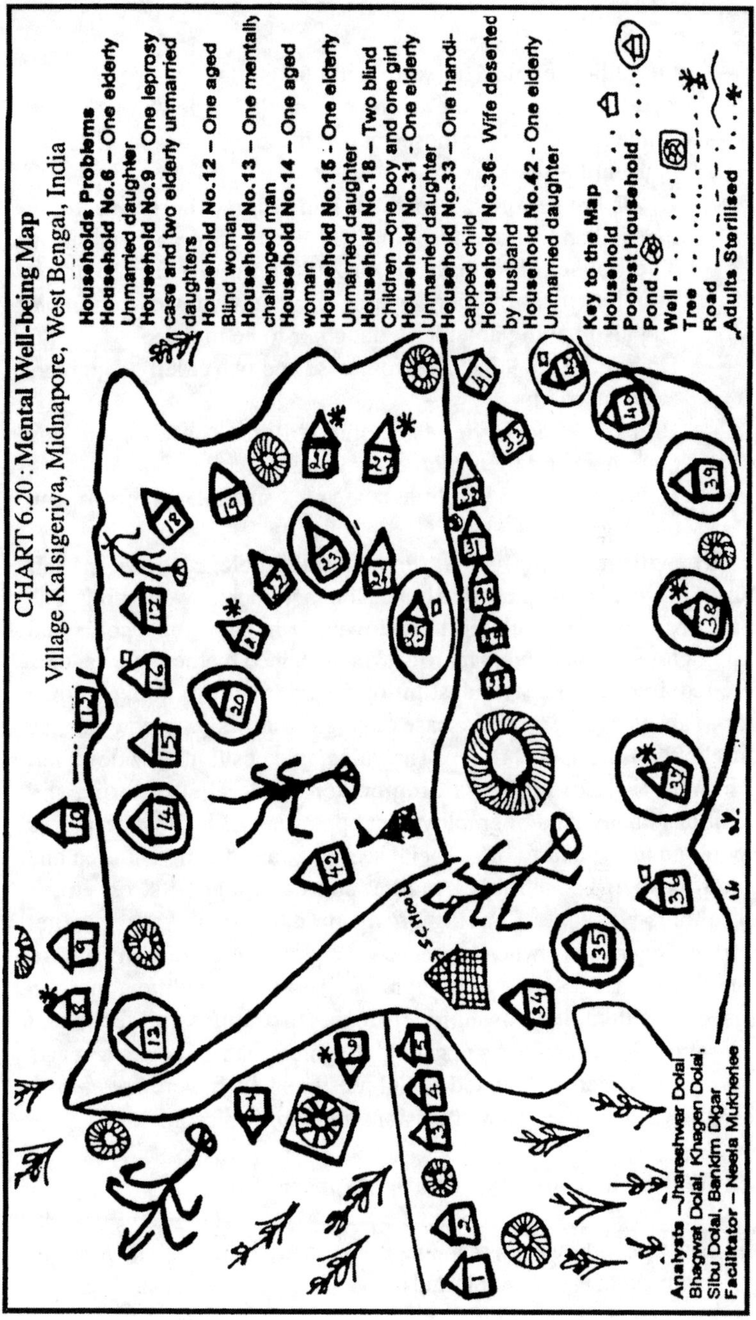

CHART 6.20 : Mental Well-being Map
Village Kalsigeriya, Midnapore, West Bengal, India

are indicated below:

— Of 42 households, 11 were without any land;
— Four households were widowed female-headed households;
— Three households of those not owning any land were widowed households;
— Of 42 households, 5 of them had elderly daughters to be married and were under considerable stress on account of it;
— The household numbering 42nd had multi-dimensional disability in terms of not owning any land, widowed household and also having an elderly daughter to be married;
— Household no. 9 had a leprosy case and two elderly daughters to be married;
— Household no.18 had two blind children (one son and one daughter) and their mother had died recently;
— Household no.35 had little land and 4 small daughters to rear.

The villagers described different social problems shown in their map, which made for a negative impact on their mental well-being. The major problems were related to widowhood in poor households and getting grown-up daughters married. As explained by the widows, they were required to cope with destitution and were mostly looked down upon. This was more so in the case of single widows or widow-headed households with small children. The vulnerable position of widows left them with little or no bargaining power to seek better terms and conditions in any kind of employment opportunity. On most occasions they found it difficult to have social security, raise young children and look after their households. Another source of mental stress in the households was that of having grown-up daughters, waiting to get married. In a society where parents are deemed to be responsible for arranging marriages for their daughters, inability to get them married caused considerable household tensions, frustrations and feeling of deprivation. Social problems of getting daughters married at the right age, dowry, wife-desertion created social tensions which were not easy to tackle, often leading to mental tensions and family discord.

6.22 Well-being/Poverty/Wealth Mapping

Well-being/poverty/wealth mapping involves mapping of all households in a locality by the local people and identifying the different categories of households—rich, poor, poorest, etc.—on the basis of locally generated criteria. The method of well-being/poverty/wealth mapping of village households and their ranking help in facilitating local communities to identify different socio-economic strata of households, rank them from the "top" or "bottom" for identifying different categories/groups of households. In this process the local communities also explain the criteria of such ranking of different households.

The method of poverty mapping was applied to some villages in Midnapore district of West Bengal. The normal process was to sit with village groups near a village school or a tea-stall or some other common location and enable the village groups to apply the mapping method for identifying the different socio-economic groups and rank them accordingly. To start with, the villagers mapped the entire village. Then they identified the bottommost poverty groups, the "poorest of the poor" households, in the village by marking the households with different colours. They also described the characteristics and the factors influencing the poorest of the poor households. After identifying the poorest of the poor group the villagers identified the next group of poor households, which had a higher rank than that of the former. They distinguished between different groups of households ranking them from the bottom and also enumerating their characteristics until all households in the village were identified.

6.22.1 Village Berapal

Village Berapal lies in the Sadar Block of Midnapore District, West Bengal. The village consists mostly of small and marginal cultivators and landless labourers. A village map (see Chart 6.21) consisting of households, roads, water sources and fields was drawn by a group of villagers amongst a large number of villagers who had gathered at a common meeting place in the village. On the basis of the village map the villagers attempted to rank the households. They marked the households, which were at the lowest strata of poverty according to their perceptions. Such households marked by the villagers were headed by widows singly who eked out livelihoods with practically no assets, no regular source of income and did not have enough to eat throughout the year. This was accentuated by the environmental degradation in terms of dwindling forest and trees in the area concerned. Others in this group included agricultural labourers neither having any land, nor any regular source of income or food. Identification of the "poorest of the poor" households

CHART 6.21: **Poverty Map**
Village Berapal, Midnapore, West Bengal, India

was followed by the villagers marking the group of households above the extreme poor group. They distinguished between the extreme poor group and the group above it on the basis of ownership of land. The households included in the higher group had some land holdings but were constrained in the presence of a large number of dependants. Between the two groups of households with the same income the one having larger number of dependants was considered to be poorer by the villagers. This meant that the number of dependants was taken as an indicator of poverty. This also showed implicitly that the villagers had some notion of average income per head per household. The group of households next identified was described as having better production from land. They had more land and were better placed as far as the quality of life was concerned despite having a large family size. The production from the land helped them in meeting their consumption requirements within the households as well as procuring income through selling a part of their produce.

6.22.2 Village Kalsigeriya

Village Kalsigeriya situated in Kharagpur Block I in Midnapore District, West Bengal, was a remote village and not easily accessible. This village grew one crop and was affected by floods every year. There were 42 households and all of them belonged to the scheduled caste category (those castes at the bottom of the Hindu caste hierarchy). On the basis of mapping of households (see Chart 6.22) the villagers distinguished between three different groups of poor households. The poorest group had no land, little food availability during the year, not many working hands and a large number of dependant family members, both young and old and not capable of productive work. Some from the group were single widows as head of households. They were deficit households with high food insecurity, which was accentuated by degradation of common property resources like forests and ponds from which they gathered food. The next poor group of households, which was, according to the villagers, slightly better off than the extreme group had little land—one or two acres. They had some working hands who contributed towards household income and after all efforts put together the households were just able to manage their consumption requirements. The next group of households was relatively "better off" with 4 acres of average land holdings of better quality. Some of their household members had jobs outside the village and they were much better off in terms of household

CHART 6.22: Poverty Map — Kalsigeriya

income, food availability and purchasing power.

6.22.3 Indigenous Criteria of Poverty

The villagers applied the mapping method for identifying different socio-economic groups of households on the basis of the characteristic features and causes of poverty prevailing in those households. Food availability during a year was a significant factor for the villagers in grouping/ranking of poor households. The size of landholdings and their productivity was another important consideration for the villagers for identifying higher groups but landholding alone was not enough, its productive capacity was equally important. The number of dependants was another consideration. The availability of food was the basic criterion and environmental degradation had accentuated the uncertainty of food availability from common property resources. The local groups explained that the common property resources were crucial to poor households. For many of them such resources formed the basis of their livelihood, for others it supplemented income, food and other requirements and also provided sustenance during difficult times. Environmental degradation had reduced the quality of life for the poor. The poor were in no position to fall back on the local resources in terms of availability of food, water, work, medicines, fuel wood and clean air especially during lean periods and in years of crop failure. The degradation of ponds, pastures, riverbeds, decline in the number of trees and shrubs, fall in the water quality and the erosion of local forest resources had adversely affected their sources of livelihood, cost of living, its standards and health. The small size of landholdings could not sustain them primarily because of the size and quality of land. Some landless households were allotted small landholdings by the State Government and had built their homesteads.

6.23 Well-being/Poverty/Wealth Grouping

Well-being/poverty/wealth grouping is a method of grouping of households on the basis of income, wealth and other local measures of well-being. Different criteria can be used for wealth grouping based on local people's perceptions. Wealth ranking is based on the presumption that the local people have the necessary knowledge to rank households, for example, they have knowledge of the kinds and position of household assets, other items and attributes of the households concerned.

This method involves identifying the socio-economic groups by the local people based on local criteria. In the villages of Berapal and Kalsigeriya, as said above, poverty mapping was followed by poverty grouping for identification of different socio-economic groups in the villages. This helps in understanding the socio-economic disparities within a locality according to the local people's criteria. An interesting aspect of poverty/wealth mapping is that points of distinction between households which outsiders' tend to overlook or miss can form an important basis for the local people while differentiating between the households concerned (Mukherjee:1992). An illustration of poverty grouping is given in Chart 6.23 as done by a village group in village Dhupaguchina in Bangladesh. The village group identified 3 socio-economic groups: "better off" households, "poor" households and "poorest" households and visually illustrated their asset positions and sources of livelihood.

6.24 Wealth Ranking—Grandin's Method

Grandin's (Grandin:1988) method of card-sorting is a method for wealth ranking where a list of households is prepared with each household having a separate number. The number of each household together with the name of the head of the household are written on separate pieces of paper which are then ranked by some key informants individually based on their criteria. The different criteria used in ranking by key informants emerges from their discussion on wealth classification which also helps in cross-checking of the list and the final wealth classes are computed on that basis. An example of wealth ranking is given in Chart 6.24 done by a village group in village Vohrakul in Bhimtal, Uttarakhand. The Chart shows the different socio-economic groups on the left side and wealth ranking of the households on the right side.

6.25 Social Matrix

Social matrix is another form of social grouping and ranking where each household has a card, which gets sorted by the local participants into different socio-economic groups based on local criteria. The household cards sorted into different groups can then be ranked within the various groups. The social matrix method not only provides different categories of households but also ranks of households within those categories. Generally such social matrix made on the ground helps in visual cross-checking and making changes as and when necessary.

CHART 6.23: **Poverty Groups**
Village Dhupaguchina, Bangladesh

Socio-Economic Group	Assets	No. of Households	Other Descriptions
Group 1 		O O O	Large land owner, many costly sarees (women's dress), gold ornaments, television, more income and power. eat good food three times a day, lesser number of family members (2 to 3) etc.
Group 2 		O O O O O O O O O O O O O O O O O O O	Owner of small land holdings, eat normal food two times a day, have two sarees (women's dress), 4-5 family members, occupation as rickshaw puller/ card puller.
Group 3 		O O O O O O O O O O O O O O O O O O O O O O	No ownership of land, live in other's land, eat only once a day, possess one saree, work as daily wage labour or maid.

Key: Group 1—Better-off households; Group 2—Poor households: Group 3—Poorest households; **Village Analysts:** Saira Khatun, Sakhna, Afroza Khatun, Shajeda Khatun, Kamala Sangma; **Facilatitor:** Syed Khabir Ahmed; **Date**—19-11-1997.

Chart 6.24: Wealth Ranking
Village Vohrakul, Bhimtal, India

Socio-Economic Groups of Households	Names of Head of Households with their Ranks within Groups
Group 1— Better of - 2 households	(1) Pratap Singh Bohra, (2) Ramesh Chandra Joshi
Group 2—Middle level - 4 households	(1) Bhairav Dutt (2) Manohar Pant, (3) Dungar Singh, (4) Kailash Pant
Group 3—Poor - 4 households	(1) Sodham Singh, (2) Taradutt, (3) Narayan Dutt, (4) Tilochan
Group 4—Very Poor - 20 households	(1) Ram Singh Bohra, (2) Khema Nand, (3) Gopal Singh, (4) Pan Singh, (5) Govind Singh, (6) Bishan Singh, (7) Lal Singh, (8) Rajendra Singh Kholia, (9) Navin Chand, (10) Gopal Singh Bohra, (11) Nandan Singh, (12) Narayan Dutt, (13) Ganga Dutt, (14) Chandan Singh, (15) Harish Chand, (16) Diwan Singh, (17) Narayan Singh, (18) Kishori Bhallav, (19) Mohan Chand, (20) Suresh Chand
Group 5—Poorest - 3 households	(1) Puran Singh, (2) Hukam Singh, (3) Navin Chand

Village Analysts: Gopal Singh, Paya Singh, Balwant Singh, Parbati Devi
Facilitator: Ajay Prakash, Date: 3-2-1995.

6.26 Social distance mapping

The method of social distance mapping is based on a comparison of a poor household with either an imaginary or an actual household, which is considered a "proper" household. Mapping or drawing a picture of a poor household under discussion would be a good starting point. This can be followed by inquiring about a "proper" household, which is reasonably out of poverty (generally it is not a fancy household — it exists either in the locality or in a nearby locality). Probing can be intensified on the basis of what are the existing conditions in a poor household, how it compares with a household considered proper in that locality or nearby locality and what are the forces explaining the difference and what can be done to bridge the existing gap. Often drawings/photos of two houses (see Chart 6.25) — one poor household's hut with thatched roof and another house in a better condition—help in facilitating the process of mapping of the two households and their comparison. This method was applied in some villages in Quang Binh Province in Vietnam during field work for problem-prioritisation and selected interventions at the household level.

Direct probing into wealth/poverty aspects of any household is avoided since it is often a sensitive topic. The above methods help in ranking of households without any discussion of the absolute level of wealth of the households concerned. Wealth ranking/grouping/mapping social distance helps in understanding socio-economic disparities amongst households and reveals local criteria for wealth/poverty classification. It helps in stratification of a sample according to wealth/poverty criteria for further study and policy-making. Wealth ranking can provide differential and perhaps better results when compared to the standard approach such as farm size analysis in rural areas where non-agriculture income has a major share in total household income (Reddy:1999). It also helps in examining survey data from local perspective (Scoones:1988).

Wealth ranking/grouping shows the patterns of wealth across households in a community as per the local people's perspective. However, such patterns may tell us little about the process of wealth creation, impoverishment and differentiation. Intra-household dynamics are also not fully reflected in such a method (Scoones:1992). This, however, can be overcome by extending wealth mapping to show intra-household differences in a historical perspective. It has been stated that the process of wealth ranking provides a wider information base, which makes the interpretation more complicated (Scoones:1999). The method

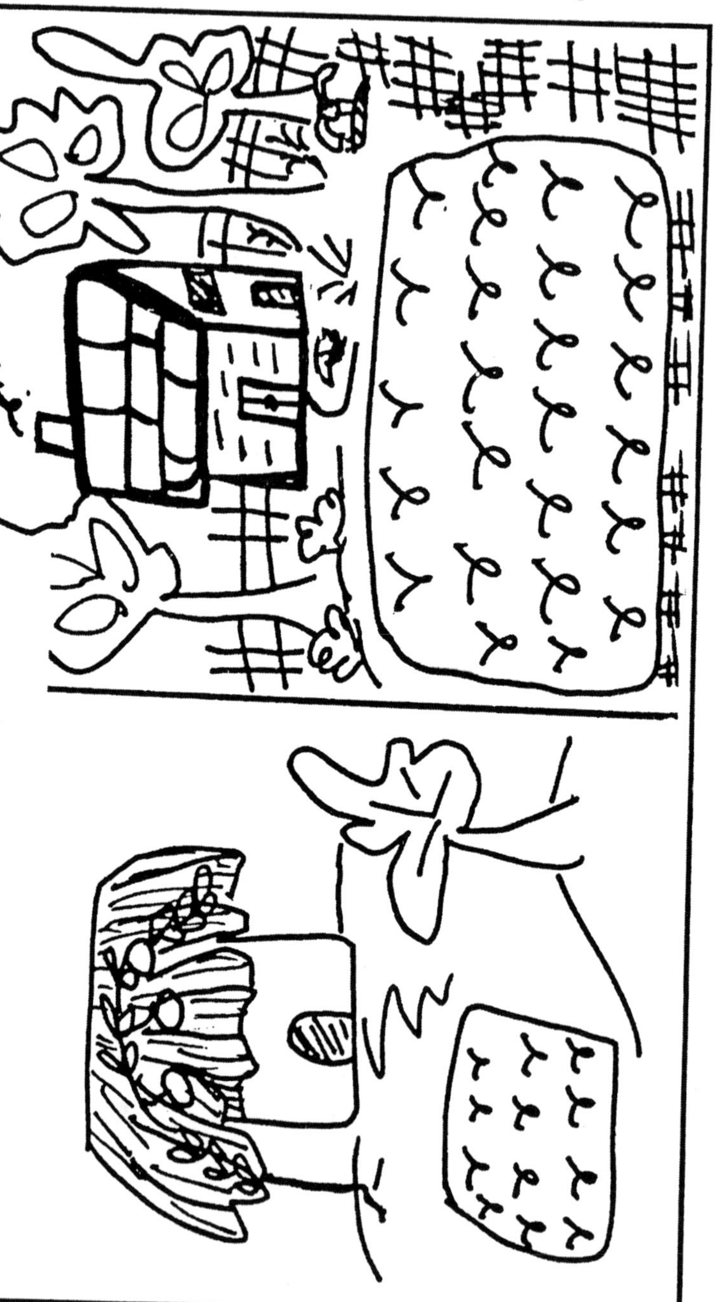

CHART 6.25: Distance Mapping of Wealth/Poverty

of wealth ranking/grouping becomes cumbersome in villages with a large number of households because it may not be feasible to have knowledge about each and every household. Grouping/ranking of households by analysts having sufficient information on all households is also not easy to find for large villages. The same is the case with wealth/poverty mapping involving a large number of households. The households are neither easy to be ranked/grouped nor efficient for group discussion on criteria used for ranking/grouping. In this context, it may be mentioned that the value of wealth ranking/grouping by the local people can be enhanced by other methods such as livelihood analysis so as to probe deeper into the issues concerned.

6.27 Participatory Concept Mapping

Participatory concept mapping (PCM) is a method to facilitate local community members to evolve/describe concepts in their own way. Any concept under reference can be elaborated with the help of local community's experience and ideas. Some examples of concept mapping are mapping of "vulnerable livelihoods", "desertification", "disaster" "child at risk", "food poor", etc. Once a concept is mapped by the local community member/s the next round of probing can dwell upon factors, which influence/determine it. In this context, some relevant questions are "what factors determine the concept", "how", "how much is their influence", "why" and "where" and "when"? Further probing can take place on what can be done to alleviate related problems/constraints, if any. In a interactive session on drought and its impact on local areas members of local communities from some villages of Western India evolved the following concept of "difficult period" (drought being a difficult period) in a brainstorming workshop.

The village participants in the workshop said that a "difficult period" is popularly known as "Akal"/ "Dushkal", which is a generic term for bad times or difficult period. According to them, "Akal" cannot be predicted beforehand and neither is it easy to escape its impact. "Akal" is dreadful because both human beings and livestock suffer acute shortage of water and food and are under severe stress. During "Akal" forests get destroyed and incidence of disease and death increases. In a historical context, the local communities have faced different types of "Akal", including dreadful ones. As per the village groups, such "Akal"/ "Dushkal" can be due to failure of rains, crop failure from pests or locust attacks, damage by floods, epidemic attacks, earthquakes, storms, etc. Such a broad connotation as expressed by the village groups imply the significance of the process accompanying "Akal"/ "Dushkal" and its resultant impacts.

Box 6.1 : What is an "Akal"?

The villagers described "difficult time" or "Akal"/ "Dushkal" as follows:

— When less rain or when rains fail "Akal"/"Dushkal" occurs;
— It cannot be predicted, it has no fixed time;
— People feel scared when they hear the name of "Akal"/ "Dushkal";
— No body in a locality can escape it;
— In times of "Akal"/"Dushkal", livestock and human beings cannot access cereal, water and food;
— The impact of "Akal"/"Dushkal" always falls on the resources for livelihood;
— During "Akal"/"Dushkal" the forests are pressurized and get destroyed; and
— During "Akal"/"Dushkal", there is spread of epidemic in humans and animals and incidence of death increases.
— During "Akal"/"Dushkal", the birds and animals become relatively quiet.

Key Analysts: Veronica, Besti, Leela and Keshar Singh, villages in Jhabua, Madhya Pradesh, India.

PCM can be used for appreciating/understanding the people's own perceptions of the issue/s under discussion. The method of PCM helps in exploring such links. It helps in identifying both causal and detailed mapping of concepts, improves upon the quality of group discussions and helps in evolving the people's own understanding of issues. Sometimes difficulties arise due to the local terminology used for concept mapping, which may not have an equivalent concept/word in other languages. For concepts, which are relatively complex, language can be a limitation. Concept mapping may also entail the need for local group/s appreciating the relevance and process of mapping such concepts. A concept mapping session becomes relatively easy when a local group mapping a concept shares a common understanding amongst themselves. Such a group can brainstorm on the relevance of the concept, its different connotations and aspects. It is useful to note/illustrate each idea/connotation on separate cards and spread them on the ground for others to see. Use of symbols often encourages the illiterate and semi-literate members to participate. Once the group ideas emerge on the cards they can be placed on the ground in a manner in which the different cards get inter-linked. Further rounds of discussion can follow such an arrangement of cards. Chalks or other markers can be used for drawing lines and showing inter-linkages amongst the different aspects of a concept under discussion.

PCM helps in group-based understanding and analysis. During the process of concept mapping it becomes much easier to discuss and analyse the "root causes/factors" and ways of resolving related issues. The strength of the method lies in providing an opportunity for group concepts to emerge and in arriving at group consensus through group interactive processes. It helps in outlining the kind of interventions, which can be addressed locally by the local communities. Where proposed interventions based on conventional research methods can also be analysed and adapted through application of the method of PCM. The method can be applied to both mapping of simple concepts and for complex concepts with multiple linkages.

Maps, models and diagrams help in visualising a future scenario. Such a scenario can be envisaged with regard to the outcome of developmental activities in a locality, changes in ecology of a locality, population changes, etc. They can be explained on the basis of maps and models of a locality through which the current position and the future possibility can be visualised and explained. This method can be used by the local people to express their expectations of the future shape of their locality and the way in which this can happen, the kind of resources which exist and the size of additional resources required in future.

These methods are basically instruments for analysis and are simple enough to be used and understood by the illiterate, semi-literate, literate and others. The methods are flexible and there are innumerable opportunities for these methods to be improvised or for new ones to emerge from the field. Output from each method can lead to the use of additional methods for further analysis. The methods are flexible and provide space to local communities to express their analysis in their own way and at the same time present it in a methodical manner. Visual methods are often self-explanatory. However, the causal forces behind the visual presentation need to come primarily from the person/persons/ groups involved in doing such "visuals". Hence semi-structured interviews generally precede and/or follow the use of any participatory method for explanation, clarification and cross-checking. Such methods are not ends in themselves. They are only a means to an end. They help in rapport building, strengthening of participatory process, analysis by the local people, creativity and empowerment. They help in their involvement and reveal their priorities, preferences, views, problems and the like. They help in identifying groups, community backgrounds, strengths, weaknesses, initiatives, talents, conflicts, wisdom and experience. They help to build action plans and also implement them.

REFERENCES

Burgess Robert G. (1990), In the Field, *An Introduction to Field Research*, Contemporary Social Research Series, General Editor: Martin Bulmer, Routledge, London.

Dewees Peter (1989), "Aerial Photography and Household Studies in Kenya", *RRA Notes*, Number 7, September, IIED, London.

Grandin Barbara (1988), *Wealth Ranking in Smallholder Communities: A Field Manual*, Intermediate Technology Publications, London.

Guijt Irene & Pretty Jules (1992), Participatory Rural Appraisal for Farmer Participatory Research in Punjab, Pakistan, IIED, London.

Jayakaran Ravi (1991), "PRA Camp at Mahilong, Bihar, 27-30, November, 1990: Krishi Gram Vikas Kendra", *RRA Notes*, Number 13, August, IIED, London.

Mascarenhas Jimmy & Prem Kumar P.D. (1991), "Participatory Mapping and Modelling: Users' Notes", *RRA Notes*, Number 12, July, IIED, London.

McCracken Jennifer A., Pretty Jules N. & Conway Gordon R. (1988), *An Introduction to Rapid Rural Appraisal for Agricultural Development*, Sustainable Agriculture Programme, IIED, London.

McCracken Jennifer (1989), "Diagrams for Participatory RRA", *RRA Notes*, September, IIED, London.

Mearns Robin (1988), "On Oral History and Local Calendars: Experiences in the Field in Papua New Guinea", *RRA Notes* Number 3, IIED, London.

Mearns Robin (1989), "Aerial Photographs in Rapid Land Resource Appraisal, Papua New Guinea", *RRA Notes*, Number 7, September, IIED, London.

Mukherjee Neela (1992), "Villagers' Perceptions of Rural Poverty Through the Mapping Method of PRA", *RRA Notes*, No.15. IIED, London.

Pretty Jules (1988), "Portraits and Stories", *RRA Notes* Number 3. IIED, London.

Reddy Ratna V. (1999), "Wealth Ranking in Socio-Economic Research: Substitute or Complement?", Research Notes, *Indian Journal of Agricultural Economics*, Volume 54, No. 1, January-March, *RRA Notes* (1991), Number 13, August, IIED, London.

Sandford Dick (1989), "A Note on the Use of Aerial Photographs for Land Use Planning on a Settlement Site in Ethiopia", *RRA Notes*, Number 6. IIED, June.

Scoones Ian (1988), "Learning About Wealth: An Example From Zimbabwe", *RRA*

Notes, Number 2, October, IIED, London.

Scoones Ian (1992),"Wealth ranking: Insights into patterns of Rural Differentiation in Southern Zimbabwe", typescript, Sustainable Agriculture Programme, IIED, London.

Shah Parmesh, Bharadwaj Girish & Ambastha Ranjit (1991), "Farmers as Analysts and Facilitators in Participatory Rural Appraisal and Planning", *RRA Notes*, Number 13, IIED, London.

Smith Kevin, Barrett Christopher B. and Box Paul W. (2000), Participatory Risk Mapping for Targeting Research and Assistance: With an Example from East African Pastoralists, *World Development*, Vol. 28, No.11, 1945-1959.

Theis Joachim & Grady Heather M. (1991), *Participatory Rapid Appraisal for Community Development, A Training Manual Based on Experiences in the Middle East and North Africa*, IIED & Save the Children Federation.

7

REVEALING PRIORITIES—RANKING AND SCORING

Prioritising issues and revealing preferences are important ways of community participation and decision-making. With resource constraints, whether in terms of funds, natural resources, material resources, human skills or social capital, all plans and actions need to be prioritised. Ranking and scoring methods help in prioritising group/individual issues/preferences at the local level and support practical decision-making within limited resources and budget. Such methods when applied "visually" become high powered than when applied verbally. They provide opportunities to deprived groups/individuals to reveal priorities and preferences, whose nuances are difficult to capture through interviews and oral talking. In this chapter those participatory methods and tools have been discussed which help the local people in revealing their priorities and preferences. Those methods and tools discussed are as follows:

- Listing
- Vector scoring
- Vector ranking
- Pairwise ranking
- Preference ranking
- Matrix scoring
- Matrix ranking
- Voting through scoring
- Livelihood activity analysis
- Wealth ranking
- Listing/scoring for participatory evaluation

7.1 Listing

Listing is a way of facilitating a list of items/criteria/activities for further analysis. Such items/criteria/activities depend on the objective/s of discussion. It is an effective way of remembering issues and highlighting them for discussion. Listing also helps in sorting out issues/criteria and arranging them in a sequence or in an ascending or descending order. A list of items/criteria can be generated at random as and when required based on which discussions can be held. Once a list of items is generated it can be rearranged on some agreed basis. A random generation of such a list can be both short and long, depending on group discussion at hand and its objective/s. Depending on the situation it may take time to generate a list of items/criteria/activities/others and then get it screened to avoid repetition. Table 7.1 provides an instance of listing of criteria from village Bhagwanpur Jullon of Dehradun in Uttar Pradesh. This is a list of benefits perceived by the women group from social forestry and flood protection measures. Once listing is done the next step is a description of those items/criteria/activities using the 8 helpers such as "why", "which/who", "how" and "how much", "what", "where" and "when". Such a list of items/criteria/activities can then be prioritised/ranked based on the selected methods explained below.

TABLE 7.1 : **Listing of Criteria by the Women Group**

Criteria
Increase in greenery
Benefit to farm
Availability of grass
Availability of leaves
Stopping soil erosion
Stopping bank erosion through embankment
Grazing of livestock
Local sight-seeing

Participants : Women group at Bhagwanpur Jullon, Kalsi Division, Dehradun, Uttar Pradesh

7.2 Ranking and Scoring Methods

The methods of ranking and scoring reveal priorities and preferences.

They provide opportunities to the local people to physically rank and re-rank selected items or preferences or benefits/costs and explain their reasons for a set of given ranking. Matrix ranking and scoring is most appropriate when outsiders wish to obtain precise information about the relationship amongst several different criteria and wish to rank some alternatives, related to uses, preferences or priorities. They can help in understanding the local people's criteria for ranking as well as the relative position of their priorities, preferences and choices in matters of occupation, food, fuel, fodder, energy use, etc. They help in easy comparison. Ranking methods include preference ranking, pairwise ranking, direct matrix ranking and wealth ranking.

7.3 Vector Scoring/Ranking

Vector scoring is a visual method and is concerned with scoring of criteria/items for assessing their relative importance so as to prioritise problems/benefits/dangers/damages/opportunities, etc. This method can be applied by the individuals as well as by the groups. In its "visual" form it involves listing of criteria on the ground with the help of symbols and scoring of such criteria/items using local materials such as stones, pebbles, seeds, leaves, etc. The methods help in decision-making by the prioritising concerned criteria/items.

Vector scoring is not a method to be applied at the beginning of community interaction. With progress in rapport-building exercises and semi-structured interviews, groups of local community interacting with outside teams generate different criteria/items, as per their perspective and subsequently score on such criteria/items. Such criteria/items can be either a set of problems, a set of benefits, a set of preferences, a set of activities/items, which a group wishes to score according to its priority. Once a tentative list of such criteria is prepared it is checked and re-checked for additional criteria, if any. The local people make further deletion or addition to the list of criteria according to their views and score on each criterion. They may choose not to score on some criteria, which they consider to be not relevant or superfluous. Such scoring can differ groupwise and individually. The scores and the list of criteria can differ with age, gender, caste, class, etc. Hence greater the flexibility in generating the criteria and the clarity in scoring, greater is the chance of attaining a realistic analysis.

At the beginning, once probing starts, it is best to arrive at an agreed theme/topic on which to generate criteria, for example, problems in a locality, problems in people-forest relationship in a locality, benefits flowing from a project, etc. It helps in focusing the topic/theme for scoring so as to have comparable criteria/items. Once such a list of criteria is generated, the list can be transferred to the ground either in small pieces of paper or with the help of different local symbols (as per the participants) generally arranged in a column. It is especially important to have agreed symbols for representing different criteria especially where group members are illiterate or semi-literate. This empowers them to understand each criterion on their own and focus their thinking before undertaking the activity of "scoring". The individual/groups may use seeds, stones, etc., to score on criteria.

The participants' scoring of criteria, whether "free scoring" (with no upper limit on scores attributed) or "fixed scoring" (with an upper limit on the scores attributed) by placing the highest score on the criterion considered to be of highest priority and placing score on other criteria according to their intensity. The participants involved in such an exercise of vector scoring may either like to score or rank the problems thus revealing their prioritisation of the locally generated criteria. At the beginning, some warming up exercises in scoring of criteria can be undertaken. For example, some local individuals in a group can score in front of others before they undertake scoring/ranking exercise as a group. This helps individuals to warm up for the exercise and start mentally comparing the set of criteria generated. This also helps in warming up for group scoring purposes.

In such a case, there often exists scope for mutual influence through individual scoring. However, individuals participating in such scoring exercise can be made to ponder that their scores/ranks need to be based on their own judgment. It is important to know the age and background of those engaged in the scoring process. This is because age, gender and experience, amongst other factors, generally influence the relative importance of each criterion. Once scoring takes place, the individuals may be approached to explain the kind of scoring that they did.

Once individual scoring takes place, group participation for group scoring needs to follow in the case of group exercises. The individuals may be requested to perform group scoring of criteria, either by the forming into one group or in different small groups as per their preference. Note of dissent can also be recorded. Much depends on how the community wishes to form into groups. In any case, it is important to encourage group interactions and a dialogue before group scoring takes place. Once group scoring is undertaken, the basis for such scoring also needs to be explained by the group. Scoring by the seeds, stones, pebbles or other local materials helps in showing the relative importance of any criterion. As mentioned above scoring of criteria can be either "free" or "fixed". In fixed scoring, a fixed number of scores, for example, 10 scores are used while in free scoring the number of scores is set free without limit. In free scoring, the relative amount of scoring for each criterion shows its importance. Fixed scoring is fixed in terms of the number of scores used and also shows the relative importance of criteria. Free scoring has no limit on scores used for each criterion. Greater number of scores means relative preference for an item under consideration. Much depends on what the local people would like to adopt. On many occasions they tend to go in for free scoring rather than fixed scoring. Much depends on their preference and convenience. Selected advantages of the method of vector scoring are as follows:

— The method of vector scoring helps in generating a list of criteria whether in terms of problems/priorities/preferences/ benefits/costs involved.
— It helps in revealing priorities from a list of criteria, which is indigenously generated, such prioritising can be both individual and group oriented.
— It helps in arriving at group consensus and also points of group dissent, if any.

Selected field exercises in the application of vector scoring are described below. Table 7.2 shows such scoring by the a women group in village Bhagwanpur for natural resource conservation by the gram panchayat. The gram panchayat was found to be pro-active in village Bhagwanpur Jullon, Kalsi Block, Dehradun District, Uttar Pradesh, for conserving natural resources, building check dams for preventing bank erosion/soil erosion, conserving natural resources and maintaining social forestry. A group of women from the village described the social forestry and flood protection measures undertaken in the village and also listed and scored criteria to assess the impact of such measures. As shown in Table 7.2 the women group allotted highest score to measures for stopping bank erosion through embankment and those for preventing soil erosion. These were followed by the benefit to the farmland from control of erosion and increase in village greenery through social forestry and tree plantation.

TABLE 7.2 : **Scoring of Benefits from Social Forestry and Flood Protection Measures**

Criteria	Scoring
Increase in greenery	7
Benefit to farm	8
Availability of grass	5
Availability of leaves	2
Stopping soil erosion	9
Stopping bank erosion through embankment	10
Grazing of livestock	2
Local sight-seeing	2

Participants : Women group at Bhagwanpur Jullon, Kalsi Division, Dehradun, Uttar Pradesh.

Note: The scoring was done by the a village group using 10 seeds for each criteria and greater the scoring the greater was the perceived importance of the criteria to the village group.

Scoring from village Khanpur

As shown in Table 7.3 a local men group listed, scored and ranked the benefits perceived from community forestry in village Khanpur in Alwar, Rajasthan. The forestry was more than 500 years old, at the top of a hill with shrubs and bushes around the slope of the hill. It harboured wildlife and a temple inside the forest which made it important from the religious and cultural perspective. The men group perceived the forestry to be of great significance as shown in Table 7.3 and criteria like "anti-pollution", "village greenery" and "prestige and show" were foremost in their consideration.

TABLE 7.3 : **Listing, Scoring and Ranking of Benefits from Community Forestry**

Criteria	Score	Rank
Anti pollution	8	1
Timber	2	6
Leaf manure	3	5
Village greenery	8	1

(Contd.)

TABLE 7.3 (Contd.)

Criteria	Score	Rank
Medicine	2	6
Water difference	5	3
Low frost	6	2
Future generation	6	2
Prestige and show	8	1
Wildlife	4	4
Religion and culture	6	2
Fodder	4	4

Participants: Men group, Khanpur Village, Alwar, Rajasthan.

Note: The men group used 10 seeds for each criterion to score. The higher the scoring the higher was the perceived importance of the criterion to the village group.

Another application of vector scoring is given in Table 7.4 where the priority health problems were assessed in a Lucknow suburb in Uttar Pradesh.

TABLE 7.4: **Priority Scoring of Health Problems**

Criteria	Score
The health facility centre is at a long distance	4
There isn't a doctor in the village	8
They do not have money to get themselves treated	5
They do not have any kind of vehicle to take patients to hospital	3
The health facility centre does not have medicines	5
They do not get the herbs they used to get earlier for their treatment	5
The doctor in the health facility centre isn't available at all times	7

Participants: Village group from Lucknow suburbs (Uttar Pradesh).

Note: The scoring for each criterion is out of a total of 10 scores.

Some of the field lessons in vector scoring/ranking are as follows:

— The greater the clarity in the discussion of issues relevant to the local people, the greater is the clarity in listing of criteria and scoring them.

- It is important to spend adequate time in conducting semi-structured interviews with different groups in learning about an issue/theme and listing the relevant criteria for their scoring.
- It is better to decide on a theme for scoring of comparable criteria. Focusing on a theme is important for arriving at meaningful results through scoring. Vector scoring focused on a comparable set of criteria helps in inter-comparisons and facilitates prioritisation at the local level.
- The method offers considerable space for group participation. It enables individuals/groups to present their views on a select list of criteria, improvise, add/delete criteria from the list and refrain from scoring, if necessary.
- It is transparent and leaves enough space for revision of scores.
- Symbols are effective if selected by the participants who actually do the scoring. It brings in familiarity, ideas, involvement and ownership.
- Experience shows that it is better to conduct such scoring/voting in an open setting/space where many can participate to offer their views and also to validate such scoring/ranking.
- Scoring on the ground helps in changing and revising them as and when required.
- In a logical sequence, criteria scoring can be a starting point for problem-based action plans in a locality, with problem-prioritisation of local communities as a first step.
- Because of group scoring and a process of group discussion, it helps in arriving at consensus within group/s and/or recording of score/rank indicating dissent, if any.
- It helps in strengthening the analytical base for development interventions in local communities and creating scope for the local people to prioritise their problems and arrive at joint decision-making.

7.4 Pairwise Ranking

Pairwise ranking which uses two items or attributes at a time for ranking can be used to explore the local people's criteria for choosing one alternative over another. A villager or a group of villagers can compare one pair at a time and give reasons for the choice made. At the end, the most favoured choice is identified if it is a question of choice. Or the major problem is identified in the case of a set of problems being ranked.

7.5 Preference Ranking

Preference ranking involves ranking of a set of problems/preferences/ priorities by a group or an individual on the basis of their criteria. An illustration of preference ranking is given in Chart 7.1 which shows the relative preference for 3 kinds of cotton varieties with 10 criteria. At the end of the matrix, the last row shows that the overall rating is in favour of the third variety of cotton.

7.6 Matrix Scoring

Matrix scoring is concerned with scoring a range of comparable items against a range of criteria. The range of comparable items on which scoring takes place can relate to a set of relevant items as decided by the local people. It can be anything, for example, a set of crops or varieties of the same crop, a set of trees, a set of animals, a set of livelihoods, a set of cooking devices, a set of trees in the home garden, a set of vegetables, etc. Since matrix scoring involves inter-comparison of items based on a set of criteria, it is important that the criteria to be scored are worthy of comparison and can lead to some meaningful analysis. For example, if the topic for matrix scoring is priority species of community fodder then the people doing such scoring will need to generate a variety of criteria for inter-comparison. One initial step is to generate a set of items on which scoring will take place and a list of relevant criteria. The method is flexible in the sense that more items and criteria can be added, altered or deleted based on group discussions. The scoring takes place in a grid-like set-up, with items on the one side and criteria on the other.

7.6.1 Facilitating Matrix Scoring

One way is to list the items/activities on the one side as a row and the set of criteria as a column. Each criterion is taken and compared across items and scored on that basis. One way for such inter-comparison is to start with the item, which has the highest preference or priority indicated by the highest score against a criterion, followed by the those items which have a lower preference against the same criterion as indicated by the lower

CHART 7.1: **Preference Ranking**
Village Meenakshipuram, Tamil Nadu

VARIETIES / CRITERIA	COTTON VARIETIES		
	KARUNGANNI	LAKSHMI	LRA 5166
DURATION	XXXX XXX	XXX XX	XXX X
BOLLS/PLANTS	[illegible]	XXXXX XXXXX	XXXXXXXX XXXXXXXX XXXXX
BOLL WEIGHT	XXX	XXX XX	XXXXX XXXXX
PEST RESISTANCE	XXXXX	X	XX
RESPONSE TO MANURING	XX	XXX	XXXX X
EASE OF BOLL PICKING	X	XXX	XXXX X
POSSIBILITY OF INTERCROPPING	X	X	XXX
PESTICIDE USE	–	X	XXX
YIELD	X	XX	XXXX
NET RETURN	X	XXX	XXXX
OVERALL RATING	(3)	(2)	(1)

PARTICIPANT: MR. PAI PANDIAN, VILLAGE MEENAKSHIPURAM; THE SIGN X INDICATES SCORING.
SOURCE: SAME AS IN CHART 4.3.

score. Such scoring is all-relative scoring, relative to the items being scored. Such scoring can be both "free" and "fixed". Scoring can be fixed out of a total of 10 (for example, a group is given 10 seeds/stones for each item to score), 20 or whatever the group decides for comparing individual items. Or, alternatively, it can be fixed for overall scoring (for example, the group is given 100 seeds/stones to score a few items). For free scoring, the output can be read and interpreted in terms of "more", "less", "high", "low", etc. Such "free" scores can be read in terms of ranking "high", "low", "medium", etc. to understand the pattern of scoring. Scoring can indicate many things. It can show the "number" of items under consideration or the "frequency" of items under consideration. It can also show the relative "quantity" of the item under consideration in relation to other items. It can represent the "quality" of the item under discussion in relation to other items.

A matrix scoring exercise on wild trees was undertaken in Nlaphwane village in Botswana (Africa). The scores are presented in Chart 7.2, in which 16 wild trees along with 16 kinds of utility were identified and a "score" for each tree was placed in the matrix according to its relative utility. For instance, it can be observed from the matrix in Chart 7.2 that "Mupani" tree had the following uses: (i) firewood, (ii) poles for making houses, (iii) fencing fields, (iv) fibre, (v) edible fruit and worm, (vi) shade, (vii) animal fodder and (vii) production of less harmful insects. Each of these uses had a separate score according to their importance to the local villagers. Chart 7.2 on utility scoring of trees provides a wealth of information. It shows how wild trees play a significant role in the lives of the local people. It also shows how the relative utility of each tree is different to the local people. The local people are conversant with the trees because they find them useful in their daily lives. At the end of the scoring the participants were given one hundred seeds to allocate amongst the different trees for planting tree saplings in a community nursery. Such allocation of one hundred seeds showed the preferred weights of different trees and the percentage of each that was recommended for plantation in the nursery.

Chart 7.3 shows the application of matrix scoring to levels of local health awareness in the village Lolai, Lucknow, Uttar Pradesh.

7.6.2 *Significance of Matrix Scoring*

Some field lessons in matrix scoring are indicated below:

CHART 7.2: Matrix Scoring

MATRIX SCORING OF WILD TREES, VILLAGE NLAPHWANE, BOTSWANA

CRITERIA FOR SCORING	1 MUPANI	2 MOSO	3 MOROTA	4 MURULA	5 MIZE	6 MBOLA	7 NSUNU	8 MUMU	9 MBGOTI	10 MPAWA	11 SWANJA	12 NTAMBA	13 NKWAKWA	14 NTHUNU	15 SKESE	16 MPANDA
1. FIREWOOD	20	4	2		1	2	1		12					3	12	
2. POLES FOR HOUSING	7				12	8	11		11							
3. FENCING FIELDS	9				5	4	5									
4. FENCING WELLS		10							8							
5. FENCING CATTLE																
6. DASHIBOMA					10			8	8							
7. FIBRE-MAKING	10														17	
8. SQUEEZING BEER								15								
9. EDIBLE	9		12	8				13		13	10	9	10			
10. SHADE	7		6	10				8		7					8	9
11. TO STRAIGHTEN WELLS									9					8		
12. TO GRIND SEEDS				12												
13. MAKING OF YOLKS						13	9								13	17
14. MEDICINES				14	6						13					
15. LESS HARMFUL INSECTS	18	12	11	13						13	10	8	9		11	13
16. ANIMAL FODDER	5	4		5		4	3	3		5		5	7	5	4	5

Chart 7.3 : Awareness Matrix on Health

Problems regarding health	Awareness among Men	Awareness among Women	Where do they have to go?	How many go? Men (Women)	Why don't the others go?
Unbalanced diet	4	2	nowhere/health centre	1 (1)	There has been lower incidence of disease
Diarrhoea	8	7	health centre	8 (7)	-do-
AIDS	2	1	big hospitals	—	-do-
Tuberculosis	9	6	big hospitals	8 (6)	-do-
Eczema	6	4	private doctor	5 (1)	-do-
Family Planning	9	8	health centre/big hospital	7 (4)	-do-
Cancer	7	5	big hospital	5 (1)	-do-

Participants: Village group from Lolai, Lucknow in Uttar Pradesh.
Note: The scores against awareness of women/men indicate proportion out of a total of 10.

- It presents an overall picture of group/individual preferences of selected items against listed criteria.
- Through the matrix scoring method, the local people can prioritise items based on such criteria.
- Such prioritisation of items at the local level can be linked directly to action plan/s.
- It helps in causal analysis of community/group/individual preferences/priorities/likes/dislikes.
- It is easy to change/revise scores when scoring takes place on the ground.
- Facilitation skills of high quality are required in order to explain the method and apply it at the local level. The groups applying matrix scoring need to be clear about the purpose of doing it and the kinds of results that they can expect from such an exercise.
- The more the comparability amongst the items in a matrix and the criteria, the easier it is to apply the method.
- It may not be feasible to extend inter-comparison of each item against each criterion especially for a matrix of a large size. A matrix scoring exercise can become complex where inter-comparisons involve a large number of items and criteria.
- After a point, the local people can lose interest in matrix scoring exercises, when they become unduly long and time-consuming.
- Tendencies to average out scores on a matrix by the outsiders can lead to misleading conclusions. If scoring involves a complex weighting pattern, the columns and rows need not be additive for arriving at total scores. Factors such as double counting, implicit weights and incomplete set of criteria need to be considered before arriving at total scores and estimation of average scores.

Matrix scoring is a powerful method for group decision-making and planning. It is an extension of the method of vector scoring whereby the scoring is not merely against a set of criteria but there are two sets involved in a grid where a range of comparable items are scored against a range of criteria. On occasions, matrix scoring may appear to be somewhat complex since the person or the group doing the scoring is required to keep track of the relative position of the scores on different criteria. In the case of a large number of items, it is possible to lose track of the relative significance of the differential score and thus impinging on quality in the process. This can happen especially in the case of a large-sized matrix undertaken for community decision-making. The danger is that one small error in matrix scoring based on relative comparisons can become cumulative through which errors in decision-making can creep in.

7.7 Matrix Ranking

Matrix ranking is similar to matrix scoring except that there are ranks in the place of scores. A field illustration given below in Chart 7.4 shows matrix ranking indicating health preferences of villagers from village Lolai in Lucknow in Uttar Pradesh.

7.8 Livelihood Activity Matrix

The local people engaged in similar livelihood sources list the stages in their livelihoods. They describe the stages in adequate detail explaining the strengths, weaknesses, constraints, bottlenecks, etc. This can be done "visually" analysed on the ground or paper. A typical activity can be considered and the stages worked backwards and/or forwards. For example, we ask about paddy stored in bags to be sold by the farmer, which we observe while visiting a farmer's household. The local people discuss amongst themselves to identify the chain of activities, the main and the sub-activities involved in getting paddy stored in bags. After identifying the whole sequence of activities, each activity can be taken up for further description for inquiring into the problems, constraints and future actions. This can be done "visually" with the help of small-sized coloured cards spread on the ground. When such problems and constraints are listed they can also be prioritised. Each activity on the card can be probed further with regard to problems/constraints and previous attempts made at solving such problems. See Chart 7.5.

Some strengths of livelihood activity matrix are listed below:

— It helps to have an overview of the sequence of activities and sub-activities—idea about the livelihood activities involved.
— It helps in identifying the length and breadth of the activities and the constraints affecting such activities, their impact, their probable sources and probable actions, if any.
— It helps in prioritising constraints related to each activity.
— It helps in planning and policy-making regarding vertical integration of selected activities for furthering benefits to local communities.

Chart 7.4: Matrix Ranking of Health Preferences

Illness/Disease	Medicine made at home	Health centre	Traditional methods	The village doctor	Medicines from the market	Not getting treatment
Fever	1	4	—	2	3	—
Headache	—	—	—	—	—	1
Malaria	1	3	4	2	—	—
Diarrhoea	1	2	3	—	—	—
Eczema	—	—	2	1	—	—
Swelling of legs	—	3	—	2	—	1
Problems women have	—	—	—	—	—	1
Tuberculosis	—	2	—	1	—	—

Participants: Village group, village Lolai, Lucknow, Uttar Pradesh.

TABLE 7.5 : **Participatory Livelihood Activity Analysis SWOL (Strength, Weakness, Opportunity, Limitation)**

Activity	Group of Women Tailors for Ready Made Garments
Activity 1	Procuring orders from market; SWOL—uncertainty of orders, orders not repeated, glut in the market
Activity 2	Procuring capital/taking loans; SWOL—small size of capital available, high rate of interest, problem of collateral
Activity 3	Procuring raw materials such as cloth, thread and others; SWOL—cloth thread, market far away, good quality thread not available
Activity 4	Getting to know popular design; SWOL—low sale for low access to popular designs
Activity 5	Cutting and stitching cloth—frocks, garments, etc.; SWOL—community machines not always available
Activity 6	Finishing stitching of garments; SWOL—finishing skills low.
Activity 7	Maintaining inventory of garments; SWOL—not enough place to stock
Activity 8	Transporting it to the market; SWOL—uncertainty of carts, high transport costs
Activity 9	Getting back unsold garments, damaged ones after some time;
Activity 10	Keeping track/realising money from the sale; SWOL—difficult to realise money from traders, many visits required, incurring transport charges
Activity 11	Incurring income, paying back loans and savings, if any.

Participants: Women group, village Chowki, Dehradun, Uttar Pradesh.

7.9 Wealth Ranking

Wealth/poverty ranking is also a form of ranking attributed to different households where some are high on the yardstick of wealth while others are low. Though this method has been discussed earlier in the chapter on mapping it is again summarised in this chapter from the point of view of participatory ranking and its applications. Wealth ranking is a method of ranking of households on the basis of income, wealth and other local measures of well-being. Different criteria can be used for wealth ranking based on local perceptions. Wealth ranking is based on the presumption that the local people have enough knowledge to rank households, thereby the implying knowledge of the kinds and status of household assets, other items, livelihoods and socio-economic attributes of the households concerned.

Grandin's (Grandin:1988) method of card-sorting is a method for wealth ranking where a list of households is prepared at the local level with each household having a separate number. The number assigned to each household together with the name of the head of the household are written on separate pieces of paper which are then ranked by some key informants individually according to their criteria. The different criteria used in ranking by the key informants emerge from their discussion on wealth classification, which also helps in cross-checking of the list and the final wealth classes are computed on that basis. One other way of wealth ranking is done on the basis of wealth mapping as discussed in the chapter on mapping. In a social map, wealth of different households is compared based on local criteria by the local groups/key informants and ranked on that basis. For specific illustrations see the chapter on mapping.

7.10 Listing/Scoring for Participatory Evaluation

Method of participatory scoring and ranking was applied for doing ex-post participatory evaluation of an Atoll development project at the Maldives (Mukherjee *et al.*:1999). A "visual" matrix was set up combining listing and scoring of criteria coupled with card-sorting. The application and the results are explained below. For setting up the "visual" matrix, group/s of participants (see illustration in Chart 7.5) were requested to remember and list the project activities on a wide sheet of paper. Each of them was provided with small cards and pens for listing/drawing/writing. After listing project activities (Column 1) and its starting time (Column 2), the participants described the type of project activities and scored each of them (Column 3) for prioritization of such impact. This was followed by the participants discussing each of such impact both in terms of qualitative and quantitative criteria and writing them on cards which led to the next column (Column 4) of the matrix. The next set of discussions was focused on the current status of the impacts and related sustainability issues, which was put in the next column (Column 5) of the PBI matrix. This was followed by the suggestions and recommendations (Column 6) by the participants, after which the results from the matrix were summarised by the facilitator/s and presented back to the participants for cross-checking of errors and omissions.

Chart 7.5 : Project-Benefit Impact Matrix

Name of Activity (Col.1)	Year (Col.2)	Score (Col.3)	Impact of Activity (Col.4)	Status and Sustainability (Col.5)	Recommendations (Col.6)
1. Health awareness programme	1993/94	10	Community awareness has grown as a result of inputs in child care, food, child spacing and family planning. Such knowledge is also getting applied.	The community with health worker's support continue to practise the imparted information.	For further sustainability the women suggest preparation and distribution of reference materials.
2. Handicraft training	1994	9	8 women took the training and can make small items like handbags, lamps and hats with local materials.	Though the women are interested they cannot practise it since there is no market for the product.	*Other recommendations :* Sewing courses should be included in any project.
3. Honey bee keeping	1993	7	The island women committee members have gained some knowledge in bee-keeping.	The members found it difficult to continue since training was incomplete. For example, when the	* There should be emphasis on planning and implementing income generating activities like shop

(Contd.)

Chart 7.5 *(Contd.)*

1	2	3	4	5	6
				bees flew away they lacked knowledge about ways to get them back.	or hotel. *Training courses in home gardening should have follow-
4. Credit scheme	1994	8	4 women borrowed money for sewing activities and still continue with loan repayment.	The scheme is useful but repayment is problematic due to no frequent local arrangement for repayment.	up sessions. * Marketing linkages should be included for handicraft training. *Island Analysts:*
5. Electricity	1995	7	24 hours electricity available to island community with manifold increase in regular income of Island Development Committee (IDC) from electricity charges.	The island women's committee helps in cleaning the power house while maintenance is looked after by IDC.	Amira, Aneesa, Faheema, Aminath, Mariyam
6. Home gardening	1993	7	A specialist taught the women and school-	The women found it difficult to continue	

(Contd.)

Chart 7.5 *(Contd.)*

1	2	3	4	5	6
			children for 8 months in preparing horticulture beds and applying fertilizers which resulted in planting banana, papaya, tomato and pumpkins.	except for growing banana plants, since they lacked knowledge on plant disease and treatment.	
7. Entrance deepening	1993	6	Has increased accessibility to the island where local fishermen are able to enter the island even after sunset.	Once a year the men clean the entrance while the women prepare special food for them.	
8. Training in electric wiring	1994	5	Only one man was trained and applies his knowledge as and when required, though he does not charge for it.	More men should be trained.	
9. Training in household	1993	8	11 men were trained who make cupboards, chairs	Men are earning good income and advance	

(Contd.)

Chart 7.5 *(Contd.)*

1	2	3	4	5	6
furniture making			and tables for income generating activity.	training course would be helpful.	
10. Training in engine repair and maintenance	1993	6	A total of 26 men participated with one person each from the local fishing vessels. They are now skilled in handling engine problems thus saving large expenses on maintenance.	The course is very useful and advance course would be an added advantage.	
11. Training in English language	1995	10	The teacher taught English for a month and left.	The community arranged for a teacher trained from India who is being paid by parents of the children.	

Participants: Women group from island Badidhoo, Dhaalu Atoll, Maldives.
Note: * Each impact was allotted a total score of 10, where a higher score meant higher impact.

One practical limitation for the outside team was that with large groups of participants there arose many views where consensus building became an arduous task. Another point observed by the outside team was that group recall of project activities took time since the project had got over. Again, since, most participants were literate, they wrote their points on the cards that were arranged in appropriate columns of the matrix.

REFERENCES

Grandin Barbara (1988), "Wealth Ranking in Smallholder Communities: A Field Manual", Intermediate Technology Publications, London.

Mukherjee, Neela, Mohammed Zahid, Aminath Lateefa and Mohammed Rasheed (1999), Project benefit-impact matrix from the Maldives—A Method for Participatory Evaluation, *PLA Notes* 34, February.

8

SEASONAL CALENDARS

Local livelihoods are integrally connected with seasonality. Each season has its specific problems and the local people have different strategies for "sourcing" their livelihoods. The seasons bear heavily on the physical conditions, which have an impact on the livelihoods and lives. Seasons bring about changes in climatic conditions, in crops grown, in prices, in physical conditions, in availability of water, food, fuel and fodder, which in turn influence the living conditions in different localities and areas. Seasonal diagramming can lead to comparisons of related aspects of local livelihoods such as seasonal variations and their linkages with food, employment, workload, disease, etc. Different aspects of local life can be reflected through seasonal diagramming. Seasonal diagrams made and analysed by the local people are comparatively richer than other methods for field inquiry such as questionnaire survey taken at two points of time over a year. In the latter case the "seasonality" factor will either tend to get neutralised by "averaging" of the outliers or conclusions can be derived based on a partial picture of one or two season/s and that too without the natural flow of the participant in describing seasonal conditions and impacts.

In seasonal diagramming, the local people prepare diagrams and charts (either with chalks or other materials) either on the ground or on paper, of various socio-economic and physical phenomena such as seasonal wages received, food consumed, prices, crops grown, rainfall patterns, sickness and others. In such diagramming, the local people construct such seasonal calendars using local materials for seasons/months/days to describe their activities, livelihood patterns, food, debt, disease patterns, rainfall, etc., as per seasons. To begin with the local people describe such seasonal changes orally followed by "visual" illustrations using local materials and explaining the nature and dimensions of such variations. Chart 8.1 presents a seasonal calendar of

CHART 8.1: **Seasonal Calendar**
North Kordofan, Sudan

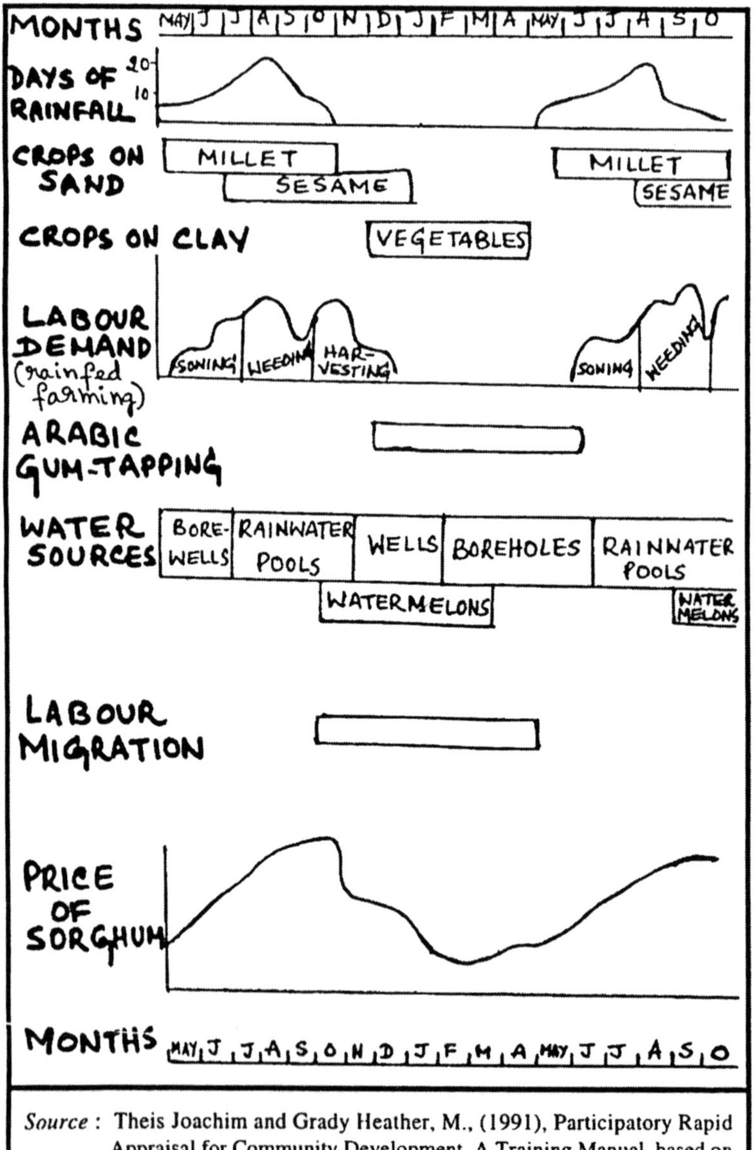

Source : Theis Joachim and Grady Heather, M., (1991), Participatory Rapid Appraisal for Community Development, A Training Manual, based on Experience in the Middle East and North Africa, IIED and Save the Children Federation, London.

peasants in North Kordofan, Sudan, which starts from the month of May. It shows the days of rainfall, crops growing on sand and clay, seasonal labour demand, allied activities like gum-tapping, water sources, labour migration and seasonal variations in the price of sorghum.

Any seasonal analysis starts with a semi-structured interview on seasons and a discussion of their impact on the community life. Once the purpose and nature of the topic is made clear to the local groups they are asked either to explain verbally each season and its impact and illustrate seasonality, visually on the ground/paper. For "visual" analysis, the different seasons can be indicated on separate pieces of paper or represented through indigenous symbols, preferably on the ground. As compared to paper, the ground gives more space for the seasonal calendars to be constructed and extended to show as many items as the local community wishes to illustrate. Such calendars can be both visual and/or verbal with verbal discussions inter-spaced with visual charts. With the help of stones, sticks, pebbles or other local materials, such changes can be described and explained. Symbolising different seasons/months by means of major activities/festivals/other symbols makes it easier for the local communities to correlate different seasons/months with the variables under consideration. On completion of a "visual" chart of seasonality, semi-structured interviews can be resumed for greater probing and clarification related to such seasonal impacts. There can also take place changes and alterations of the "visuals" depending on the participants who do it.

8.1 Seasonal Disease Calendar

Like seasonality of food and livelihood, the local communities are also faced with seasonal diseases. Chart 8.2 is a seasonal analysis of nine diseases in Udaanampatti villages in India. It shows seasonal frequency of local diseases of which, for example, headache is a frequently occurring disease while the frequency of diarrhoea is largely concentrated in the months of April, October and November. The chart can be directly linked to health intervention measures in terms of strengthening of primary health care depending on the frequency of the disease in the period concerned.

Another seasonal disease calendar is illustrated in Chart 8.3. The pattern of seasonality is as follows:

CHART 8.2: **Seasonal Health Calendar**
(Seasonality with Scoring)

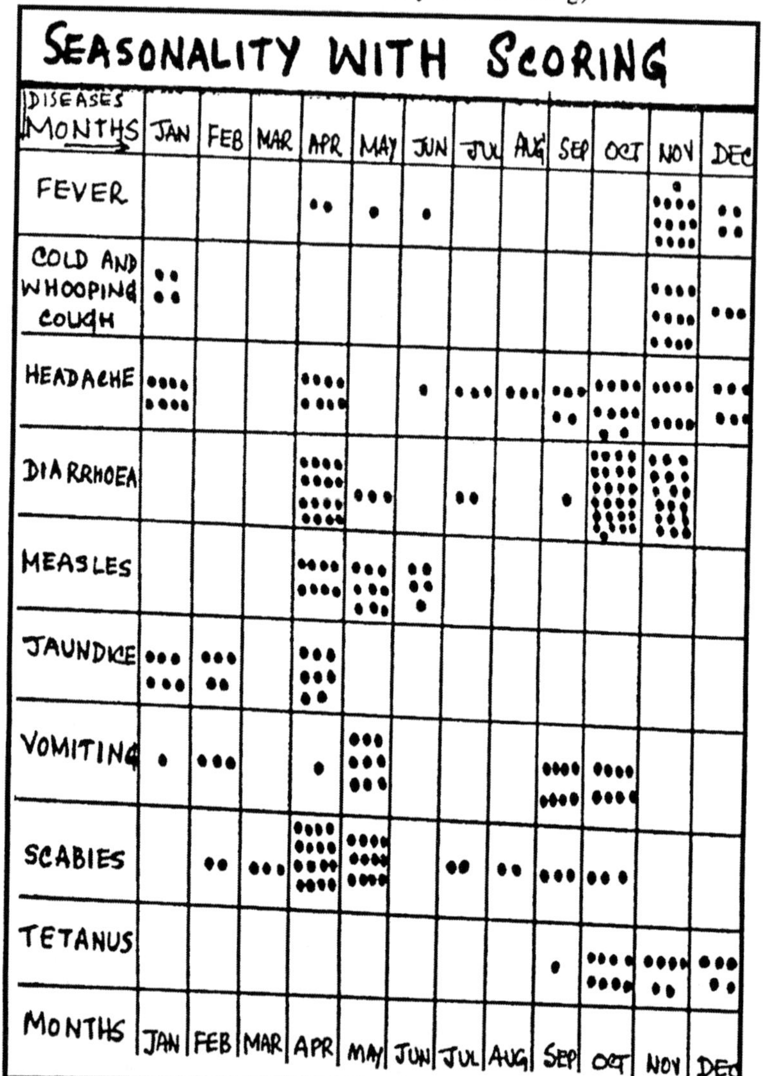

Note : Seasonal Health Calendar of Nine Diseases, Udayanampatti Village; Villagers Used Stickers to Depict Frequency of Disease.

Source : Devavaram Joh et al.(1991), 'PRA for Rural Resource Management', RRA Notes, Number 13, August, IIED, London.

Chart 8.3: Seasonality in Disease/Illness

Seasons (months)	Type and frequency of disease/s
Baisakh (April-May)	They contract dysentery due to polluted water by drinking water without boiling it. There are no containers to keep boiled water. The excreta has blood and mucous.
Jyaistha (May-June)	Mainly intestinal diseases occur such as gastroenteritis, diarrhoea, common cold, cough, fever, headache, etc.
Srabon–Bhadra (July-September)	The local women and men generally have fever, forced to eat less, have malaria attacks and go to the doctor for medicines.
Aswin (September-October)	The local women and men have occasional fever, they treat themselves with their own medicines and go to the doctor if illness persists.
Kartick (October-November)	They often have fever and headache, mainly the women. Those women having stomach problems with watery excretion and occasional fits take traditional medicine.
Agrahyan (November-December)	Both local women and men have fever, cough and cold.
Magh (January-February)	The local women and men have fever due to cold. They also have problems with their stomach. Some of them have itches and boils. They apply their own medicines.
Phalgun (February-March)	People suffer from fever. Some have chicken-pox. They pray to God and make offerings.
Chaitra (March-April)	They have diarrhoea but if they drink boiled water they can avoid it.

Note: Women and men participants, Krishna Rakshit Chak, Midnapore, West Bengal.

Chart 8.3 shows that there are changes in the pattern of diseases over seasons and fever is quite a common seasonal occurrence. Over the months of Baisakh, Jyaistha and Chaitra diarrhoea and dysentery are quite common while Phalgun onwards the occurrence of fever is high.

8.2 Seasonal Livelihood Calendar

Chart 8.4 illustrates a seasonal livelihood calendar, indicating the source of livelihood for women and men against different months. The calendar clearly shows that in certain months such as Baisakh and Jyaistha women have no sources of livelihood to fend for themselves while men have better opportunities in most months. The wage rate also discriminates against women while the work available is not gender-neutral.

Chart 8.4 : Seasonal Livelihood Calendar

Months	Sources of Livelihood – Women and Men
Baisakh (mid-April to mid-May)	Work available for men for 5 to 6 days, nature of work—catching fish, blasting sites through applying dynamite, applying gravel to roads.
Jyaistha (mid-May to mid-June)	Work available for men for 1 or 2 days, nature of work—men called by farmers to cut wood in small pieces for collecting and storing fuel for rainy season.
Ashar (mid-June to mid-July)	Work available for 1 or 2 days for men, nature of work for men—they are called by farmers to prepare field, women sell mushrooms, men/ women also sell fish.
Srabon (mid-July to mid-August)	Work available for 15 to 16 days, men get work in the field; women get transplantation work, some of them sell vegetables from homestead/ home garden.
Bhadra (mid-August to mid-September)	There is no work available, so they take loans and have high indebtedness during this period and return the money after 1 or 2 months. Fish availability is high so they catch fish. Some of them sell vegetables from homestead/home garden.

(Contd.)

Chart 8.4 *(Contd.)*

Months	Sources of Livelihood – Women and Men
Ashwin (mid-September to mid-October)	There is little work available, some harvest work for men and 4 to 5 days' work for women to remove weeds from fields. They catch fish, if the catch is high they sell more and/or eat themselves. Some of them also sell vegetables from homestead/home garden.
Kartick (mid-October to mid-November)	Some work is available for women in paddy harvesting (Rs. 25 plus puffed rice), the harvested paddy is arranged and tied by the men and also sized through machines by men (Rs. 30 plus puffed rice). The men also carry the paddy to the farmer's house to the place of storage, some female also carry them (Rs. 30 plus puffed rice). All able-bodied women and men do not get work. Such work is available on an average for 5 to 10 days. They also do weeding in the paddy fields on their own (not paid), such weeds can be used for feeding livestock.
Aghrayan (mid-November to mid-December)	Paddy harvesting (women do for Rs.30 plus some puffed rice, sometimes the wage is also Rs.20) and men also do such work. The harvested paddy is arranged and brought from the field for storage purposes, both by men and women and also cleaned through machines. (women's wage is Rs.30 plus puffed rice for carrying headload of harvested paddy while men carry more of it sideways and they get Rs. 50 plus puffed rice).
Poush (mid-December to mid-January)	No work available for women. They collect the wasted paddy scattered around the fields while harvesting and arranging it for storage. In the evening they generally do this job and are able to collect 3 to 4 kg of paddy. Around 15 days work is available for men, which is paddy husking (Rs. 30 plus puffed rice). Those who have little land do cultivation and earn some income. Those

Chart 8.4 *(Contd.)*

Months	Sources of Livelihood – Women and Men
	not having any land buy paddy/rice during Aghrayan. The festival of "Tushu" also falls in the month of Poush for which they buy new clothes.
Magh (mid-January to mid-February)	They do winnowing. Some work left. Women find work in Boro paddy sowing for 10 to 15 days. Some work is also found in winnowing by both women and men (Rs. 30 plus puffed rice). Sometimes men get to do earthwork at Panchayat. In Magh if it rains the men get to do earthwork in Magh. Everyone does not get work. Such work is available for 2-5 days, sometimes for 10 days. Those who have facility of water cultivate their land and with the income buy vegetables. No items are collected as food in this season.
Phalgun (mid-February to mid-March)	There is plenty of fish in the lake called Rajbandh. This provides some avenues for employment and income. There is also digging work done by men. The men do it and the women do the carrying. They get Rs. 20/30 per sq. ft or even Rs.40 per sq.ft. Not everybody can find work. For cutting 100 boulders they are paid Rs. 80. They explode the site with dynamite. After that within 2 to 3 hours they dig the boulders out for which they get Rs. 80 per 100 boulders. They also catch fish and eat. They also grow vegetables. They eat jhinuk, shamuk and fish.
Chaitra (mid-March to mid-April)	The men go to catch fish. They also get employment in private eucalyptus farms by the contractors to do the felling. After 15 days of Chaitra women get some work—Boro paddy harvesting. 15 to 20 people migrate temporarily to a far off village to harvest Boro paddy.

Note: Women and men participants, Krishna Rakshit Chak, Midnapore, West Bengal.

8.3 Seasonal Food Calendar

Seasonal food calendar is a specific use of seasonal diagramming. Seasonal variations in food availability constitute an integral part of rural life and the PRA method of food calendar can illustrate food availability in different seasons. Both the quantum and the kind of food availability over different seasons or months can be shown through a food calendar. For a meaningful analysis in seasonality, it is important to connect items of seasonal food calendars with their magnitude to the extent possible. Such magnitudes can be both qualitative and quantitative, such as the number of people sharing a particular food item, whether in household/ group/community and the amount available from production, collection, purchase, etc., whether measured in terms of indigenous measures or others. Since the kinds of food consumed give only an indication of its variety and quality, it is important to include the volume of food to the extent possible.

In a PRA session in Nlaphwane which is resource-poor and drought-affected village near Francis town, Botswana, the villagers made a food calendar as shown in Chart 8.5 and explained their seasonal food availability in a normal year. They drew a food calendar to describe the availability of food stocks, their staple food in different months and how they supplement it with other kinds of food. They started with the month of July in a normal year with adequate rainfall when they indicated that after the harvest they have 30 bags of staple food. The food availability dwindles slowly over different months and reaches only 7 bags in June after completion of a full year. It is supplemented through a wide variety of food items from the "wild" and other sources.

The food calendar in Chart 8.5 depicts food in a period of normal rainfall. Besides staple food like maize, millet and sorghum they also grow other crops. In March-April, they have a variety of supplements to balance the declining food stocks like watermelons, pumpkins, green maize, yums, groundnuts, cowpeas, bambara nuts, sweet reeds and sweet melons. They also ate chickens, goats and beef any time of the year. In addition, they also had "biltong" or dried meat of cattle. Wild food like "moroja" supplemented their diet during the period of January to April. Few farmers had them growing in their homesteads while others went to collect them in the wild. Wild nuts from "murula" tree supplemented their diet during May, June and July. The months of December and January were not easy in terms of food availability when they had less scope to supplement their diets through wild fruits and other vegetables.

CHART 8.5: Food Calendar, Village Nlaphwane, Botswana

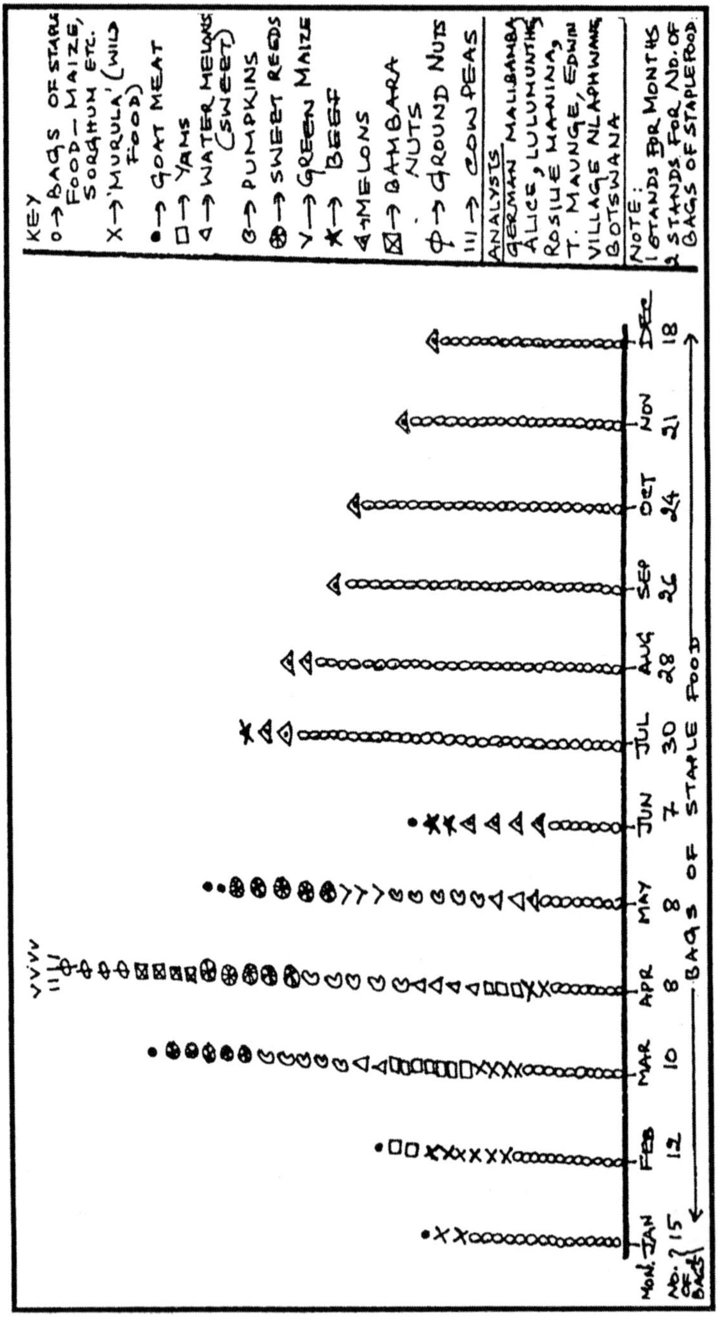

Chart 8.6 depicts seasonal survival strategies of rural women and seasonal livelihoods in a remote and poor village named Benageriya in Midnapore, West Bengal. In most seasons, the poor women have enormous difficulties in coping with the local conditions and suffer acute food insecurity.

Chart 8.6: Seasonal Survival Strategies of Rural Women and Livelihood

Months	Livelihood of Women and Vulnerability of Forest	Food Availability and Survival Strategies
1	2	3
Baisakh (mid-April-May)	For most women, agriculture or other jobs are not available. However, very few go with their husbands to harvest paddy for 8 days. The women stitch Sal leaves for making plates and also collect few bags of dry leaves/twigs for selling.	Often they are forced to have empty stomachs due to incapacity to access food.
Jyaistha (mid-May-June)	Between 2 and 4 days of work is available for few women related to collecting earth dug by men and carrying it as a headload for transferring it elsewhere. Women are paid at the rate of Rs. 10 per day plus a bowl of puffed rice.	They eat less rice (they buy rice at Rs.7 or 8 per kg).
Ashar (mid-June-July)	The women get trans-plantation work for 10-12 days at a daily wage of Rs. 21 plus some puffed rice, for which they need to travel far. (This year some forest-related work was available under JFM).	They are able to buy vegetables and rice, and collect small sized snails to eat.
Srabon (mid-July-August)	Some women are engaged in weeding out grass/weeds on	They are able to buy vegetables and rice.

Chart 8.6 *(Contd.)*

1	2	3
	agricultural land for 2-10 days at a daily wage of Rs. 21 plus a bowl of puffed rice. (Some forest-related work under JFM was available in 1998).	
Bhadra (mid-August-September)	No agricultural work is available. The forest is in danger since no work is available. There is not much sunlight and no work can be done related to Sal leaves. The women try to sell leaves of "Atandi" to farmers who use them as fuel and pay Rs. 5 for one bundle of leaves. For selling such leaves they walk for at least 2 miles besides collecting it.	Some women try to survive on money earned by men and also draw upon the savings done during Ashar. They try to keep some cash for medical treatment since illness is rampant during monsoons. This also makes them eat less.
Aswin (mid-September-October)	Very few women get 2 to 10 days work related to the harvesting of "Khudi" paddy at a daily wage rate of Rs. 21 plus one bowl of puffed rice. The forest is in danger due to little availability of work and higher incidence of seasonal disease.	Many of them also fall sick and have fever for 15 days at a stretch. This also increases their medical expenses. For supplanting food, they also try to catch some fish from the agricultural land once the rain water recedes.
Kartick (mid October-November)	Some women get 8 to 15 days work relating to harvesting of paddy and threshing it at a daily wage rate of Rs. 21 plus a bowl of puffed rice.	This month is relatively better than the previous month.
Agrahyan (mid-November-December	Some women are engaged in harvesting of paddy for 8 days. They approach the farmers for work and some of them	The survival strategy is one of beg and borrow from people or steal from the forest.

(Contd.)

Chart 8.6 *(Contd.)*

1	2	3
	also get engaged in threshing of paddy. This work is mainly of men but few women do get a chance. The forest is in danger.	
Poush (mid-December-January)	There is no work available for women. In the past years, the women used to arrange straw during Poush, Magh, Phalgun (at a daily rate of 50, 75, 25 paise). Now this work is no longer available. Some work related to rice husking and winnowing is available for 2 to 4 days at a daily wage rate of Rs.21 plus a bowl of puffed rice. The forest is in danger.	Mostly the same strategy as in the earlier month.
Magh (mid-January-February)	No work is available for women. So some of them cut trees in the forest, sometimes caught by forest officials and fined. Often the fine is made good by cutting more trees.	Survival is harsh.
Phalgun-Chaitra (mid-February-April)	No work is available. Their work gets over by Magh and Poush because most farmers grow one crop. The women go to the forest and collect fuel and sell them at Re. 1 per bag, by which they earn around Rs. 5 per day. Some women are also forced to cut trees.	Survival is harsh.

Participants: Women analysts—Kulmoni Rout, Netri, Phula Rout, Gulapi, Sandhya, Bharati, Brindabati, Giribala and others, village Benageriya, Durganhari FPC, Sankrail Beat, Kalaikunda Range, Midnapore, West Bengal.

8.4 Seasonal Food (Discrimination) Calendar

The method of seasonality has been applied to food discrimination practices on a seasonal basis. Discriminating food practices may be on account of different reasons such as poverty in a household with women eating less, cultural perceptions that men are superior to women and hence should eat more, higher food requirements of men, etc. Charts 8.7 and 8.8 provide an illustration of food discrimination practised in village Banstaol in Tangail District of Bangladesh. Seasonal food calendars comparing quantum of food intake by an adult man and an adult woman as in Chart 8.7 and that of a girl child and a boy child as shown in Chart 8.8 were prepared by a group of women villagers of village Banstaol. The calendars give an idea of what kind of discrimination is practised and how it varies seasonally. Such discrimination is present in almost all items of food and gets pronounced with better quality food. The food calendar for adults as shown in Chart 8.8 shows food intake by a man and a woman on 8 items—rice, chappati, vegetables, pulses, eggs, fish, milk and fruits. The calendar was constructed on the ground using different kinds of seeds representing different food items. In the interview, which followed once the calendar was constructed the women explained that for certain items like rice, vegetables and pulses, the seeds represented weights while for others, such as eggs, fish, milk and fruits, the seeds showed frequencies of consumption of those items. The calendars relate to all the 12 months. In Chart 8.8 seasonal food discrimination has been shown for a one-year-old girl and a one-year-old boy. The number of seeds used to score on the food calendar depicts both weight and frequencies similar to the food calendar for adult man and woman. The food taken by children increases as their age increases from one year to two years yet the girl child gets relatively less than the boy child and such societal discrimination continues even during their growing years.

8.5 Seasonal Calendars: Selected Lessons from the Field

Selected lessons on the method of seasonality are listed below. They are based on field experience in different areas.

— Too many items included in one seasonal calendar, at one time, can make the analysis complicated and tiring for the local people. Seasonal calendars focused on related issues

CHART 8.7: **Seasonal Food Calendar—Food Discrimination (Children)**

SEASONAL FOOD CALENDAR – GIRL CHILD/MALE CHILD - ONE YEAR OLD

MONTHS / ITEMS	CHAITRA		BAISAKH		JAISTHA		ASHAR		SRABON		BHADRA		ASWIN		KARTIK		AGRAHAYAN		POUSH		MAGH		PHALGUN	
	M	F	M	F	M	F	M	F	M	F	M	F	M	F	M	F	M	F	M	F	M	F	M	F
RICE	2	1	3	2	5	3	6	4	6	5	7	6	8	7	6	5	7	6	8	7	9	8	6	5
PULSES	7	6	6	5	4	3	6	4	5	4	7	6	7	6	6	5	6	5	6	5	5	4	7	6
VEGE-TABLES	3	2	4	3	3	2	4	4	4	3	6	5	7	6	5	3	4	3	7	6	6	5	5	4
FISH	2	1	2	1	2	1	3	2	3	2	4	3	5	4	4	3	4	3	5	4	6	5	4	3
EGG	6	4	4	3	3	2	3	2	4	3	5	4	6	5	4	3	7	5	8	7	4	3	10	9
MILK	9	7	4	3	5	3	4	3	4	3	5	4	6	5	6	5	6	3	8	7	6	5	7	6
BANANA	7	3	6	4	4	3	3	2	4	3	5	4	7	6	6	5	4	4	6	5	5	4	8	7
ORANGE	4	3	4	2	3	2	2	1	3	2	2	1	4	3	4	3	4	4	5	4				
MANGO							3	2																
JACK-FRUIT							4	3																
PINE-APPLE											2	1	1		3	2	4	3	5	4				
APPLE													2	1	4	3	4	3			5	4		
PAPAYA											4	3											6	5
BISCUIT	3	1	2	1	2	1	3	2	3	2	2	1	5	4	5	4	5	4	6	5	[illegible]	[illegible]	[illegible]	[illegible]

Village Analysts : Rehana Parvin and Ferdusi Begum *Village Banstaol*, District Tangail, Bangladesh

CHART 8.8: Seasonal Food Calendar—Food Discrimination (Adult)

SEASONAL FOOD CALENDAR– MALE ADULT / FEMALE ADULT

MONTHS / ITEMS	CHAITRA		BAISHAK		JYAISTHA		ASHAR		SRABON		BHADRA		ASWIN		KARTIK		AGRAHAYAN		POUSH		MAGH		PHALGUN	
	M	F	M	F	M	F	M	F	M	F	M	F	M	F	M	F	M	F	M	F	M	F	M	F
RICE	2	2	6	5	7	6	9	8	9	8	7	6	6	5	5	4	8	7	6	3	6	5	6	5
CHAPPATI	5	4	0	0	0	0	0	0	0	0	0	0	0	0	2	2	0	0	0	0	3	2	3	2
VEGETABLES	1	1	2	2	6	6	10	10	7	7	5	5	4	3	6	4	3	3	3	2	2	2	2	2
PULSES	10	10	5	5	4	4	2	2	3	2	6	6	7	7	7	6	7	6	9	7	8	8	9	9
FISH	1	1	5	2	4	3	2	3	5	2	3	3	8	3	8	2	5	2	4	2	1	2	2	2
EGG	3	2	4	2	3	2	3	2	4	1	4	2	8	3	10	4	9	9	10	9	8	7	7	6
MILK	11	10	5	5	4	4	3	3	3	2	3	3	4	3	2	2	2	2	2	2	2	2	8	8
MANGO	-	-	-	-	4	4	-	-	-	-	-	-	-	-	-	-	-	-	-	-	-	-	-	-
JACKFRUIT	-	-	-	-	9	6	8	5	-	-	-	-	-	-	-	-	-							

VILLAGE ANALYSTS – REHANA PARVIN AND FERDUSI BEGUM
VILLAGE BANSTAOL, DISTRICT TANGAIL, BANGLADESH

can provide a rich and meaningful picture of local seasonal diversities.

— Use of local symbols makes "visual" more meaningful, culture-based and also creates space for illiterate and semi-literate to participate. For items like trees, vegetables, fruits, flowers and others, some actual symbols can be used for directly representing these items, for example, in the case of seasonality of produce from a set of trees, leaves/fruits of such trees can be used as symbols for scoring and discussion. This helps in better recollection of seasonality forces and patterns associated with specific items.

9

VISUAL DEPICTION—DIAGRAMS AND FLOW CHARTS

In this chapter, selected field methods related to diagrams and flow charts have been discussed based on field illustrations from different countries. The "diagramming" methods described in this chapter are as follows:

— "Chappati" (Venn) diagram
— Communication linkage matrix
— "Chappati" (Venn) ranking
— Link/anchor person "chappati" (Venn) diagram
— Support system's diagram
— Source diagram
— Pie chart
— Livelihood analysis
— Ratio analysis
— Impact flow analysis
— Impact diagram
— Flow chart analysis
— Comparative flow chart
— Visual trend analysis
— Diagram of income generating activities
— Causal tree analysis
— Demonstration pack
— Live sample method.

This chapter also has a discussion of the importance of "diagramming" and its limitations. Diagrams drawn are "visual" methods and provide a tangible basis for any discussion and thereby enrich participatory process. In PRA/PLA such diagrams form the basis of discussion and help in clarity and "visual" details. Physical sample method is also included here, which helps in providing a basis for discussion on the related issues.

9.1 Diagramming: Its Significance

Diagramming is a "visual" activity and is an important part of participatory learning and action. Diagrams are "visual" and help in providing a tangible base to any discussion and thereby enrich the process. They present "visual" details and complement and supplement verbal discussions. They help in flagging issues, which are important to the local communities, both literate and illiterate. The help in clarifying issues by providing details through visual pictures. They make the "insiders" feel interested and involved in issues under discussion. They are more objective in nature than verbal methods since they provide a tangible base and change can be incorporated in them in the presence of all concerned..Diagrammatic error can be easily recognised. They are forms of "visual" documentation and record of discussions.

Diagrams help in building consensus and can form a basis for resolving conflicts and differences of opinion. They help in cross-checking of information and cumulative build up of knowledge on that basis (RRA Notes:1991). Diagrams also facilitate exchange of views on the basis of information presented in them. The diagrams make space for those who are relatively silent and find it difficult to participate in discussions and present their views. When people have the entire "visual" set in front of them they can get into finer details without missing any important point.

Diagrams can be made of anything and anywhere with or without drawing capabilities. Often, it is enough to have a rough sketch of the object/issue in front of local groups as a basis for discussion. Those participating can have a visual impression of the object/issue under discussion. On many occasions, diagrams and flow charts also help in rapport-building exercise for establishing goodwill. The form a diagram takes is contextual depending on perspectives, cultural perceptions, gender and other factors. They help in revealing perspectives and preferences, which are otherwise hidden and obscure. They form bases for process building, data generation, planning, implementation, monitoring and evaluation.

9.2 "Chappati" (Venn) Diagramming

"Chappati" (Venn) diagrams are visual methods to represent the role of individuals/institutions and the degree of their importance in decision-making. In such diagrams circles of different sizes represent an individual or an institution, whose size shows its degree of importance in decision-making in a local community and the overlapping of circles indicates overlapping in decision-making. Overlapping of circles arises due to one institution/individual interacting with another institution or individual in which case the circles overlap on one another. Such overlaps may be large or small depending on the extent of interaction. If the circles are separate, the institutions have no contact and if they touch each other there is information-passing between institutions. Strong/weak linkages between two institutions represented by two circles can also be shown by steady/broken lines/arrows.

Venn diagrams can be useful in the study of relationships of institutions/individuals with local communities. For the local community members Venn diagrams would reflect the kind of communication between the local community and different organisations including governmental organisations and NGOs. Different aspects of local life can be taken up to see their interaction and their role in decision-making involving local-level planning, in running of projects, in distribution of land, credit, water and other assets, in the construction of roads, school buildings, dams, etc.

Chart 9.1 shows the key institutions, which play an important role for those households raising livestock in village Tien Phong of Vo Ninh Commune at Quang Binh Province of Vietnam. It identifies the degree of contact and overlap between them in terms of provision of service. The institutions identified are the People's Committee of Commune, Village Farmers' Association, Commune Farmers' Association, People's Committee of Districts, Women's Union of Commune, Veterinary Service, Extension Service and District Agriculture Unit. All institutions are of equal size meaning thereby that they are equally important, however, some are close to the community while others are far away in terms of mental distance. This is reflected in the "distance" of the institution from the community. For example, as shown in Chart 9.1, the village farmers' association is closest to the livestock community of Tien Phong village while district agriculture unit is farthest from the community. This also implies perceptions of the community regarding provision of services in the area of livestock.

CHART 9.1: Chappati (Venn) Diagram
Village Tien Phong, Quang Binh (Vietnam)

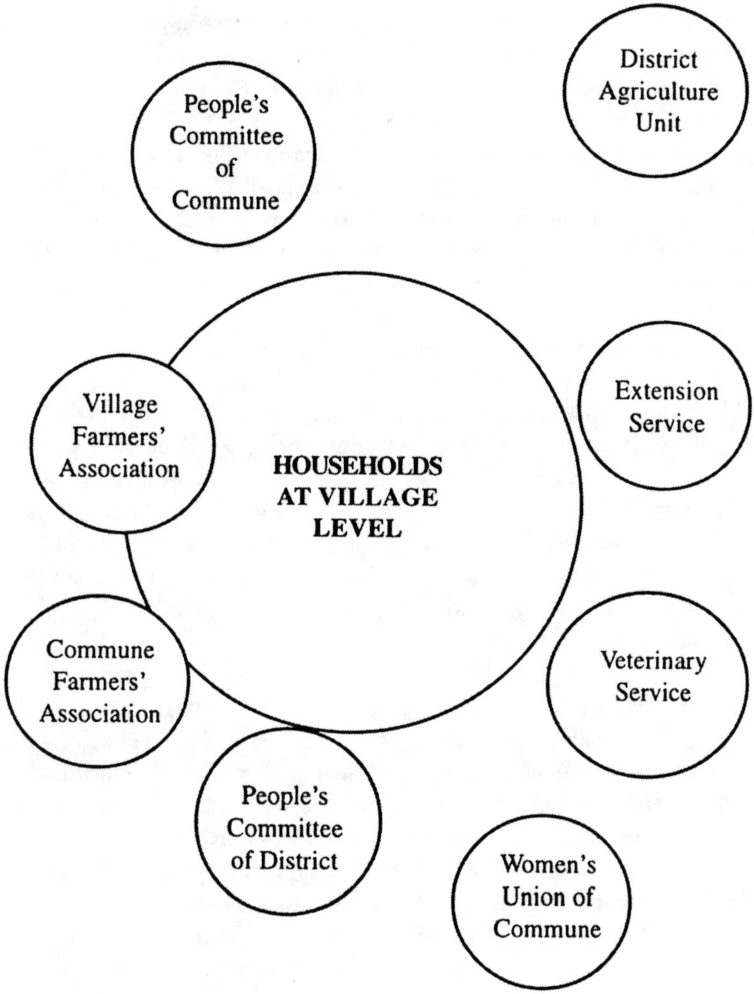

9.3 Communication Linkage Matrix

Communication linkage matrix indicates the level of communication between different individuals and institutions assessed on the basis of multiple criteria. The Venn diagram can be extended and analysed through communication linkage matrix as shown below in Chart 9.2. In the Venn diagram, those village households raising livestock were placed at the centre while their relationships with different service-providing institutions were shown through circular-shaped papers of different size and distance, either kept on the ground or pasted on the paper. These institutions are shown in the matrix given in Chart 9.2. Through the communication linkage matrix the village groups further analysed aspects of communication with the institutions against selected criteria such as "behaviour", "timeliness", "information exchange" and suggestions for improving communication. This matrix given in Chart 9.2 was done by a village group through group discussion upon completion of the Venn diagram.

9.4 "Chappati" (Venn) Ranking

The different institutions depicted in a Chappati (Venn) diagram can also be ranked in order of their perceived importance. An illustration on such a "visual" method is given below on the basis of "Chappati" ranking and diagramming done by a village group from village Karambelli in Raigad district, Maharashtra. The illustration shows how the participants can move with ease from "Chappati" (Venn) diagramming to ranking (and *vice versa*) to depict the relative significance of institutions in their sphere of social interaction.

The village group began by working on an institutional diagram. The process was as follows. The group wrote down the names of all the institutions, which had a bearing on their lives and their village. After consulting among themselves, they listed down eleven such institutions. Names of the institutions were written by a young man on separate pieces of paper, making sure that one piece of paper bore just one name. The outsiders then requested them to rank the institutions in the descending order of their importance to the community according to their best judgment. The pieces of paper with names of the institutions on them were first arranged in one row on the floor. The group then indicated their importance by placing stones against each of the institutions: the most important institution having the largest stone against it and the least important institution had the smallest stone to its right. We thus had two rows. Row one had slips of paper with names of institutions written on them and the row two had stones of different sizes indicating the

CHART 9.2 : Communication Linkage Matrix

Institutions	Behaviour	Timeliness of Service	Information Exchange	Suggestions
HH-Extension Service	Strong bond	Regular	Receive Information from villagers	More training courses required
HH-Veterinary Service	Good linkage	Frequent	Fast, punctual	Provision of medicine should be in time
HH-People's Committee of Village	Strong bond	Regular	Fast	Can provide information on good techniques, disease and its treatment, marketing
HH-People's Committee of Commune	Good linkage	Irregular	Fast	Officials must visit HH more often on a regular basis
HH-Commune Farmers' Association	Strong bond	Regular	Fast, punctual	Can provide regular information on economic benefit of farmers

(Contd.)

Chart 9.2 *(Contd.)*

HH-Village Farmers' Association	Strong, cooperative bond	Regular	Good linkage	—
HH-Women's Association	Good linkage	Regular	Fast	Awareness creation on ways of livestock raising and application of new techniques required
HH-District Agriculture Unit	Weak bond	Irregular	Slow	Livestock-raising programme inputs should be provided in time

Note: HH stands for households raising livestock in village Thon Trung in Vo Ninh Commune, Quang Ninh District, Vietnam. The above matrix was done by women group from the village on 19th December, 1997 after completion of a Venn diagram showing relationship of different institutions with households raising livestock.

importance of the institutions. The ordering of the institutions was like the one showed in Chart 9.3.

The ranking was then interviewed. The importance of institutions was on the basis of their potential to be of use to the community. Thus though the inhabitants of the village belonged to the tribe known as Katkari, the Adivasi officer (Officer in Charge of Tribal Development) of the District was ranked lower down in the order. This is because the community saw no benefit to them from the officer, despite the fact that she/he operates the Tribal Sub-Plan, which has a huge sum of money for development work, as government officers did not care for the poor. Contrast this with local NGO and Zilla Parishad's rank at I and II respectively. Functionaries from these institutions care for the poor and there was a possibility of being benefited from them in the future. The police station was ranked at VIII, because the villagers opted to solve their own disputes within the community, rarely referring to the police. The relationship of apparent mistrust between the community and the police station seems to be mutual. While the Katkaris avoid the police, the police call them a criminal tribe.

The Talati Office (local revenue office) was ranked fourth in the order of importance, because the power to issue "Sath Barah" (literally meaning *Seven Twelve*), an official notification of sorts, which proved ownership of land, vested with the Office. Most of the tribes cultivate land under their possession as handed down to them from their fathers and forefathers for generations, having no title deed to celebrate ownership. In consequence, they depend on the discretion of the officer in the Talati Office to establish their title to the land they cultivate. Curiously enough the Jangal Samiti (Forest Society) with whom the tribal people ought to have good interface was placed at the lowest rung of the ladder, for the simple reason that the office does not function at all.

Having ranked the institutions and having explained the rationale for the ranking, the outsiders asked the village group whether they could now place them in order of their usefulness by placing that institution which is least useful to them, irrespective of its importance, farthest from the point which represents the community at the centre. And in contrast place that institution which is most useful to them nearest to the point representing the community at the centre, irrespective of its importance. The outsiders further clarified that the distances they were talking about now were not physical distances but psychological distances. The outsiders helped them put up a pile of stones in the middle of the room, representing the village. The village group reversed the process. They

Chart 9.3: Ranking of Institutions by Village Group, Karambeli, Penn Taluka, District Raigad

Serial Number	Name of the Institution	Stone Placed	Rank
1	Local NGO		I
2	Zilla Parishad Office		II
3	Panchayat Office	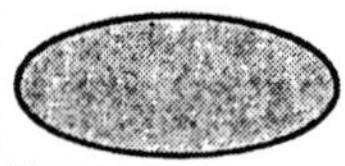	III
4	Gram Panchayat		V
5	Talati Office	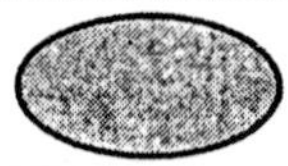	IV
6	Tribal Welfare Office (Adibasi Office)		VII
7	Tahsildar's Office (Local Revenue Office)	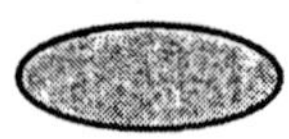	VI
8	Samaj Kalyan (Social Welfare) Office		X
9	Jangal Samiti (Forest Society)		XI
10	Police Station	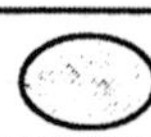	VIII
11	Credit Cooperative Society		IX

Notes: Village Analysts: Maruti Pawar, Ram, Pai Ram Pawar, Sonoo Pawar, Rama Wadmore of village Karambelli, on 13-2-2001. Facilitated by Amitava Mukherjee.

placed the local NGO and Zilla Parishad nearest to the community and then placed the other institutions at suitable distances representing their usefulness to Karambelli. The institutional diagram of Karambeli village thus emerged is shown in Chart 9.4.

The nearest institutions to the community were the local NGO or the "Sangstha" as they call it, followed by the Zilla Parishad and the Gram Panchayat office. Talati office came next. Rest of the institutions were far away in the psychological map of the village group. Thus it seems that most of the institutions which have accountability in one form or the other to the community are considered more useful than the appointed institutions which have virtually little or no accountability. Thus the tribal welfare office, the police station, social welfare office, forestry society, cooperative society, tahsildar's office are far away from the community in its mental configuration, in spite of recognising them as important to the village. The outside group did present this interpretation to the villagers and they confirmed that indeed that is the case, adding in the same breadth that accountability of the local NGO and Panchayati Raj institutions is reflected by the fact that the functionaries from these institutions come to the community. Whereas in contrast, in the case of the Tribal Welfare Office, Police Station, Social Welfare Office, Forestry Society, Cooperative Society and Tahsildar's Office, either the villagers travel there for a hearing or they do not function at all. The picture here conforms to what is seen elsewhere that where government offices do not function, the role of non-government offices and institutions is greatly valued.

9.5 Link/Anchor Person "Chappati" (Venn) Diagramming

The method of identifying link/anchor person/s by using "Chappati" (Venn) diagram is a way to identify actual or potential catalysts/anchor person and other communicators at the local level. It is a way to identify person/s who possess the ability or play the role of anchoring others for different activities and initiatives and also those who play supportive roles in spreading messages. The method can help in probing about who plays a key role in local decision-making ?

- — Who all support the anchor person?
- — Who spreads the messages to others?
- — Who is more sociable than others and holds others together?
- — Who can influence decision-making, community views?

CHART 9.4: **Institutional Diagram by Village Group, Karambeli Village, Raigad District**

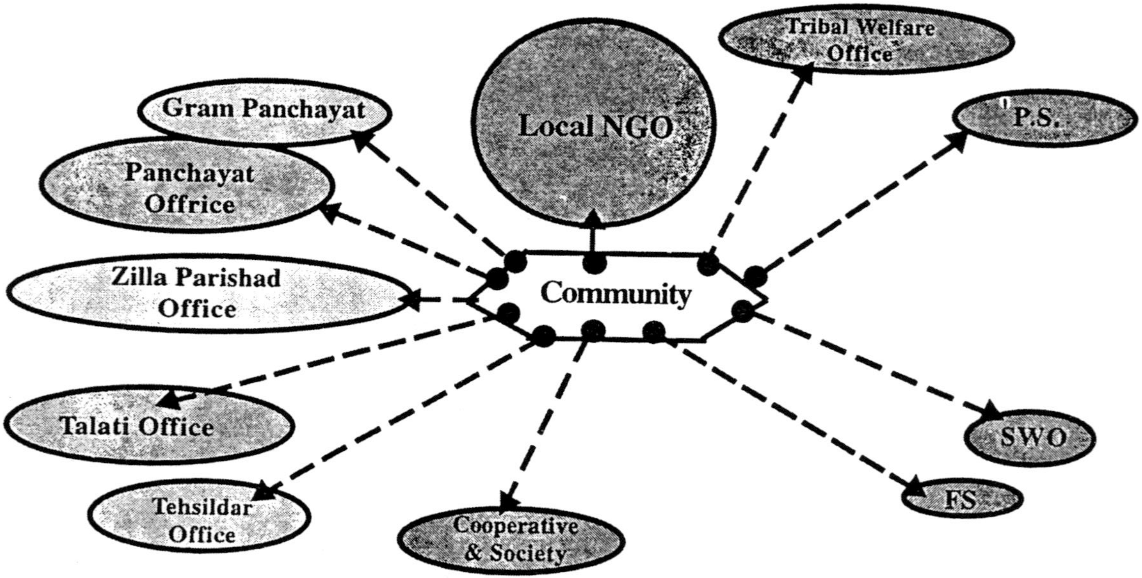

Note : PS= Police Station, FS = Forest Society, SWO= Social Welfare Office.
Village Analysts: Maruti Pawar, Ram, Pai Ram Pawar, Sonoo Pawar, Rama Wadmore.
Facilitator: Amitava Mukherjee. Date: 13-02-2001.

— Who listens to whom?
— How many act on such listening, etc.?

This is an important aspect of participatory inquiry because it can provide clues to important aspects of local relationship and communication. There can be a catalyst in a local community who has the qualities to urge people to do things, to make things happen. There can be a anchor person who holds others together and is socially interactive with a large segment of the community and for whom people have respect and listen to. Such a person can be a catalyst, somebody else can be good at spreading messages and some have more knowledge and experience than others and advise others. Some yield more social power and command social space than others. It is potentially useful to learn about

Chart 9.5: Link/Anchor Person "Chappati" (Venn) Diagram (Women)

'Chappati' Diagram of Village Communicators (Women), Village Baruabagh, Haldwani, India

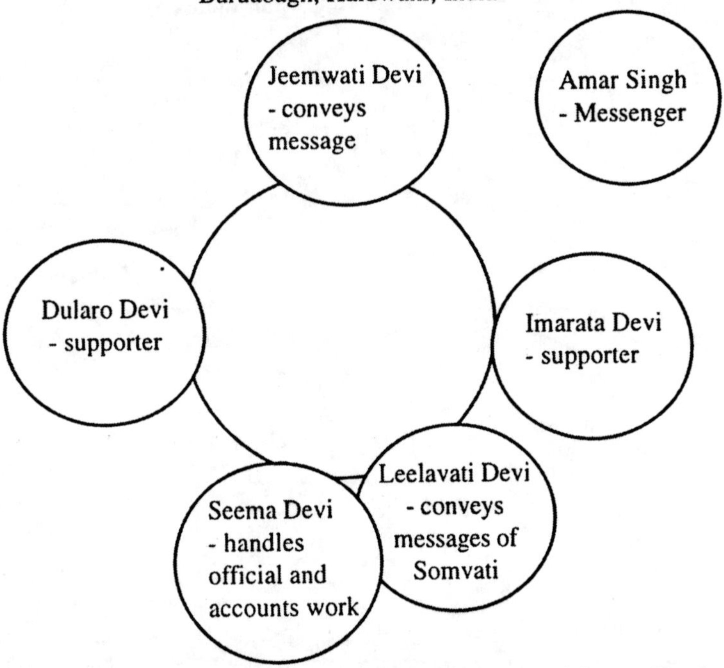

Village Analysts : Rajvati, Meenavati, Dulari Devi and Seema Devi. *Facilitators :* Ramesh Chandra Shukla, Vimla Bisht, Nimmi Kukreti and S.C. Sirohi. Date : 11-3-2000.

the communication set-up, formal or informal, of a local community.

Chart 9.5 is a "Chappati" (Venn) diagram on link/anchor person as done by women group in village Baruabagh in Haldwani, India. It shows formal communication structure within women's group. The President of the women's group is in the middle and Dularo Devi and Imarata Devi are the two main supporters of the President. Two women Jeemwati Devi and Leelavati Devi convey message to be further conveyed by Amar Singh to others. Seema Devi keeps official records and accounts.

Chart 9.6 is a "Chappati" (Venn) diagram on link/anchor person as done by men group in village Baruabagh in Haldwani. It shows the set-up of communication structure within the men's group. Sugriv Singh is key to decision-making though Puran Singh, the Village Chief (Gram Pradhan) formally communicates decisions. Sugriv Singh has two supporters, Karan Singh and Suresh Singh. While Khadag Singh reads

Chart 9.6: Link/Anchor Person "Chappati" (Venn) Diagram (Men)
'Chappati' Diagram of Village Communicators (Men), Village Baruabagh, Haldwani, India

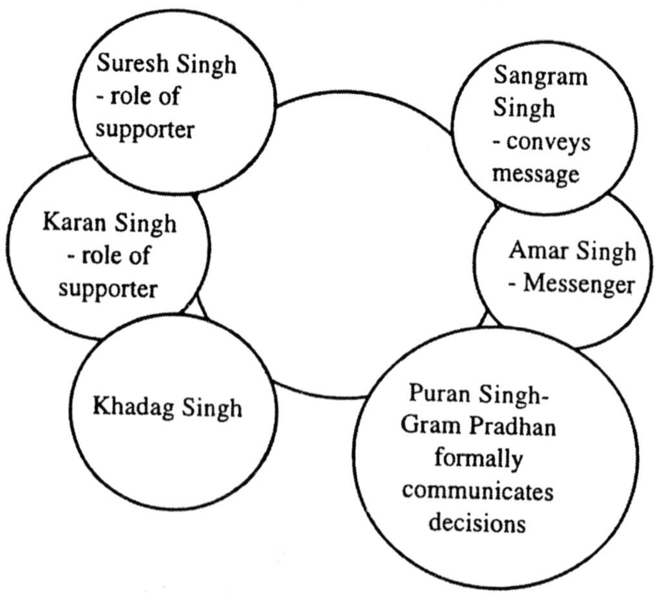

Village Analysts : Bhajan Singh, Kripal Singh, Dhani Ram, Virendra Singh.

Facilitators : Ramesh Chandra Shukla, Vimla Bisht, Nimmi Kukreti and S.C. Sirohi. Date : 11-3-2000.

out decisions, Sangram Singh conveys messages through messenger Amar Singh.

Such "Chappati" diagrams give useful insights into the local communication set-up and power relations and pockets of inclusion and exclusion in normal communication channels. This can also form the basis for improving communication flows at the local level.

9.6 Support System's Diagramming

A systems diagram depicts a system underlying some activity or a group of activities of a person or a group concerned. It helps in understanding the effectiveness of the constituents of the system, its strong points, problematic areas and constraints. Such a diagram for support system, as in Chart 9.7, drawn by a farmers group from village Maraon in Varanasi

Chart 9.7: Support System's Diagram
Farmers' Support System at Village Maraon, Varanasi, India

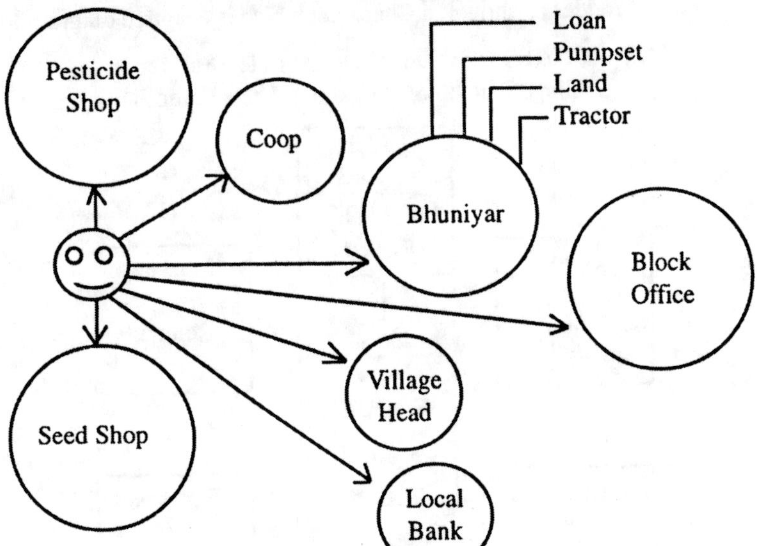

Village Analysts : Pratap Patel, Radheyshyam, Hiralal, Ashok and Munna Lal, Mahato Basti.

Facilitators: Sudipta Ray. Date : 11-3-2000.

Note : The participants assigned circles for each organisation with size implying the degree of importance. The distance of the circles from the farmers shows the level of support actually received by them.

illustrates a farmer's relationship with the various identified organisations such as block development office, seed shop, pesticide shop, cooperative, village head, local bank, etc. The input traders—the seed and pesticide shops—hold important place as they act as sources of information. Though the block development office is an important organisation as shown by its size, its role is not as effective as shown by the distance from the farmer. The farmers' cooperative, though small in size due to its limited resources, is closer to the farmers than the local bank.

9.7 Source Diagram

This method helps in identifying sources of any activity, items, issues and other criteria. It also provides scope for ranking/scoring of such sources according to their importance. This method is handy especially in the case of multiple sources and helps in comparing such sources in terms of their significance and availability. Local community members of village Panchma of Gorakhpur District in Uttar Pradesh, identified and ranked sources of fodder as shown in Chart 9.8, which is a source diagram for

CHART 9.8: Source Diagram for Fodder
Village Panchma, Gorakhpur, Uttar Pradesh

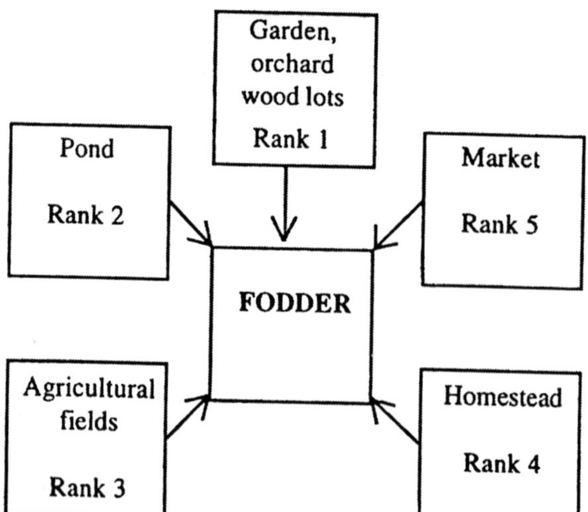

Note : Sources of fodder identified and ranked in village Panchma by a group of local villagers.
Facilitators : Jamal.

fodder. The chart shows that fodder is still available from resources within the community and some little fodder is purchased from the market, which is fifth in rank. It also shows that gardens, orchards, wood lots and ponds are more important sources of fodder than agricultural fields and homesteads.

9.8 Pie Chart

Pie charts indicate parts of a whole in proportional terms. A pie-chart method can be applied to illustrate relative shares of any item concerned. The method comes handy when comparative shares of different items/ factors are brought into discussion for further probing. Pie diagrams show the importance of relative items in the lives of local communities. They can show the use of land, water, credit and patterns of income, consumption and expenditure, sources of debt, medicines, kinds of trees, etc., in the lives of local communities. In Chart 9.9, the pie chart as done by the women group of village Sagarpur in Faridabad of Haryana is a comparison of yield loss in three crops—wheat, mustard and vegetables—caused by different factors, for two years—1998 and 1999. Such yield loss is 4 "anna" (or per cent) in wheat for both 1998 and 1999, for mustard it is 15 "anna" (or per cent) in 1998 and for vegetables it is 12 "anna" (or per cent) in 1998 and 1999. The yield loss was quite high in case of mustard in 1998 and also in vegetables in both the years.

One way of explaining pie chart as a method is to relate it to the currency and its part, which they use for the local payments. For instance, the Indian rupee is made up of 16 "anna" or 100 new "paise" and it becomes easy for participants to indicate what proportion of the rupee they think would constitute any factor responsible for the yield loss. Once the share of, say, the major factor gets determined by the participant/s, share of other factors can be estimated accordingly. The method of pie diagram is easily understood by illiterate/semi-literate especially when it is linked in terms of some local medium of payment, say, a currency or some other measure used locally for weighting. When a group participates in preparing pie diagrams, estimates of the share get naturally cross checked within a group of participants through mutual discussion.

9.9 Livelihood Analysis

Livelihood analysis method would consist of (a) listing of livelihoods; (b) description of livelihoods; (c) relative share of livelihoods—pie chart;

CHART 9.9: **Pie Chart**

Village Sagarpur, Faridabad, Haryana, India
Factors Causing Yield Loss in Agriculture

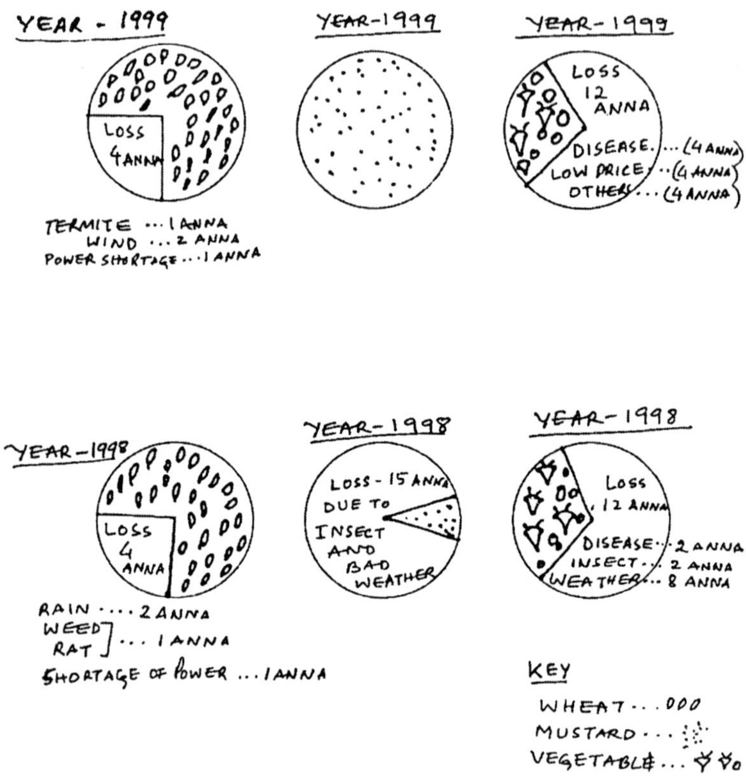

Village Analysts : Women group—Rajwati, Prem, Bhagwati, Purandei.

Facilitator : Meera Jayaswal. Date: 5-4-1999.

Note : The pie charts are a comparison of factors causing yield loss for two years 1999 and 1998 for three crops, wheat, mustard and vegetables.

(4) resource base for livelihoods; (5) livelihood constraint, problems and returns; (6) gender issues in livelihoods; (7) livelihood systems and strategies.

One application of pie diagram can be for analysing livelihood through the help of pie charts. This depicts the behaviour and adjustment strategies of households with different socio-economic characteristics. Each household has a strategy or strategies to cope with difficult situations and periods which arise from time to time. Such an analysis could take into account the size of the household, age and gender composition, wealth, assets, livestock, income and expenditure patterns, debt pattern, consumption pattern, seasonality, income by sources, disease and social obligations. Chart 9.10 on livelihood analysis presents a livelihood source analysis of village Mahilong (Bihar) with the help of pie-charts (Jayakaran:1991). In 1970, the livelihood analysis was less diversified with 75 per cent of the total number of households dependant on agriculture, while the rest 25 per cent were dependant on the service sector. This scenario underwent considerable change and by 1990 livelihood sources became quite diversified for the households in question. Of the total number of households around 80 per cent of the households referred to as Group A had a different pattern of livelihood in comparison to Group B, the rest constituting 20 per cent. Of the people in Group A, around 75 per cent were engaged in the service sector and 20 per cent in paddy cultivation together with 5 per cent in growing of vegetables. As far as Group B was concerned the distribution of sources of livelihood was as follows. Agriculture was the source of 45 per cent of the livelihoods followed by casual labour (40 per cent), vegetable growing (10 per cent), business (3 per cent) and others (2 per cent).

9.10 Ratio Analysis

Another method similar to pie chart for learning about proportionate share is the ratio analysis. For comparing proportionate shares, the total number of units is made divisible into discrete units, which are then considered for comparison. As shown in Chart 9.11, the total of crops grown in winter is divided into16 discrete units, of which the share of wheat is shown as 15 units. The way the ratio method has been explained in this context is by drawing its semblance to the Indian rupee consisting of 16 "annas" (its smaller denomination). The 16 "annas" are the discrete units by means of which such comparison has been done. Of

CHART 9.10: **Livelihood Analysis**
Village Mahilong, Bihar (India)

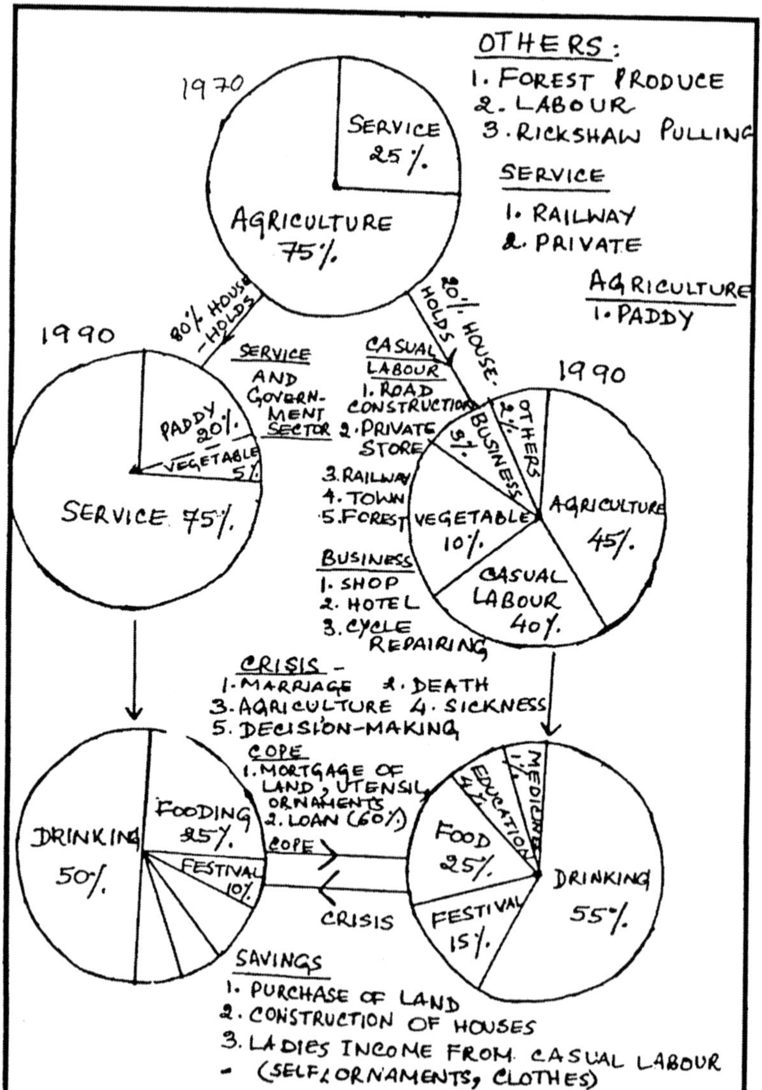

Source : Jayakaran Ravi (1991), PRA at Mahilong, Bihar, 27-30 November, 1990; Krishi Gram Vikas Kendra, RRA Notes, No. 13, August, IIED, London.

CHART 9.11: Ratio Analysis

Share of Wheat Crops in Winter Crops, Sagarpur, Faridabad Haryana, India

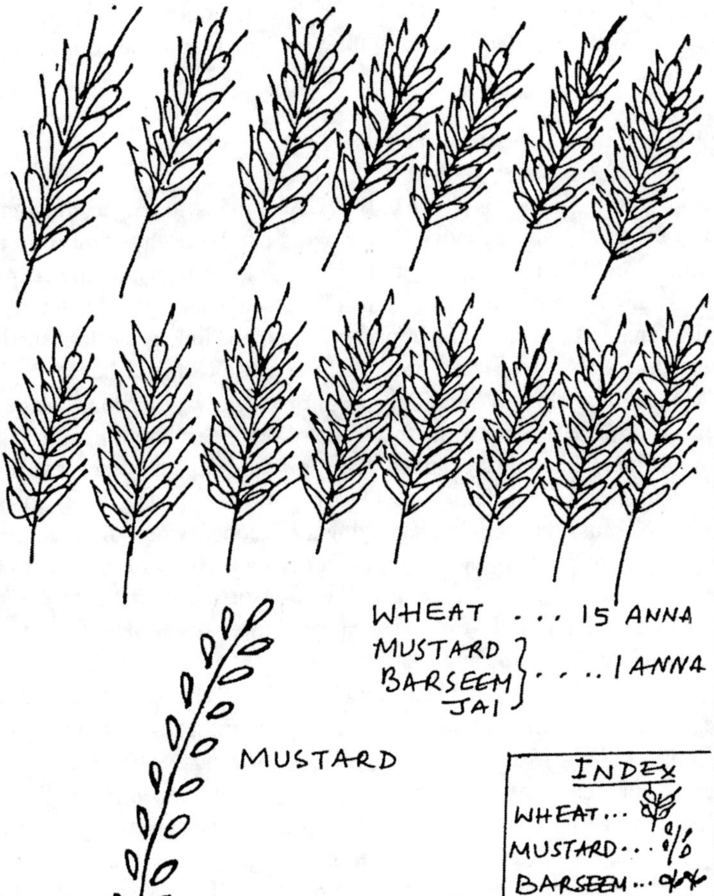

Note : 16 Anna of a Rupee = 100 per cent

Village Participants : Bhagwati, Prem, Pyari, Prem, Saroj, Shant, Vimla, Santosh.

Village : Sagarpur.

Facilitator: Meera Jayaswal. Date : 27-3-1999.

16 "annas", only 15 "annas" are wheat crops and one "anna" is fodder crop. Both methods of pie chart and ratio analysis are easy to be understood provided they are explained in simple terms with reference to some unit of measurement which people commonly use. Both methods indicate proportional shares and the choice of methods can be left to the insiders, the way they prefer to represent proportional shares.

9.11 Impact Flow Analysis

Impact flow analysis is a type of flow diagram. It is an impact diagram of the effects of any activity. The effects can be both favourable and unfavourable on the local communities. Impact flow method helps in analysing a chain of impacts of any event, activity, asset, etc. The impact flow analysis can show the impact point and the linkages established (or disrupted) as a result of interventions made (Shah, Bharadwaj and Ambastha: 1991). While analysing impact flows, a primary or direct impact can be listed leading to a chain of secondary or indirect impacts. While literate people are able to write down the impacts, others can make drawings to show such impacts. Once the primary impacts are listed, then group discussions help in identifying the secondary or indirect impacts. One way of probing into the impact of any activity or asset is to ask whether that activity or asset has made any difference in the day-to-day living and livelihood. And, if so, what are those differences which have come about. Once the impacts are listed, use of 8 helpers "why", "what", "which/who", "how" and "how much", "where" and "when" can be used for deeper probing into the impacts and also in listing of the follow-up impacts, if any. In Chart 9.12, one group from village Salri near Dehradun has described 5 beneficial impacts of the thresher machine on different aspects of local livelihoods such as reduced costs, saving of animal power, saving of time, better grinding and monetary benefits by outsiders using the machine. Such primary impacts also have a range of indirect impacts like saving money, good health of livestock, more time, better fodder, improved quality of life, more good milk and more income.

Similarly in Chart 9.13, the impact flow analysis of the physical productive infrastructure, such as a dam has been explained. A range of impacts has been covered, such as availability of water for domestic use, improved environment and water for irrigation. Each impact has led to further impacts as listed by the village group. The trend of the impact is from physical impacts to social ones.

CHART 9.12: **Impact Flow Analysis**

Impact of Thresher Machine, Village Salri, Dehradun, India

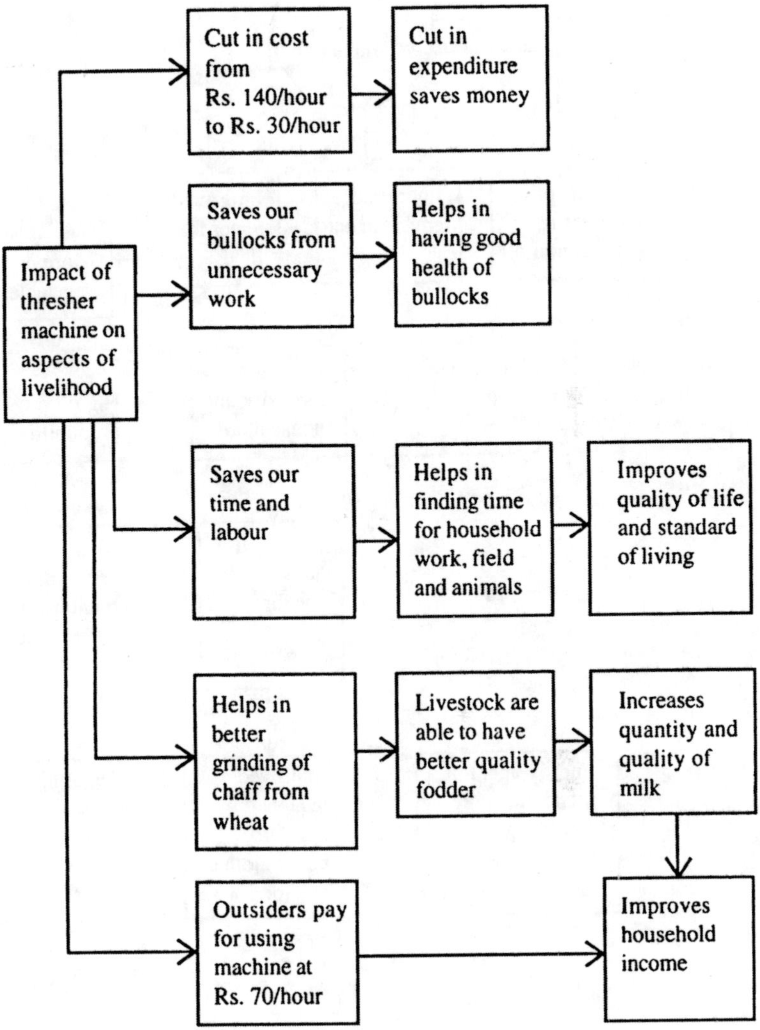

Village Analysts : Padmadutt, Ramesh Chand, Narayan Dutt, Ramesh Belbal, Preya Devi, Ganga Devi, Bhagwati Devi, Ganga Dut.

Facilitator : Tiger Group. Date : 5-2-1995.

Chart 9.13: Impact Flow Analysis

Impact of Dam, BO Track, Quang Binh, Vietnam

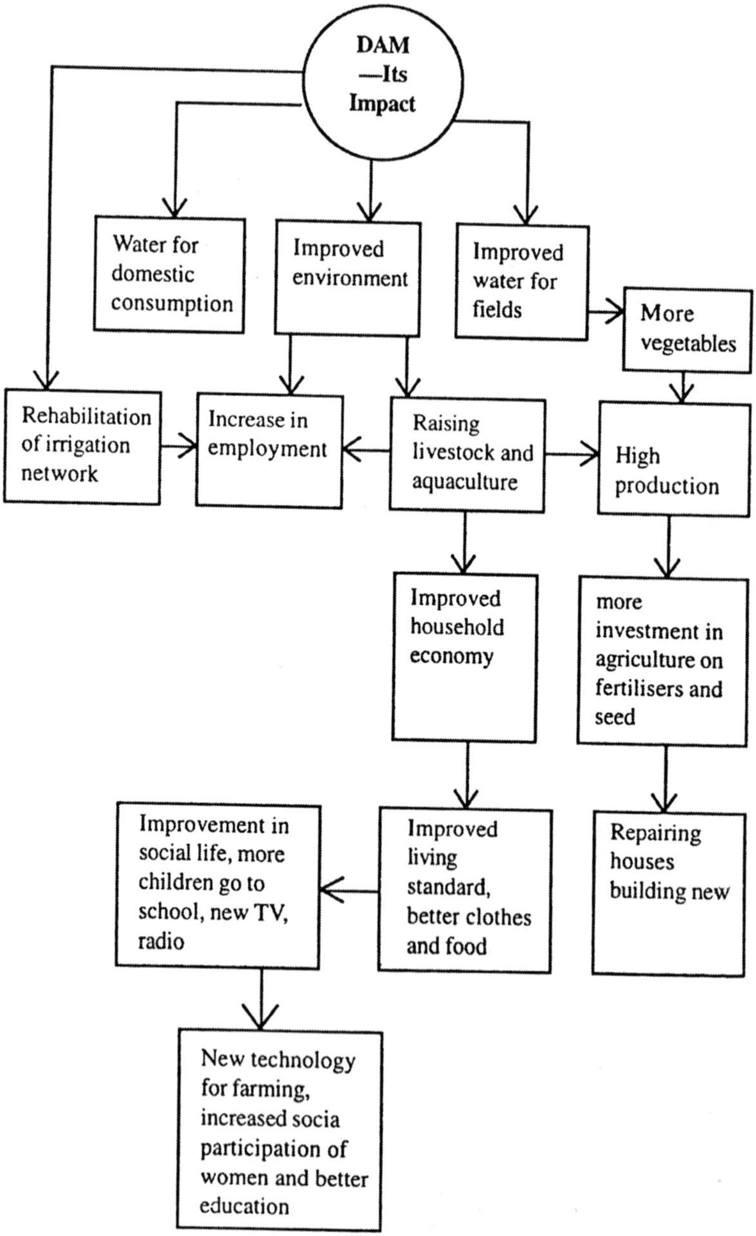

9.12 Impact Diagramming

Impact diagramming is a method involving illustration of impacts through drawing. Each impact is visualised through illustrations. In Chart 9.14, impacts of Con Ruong reservoir in Tien Phong village of Quang Binh of Vietnam has been illustrated. Such impacts consist of livestock raising, growing staple crop and fruits, two crops of high-yielding variety, fish-duck raising, fish cultivation, flower plantation, bathing, drinking water, etc. These have led to improved living standards, more savings, consumption, recreation, more investment and building of new schemes and their upgrading.

9.13 Flow Chart Analysis

They show the cause-effect relationship amongst different factors and can be effective for understanding the inter-linkages amongst different aspects of local community living. The local groups of women and men can be asked to identify different causes of a problem which they are facing and then asked to inter-connect the different aspects so as to have a causal analysis of the problem at hand. They can help in identifying the problems, the determinants, their nature and linkages. This can help in suggesting policies for minimising constraints and other bottlenecks and can also help in framing of feasible options. For instance, the flow diagram as in Chart 9.15 is of a village named Krishna Rakshit Chak in Midnapore, West Bengal which shows how two factors—crop failure and agricultural pollution—have led to increased impoverishment and decreased food availability in a resource-poor village. Lack of rain has led to crop failure, which has lowered the availability of food/income. This, in turn, has led to increased dependence on common property resources, some of which have been affected by agricultural pollution leading to lower availability of food and increased starvation.

9.14 Comparative Flow Chart Analysis

Drawing from the flow chart method, comparative flow chart is a method of comparing two separate flows. The method helps in identifying and developing criteria for two similar flows, which are comparable. As in Chart 9.16, oxen-tilling and tractor-tilling have been compared step-by-step in terms of usage, benefits and limitations. The flow chart of oxen-tilling is mainly in terms of activities in a sequence and primary and

CHART 9.14: **Impact Diagram**
Impact of Con Ruong Reservoir on Life at Village Tien Phong, Quang Binh, Vietnam

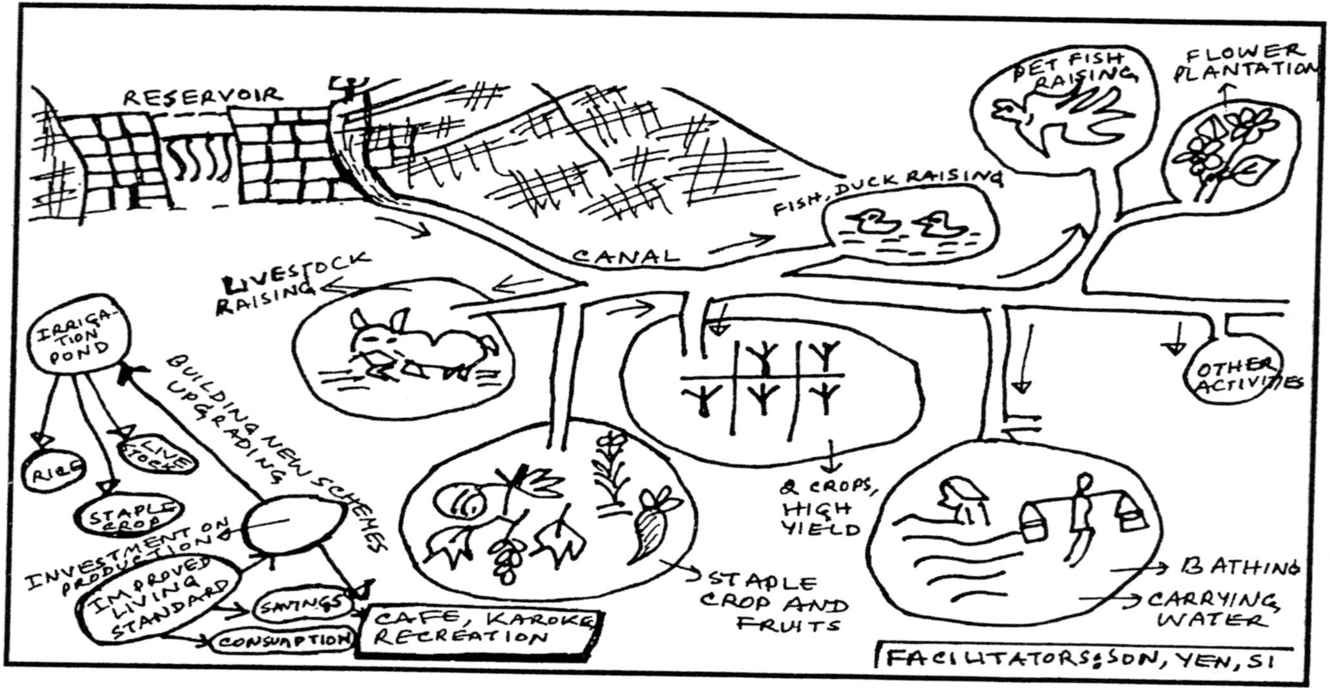

Chart 9.15: Flow Chart Analysis

Impact of Drought and Pollution on Village Krishna Rakshit Chak, West Bengal

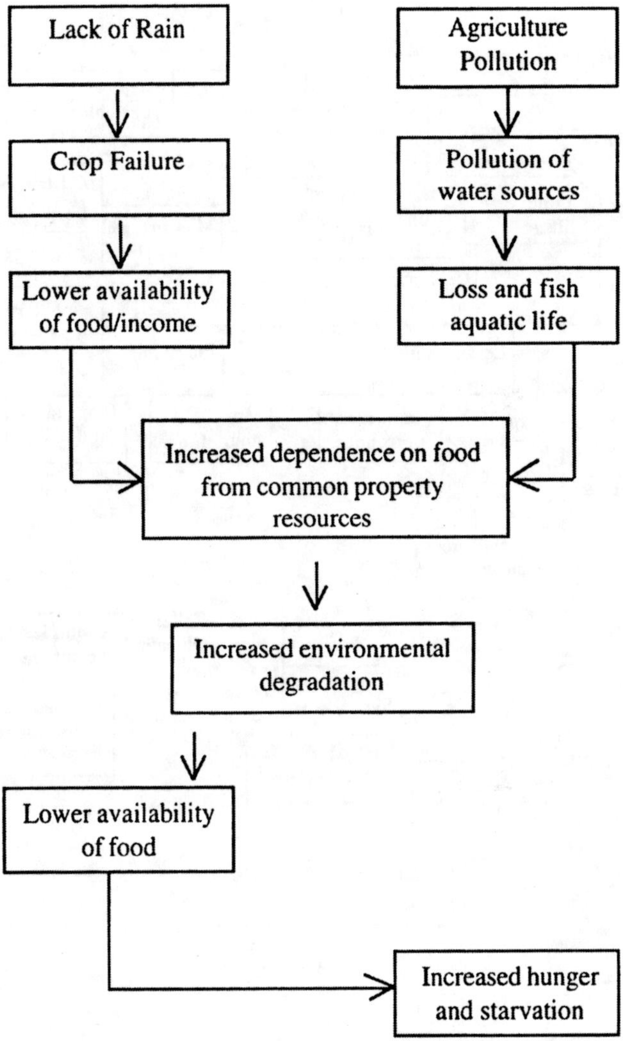

Village Analysts : Buddeshwar Dandapat, Mathur Mallik, Manmatha Mallik.

Facilitator : Neela Mukherjee.

CHART 9.16: **Comparative Flow Chart**
Oxen-Tilling Vs. Tractor-Tilling : Village Nuaon, Varanasi, India

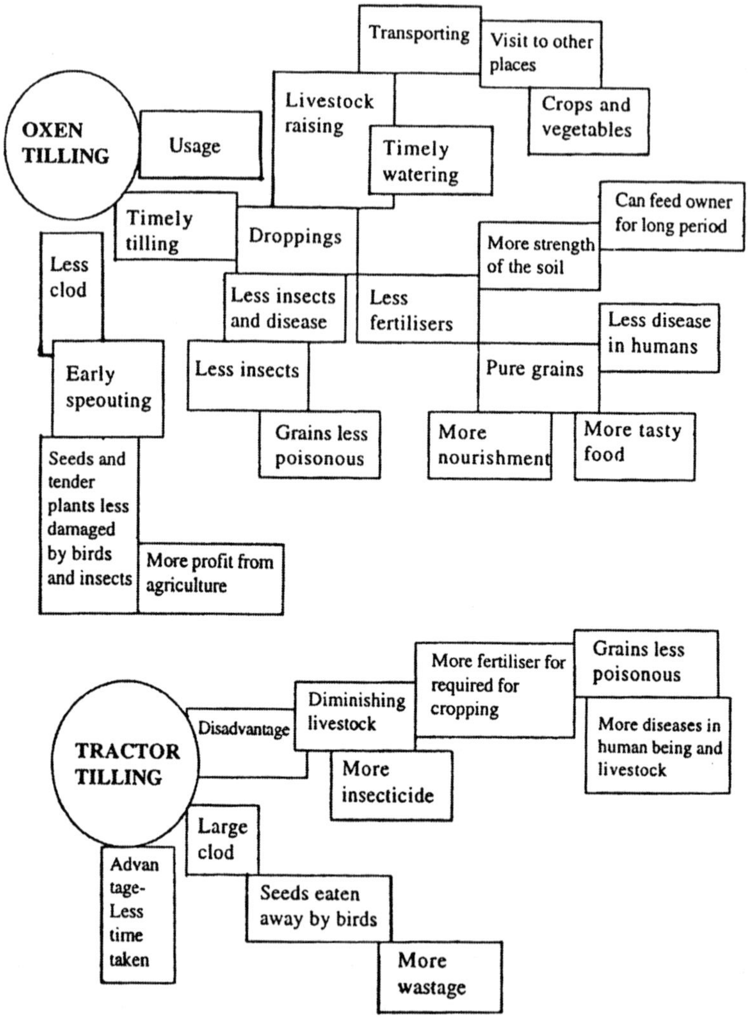

Village Participants: Awalakhi Devi, Manti Devi, Sabita Devi, Dhankesra Devi.
Village : Nuaon, Varanasi, Uttar Pradesh, India.
Facilitator : Meera Jayaswal. Date : 5-4-1999.

secondary benefits while the flow chart of tractor-tilling is more in terms of disadvantages. The visual depiction of flow charts of both oxen-tilling and tractor-tilling show clearly that as per village group of Nuaon from Varanasi, the former is clearly superior to the latter, whose benefits are greater.

9.15 Visual Trend Analysis

This method shows quantitative changes over time in different aspects of village life such as yields, population, livestock population, number of trees, area under cultivation, rainfall, time and distance to collect fuelwood and fodder, prices, etc. With the help of this method one can directly or indirectly see the increase or decrease of hardship in the poor people's lives. A time trend is different from a historical transect or a time line where the former is more precise giving indications of change (an increase or decrease) whereas, the latter can show broad movements of different aspects of village life rather than their precise shifts. Any local group, who are long-term residents of a locality, can be approached to show such a trend visually, preferably on the ground with indigenous materials such as sticks, seeds, stones, piles, etc. and then asked to explain such a trend. It is a way of visualising changes over time on the basis of information with the local community members.

Chart 9.17 illustrates the trend in tree population over a period of 25 years in village Nlaphwane in Botswana. The scoring by the village group shows how amidst a declining trend, local tree population reduced drastically between 1975 and 1980.

9.16 Diagramming of Income Generating Activities

Income generating activities, which are of crucial significance for the local livelihoods, can be portrayed through different diagrams, based on which discussions can proceed. This method is effective in focusing on income generating activities, existing ones and those proposed in future. Such activities are intrinsic to living and livelihood. Drawings of income generating activities illustrate many subtle points, which mere discussions can hardly help in highlighting. The kind of income generating activities and location can be learnt through holding conversations with "insiders" but visual depiction helps in highlighting quality and other nuances of the issue at hand. Such an income generating activity can be any activity, which gives rise to income. In Chart 9.18, a

CHART 9.17: **Visual Trend Analysis**
Village Nlaphwane, Botswana

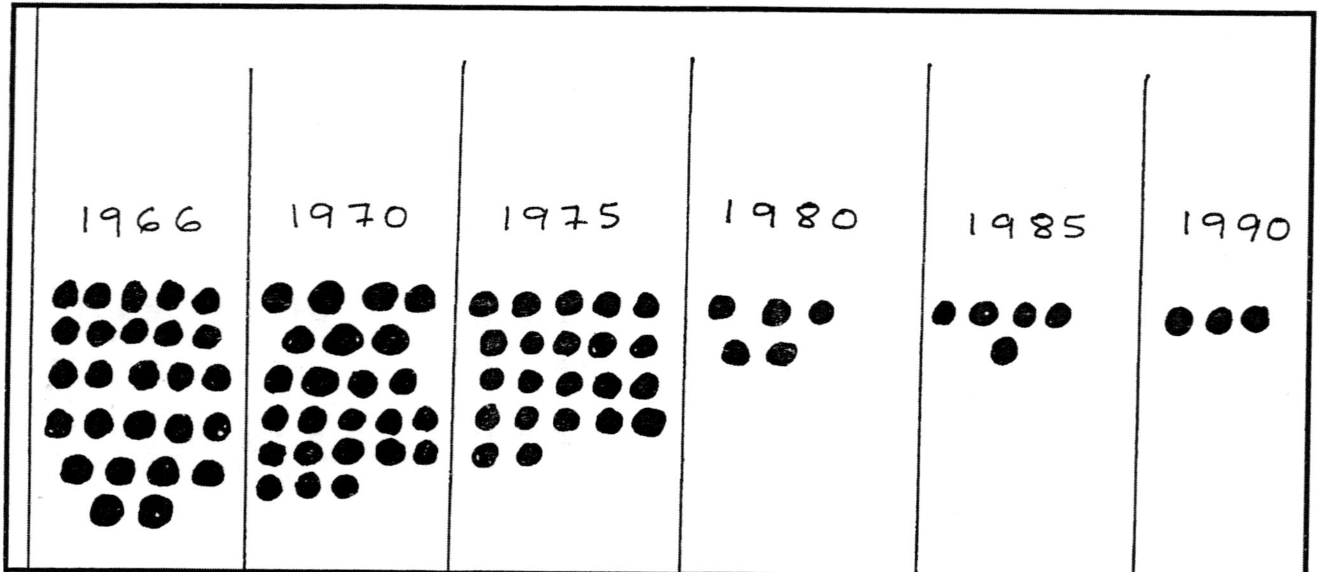

Note : "Free" Scoring shows the Change in Tree Population over a period of 25 years in Village Nlaphwane, Botswana.
Facilitator: Rhino Group, PRA Workshop, FSP-FAO, Gaborone.

CHART 9.18: **Diagram of Income Generating Activity**
Ha Giang, Vietnam

farmer from Ha Giang Province of Vietnam has drawn the existing livestock as means of earning income. He has also emphasised that such activities are adversely affected due to a sudden attack of diseases on livestock, little money to buy good quality livestock, no proper structure for livestock, shortage of capital for rearing more livestock. The diagram can be the focal point of discussion. It can be the starting point for participatory micro planning in income generating activities.

9.17 Causal Tree Analysis

Causal tree analysis is a "visual" method in which issues are identified as generic clusters and analysed in terms of branches of a tree, while the causes are thought as part of the root of the tree. A tree can also help in gaining an idea of costs and returns from any activity, where the roots are the costs while the branches are the returns. It helps in visualising a tree with different branches representing different problems and hence, implying varied solutions. Once the generic problems are identified as different branches of a tree, the specific problems within those generic clusters are identified, listed and analysed.

Chart 9.19 provides an illustration of a simple investment and return tree analysis as done by a women group from village Sahupura in Haryana as facilitated by Bratindi Jena. Jena writes that while discussing the investment and return pattern in agriculture the women drew a tree, in which the roots represented the return and the branches represented the investment. They believed that if the returns were low then they would abstain from investing in the next crop. The branches of investment were investment in land cultivation, fertiliser, pesticide, and seed, irrigating of the land and labour for weeding and harvesting the crop. The roots of the tree or the returns were crops worth 2,800 kilogram, fodder of 2,000 kilogram, sale of cash crop and extra foodgrains and seeds stored for the next year. During the exercise it became clear that investment was more than the return in the case of crop failure. Food requirement was partially fulfilled, they also got fodder for livestock and crop waste for meeting fuel requirements.

9.18 Demonstration Pack

Sometimes for conducting field inquiry, the outsiders carry a pack of cards in which some activity, item or event/process is already illustrated. They are generally common illustrations, which fit with local ethos and cultural perceptions, easily understood by the local community members. Certain

CHART 9.19: **Causal Tree Analysis**
Village Sahupura, Faridabad, Haryana, India

Facilitator : Bratindi Jena

CHART 9.20: **Demonstration Symbols**

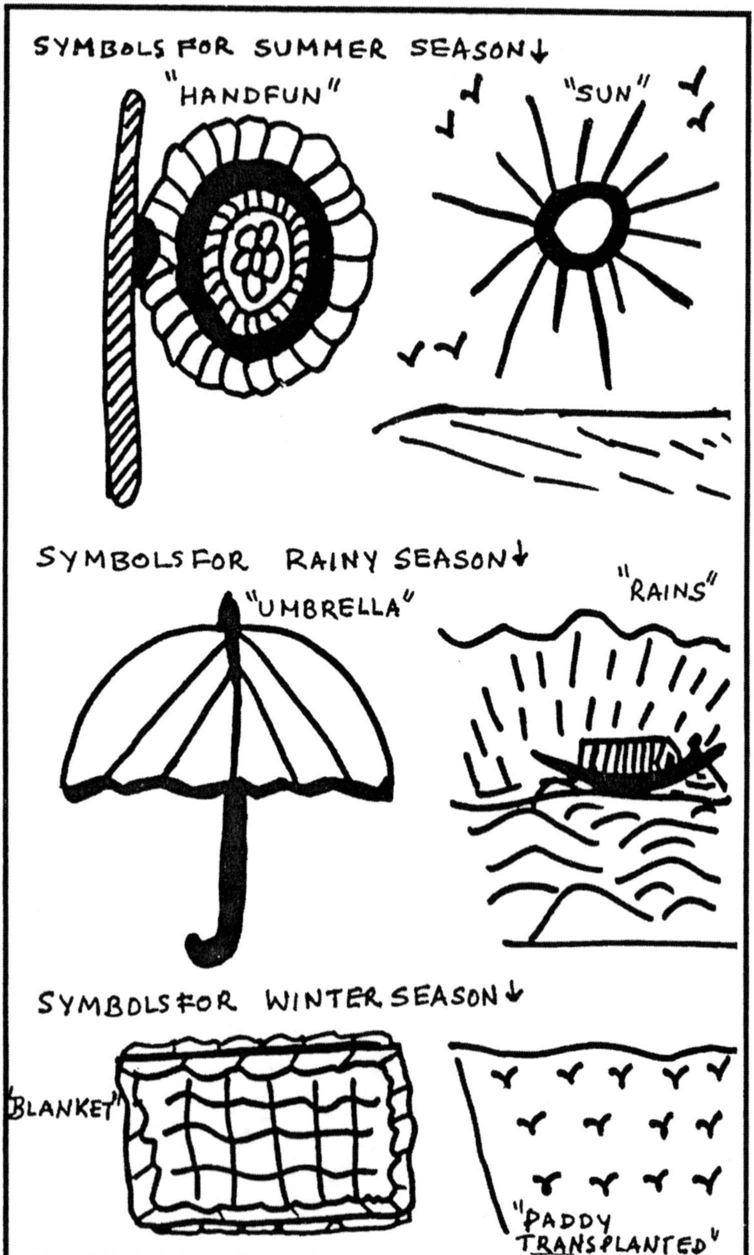

demonstration symbols are given in Chart 9.20, where symbols for three seasons have been shown. For example, for summer there are the symbols of "sun" and "hand fan" (locally used), for rainy season there are the symbols of "rain" and "umbrella" and for winter the symbols are "blanket" and "paddy transplanted". These symbols on cards were used during Participatory Rapid Rural Appraisal sessions for conducting field inquiry in 10 districts of Bangladesh in 1996 for the Human Development Report of Bangladesh (UNDP:1996).

9.19 Live Sample Method

In the live sample method, a little sample is obtained of a plant, a flower, fruit or a leaf or an insect-damaged root and other items important for further discussion and record. The insider/s identify some problem or constraint, which need to be explored further. Having tiny samples for discussion help in focusing on selected issues and in having a better participation with the "visual" sample placed in front of all for discussion. Such a sample provides clues to many useful points, which are then listed and discussed. This method also helps in larger groups' participation with common problems to solve. It makes planning easy and realistic. This method was used extensively for participatory action research during 1998-99 in a DFID funded project on community perspectives on the impact of air pollution on agriculture in Varanasi and Faridabad.

Box 9.1: Showing Sample of Brown Plant Hopper from Paddy Field to Scientists

"The team proceeded to Chitaipur to see the sample of brown plant hopper in paddy. Since it occurred for the first time, most farmers were not able to differentiate between blight and this. Further, such crops were harvested by many farmers. After visiting six sites of the standing paddy crop, we were able to see the sample..... Later, the team met two senior members of the Department of Mycology and Plant Pathology in the Banaras Hindu University, to obtain technical clarifications on the constraints reported by the farmers. All the samples collected during the field work were shown to them for their opinion."

Source : Field Report (1999) on "Community Perspectives on Agriculture and Air Pollution", Varanasi, by Action Aid, India.

The use of diagrams, however, has some limitations. Some diagrams drawn are too complicated to be widely understood. This can be avoided by encouraging simple diagrams, easily understood by people around. Appropriate notes need to be taken as and when local people explain their own diagrams. Sometimes it may become difficult to explain all parts of a diagram due to lack of space. The scope of a diagram becomes limited in the case of large gatherings. Diagrams drawn on the ground using local materials, unless translated into paper or retained through photographs, can be easily damaged and destroyed.

Diagramming is an integral part of PRA. Diagrams enrich discussions, help in revealing perspectives/priorities and in cross-checking of information through group interactions. Each method can be used in its own way to approach rural issues.

10

APPLICATIONS OF AND REFLECTIONS ON PRA/PLA

In this chapter I have compared the different methods that have been discussed in the earlier chapters and I have also discussed the different types of PRA/PLA activities and the issues related to the methodology and approach of PRA/PLA-type activities. Such issues help us in reflecting on PRA/PLA and remind us that each methodology has its own share of limitations and no methodology in this world can be considered as perfect. Such reflections can help us in finding ways to overcome such limitations and constraints from time to time. Again there are no set formulae to overcome the limitations and the constraints. Much depends on the issue, the situation and the context under reference.

10.1 Inter-Comparison of Methods

The methods and tools for PRA/PLA are a basket of basic, complementary and supplementary methods and tools, which can be combined in different ways depending on the purpose at hand. To start with there are the basic methods and practices for improving one's personal qualities, behaviour, approach and analysis. These have been discussed in Chapters 2 and 3. Such basic methods help in deconstructing mindsets, stimulating individual faculties, inculcating team spirit and augmenting analytical skills. These methods support PRA/PLA-type activities and do the spadework for approaching field and establishing positive and fruitful relationships with the local communities and groups. Only when such personal capabilities have been addressed can PRA/PLA-related field work become meaningful. Hence, in a PRA/PLA-type approach, mere acquisition of skills in participatory methods without appropriate mindsets is not in tune with the principles of PRA/PLA and is not enough for envisaging the participatory process, which PRA/PLA visualizes. Hence the "visual", "verbal" methods and the other participatory methods for conducting field inquiry are definitely important but the methods for influencing the mindset are those to start with. For PRA/PLA-type activities appropriate mindsets of outsiders are crucial though bringing about a change in the mindset is not easy. Considerable efforts are required for having an open and flexible mind, a learner's mind, a forward looking and positive synergistic mind, which helps in PRA/PLA-type approaches and activities.

The local knowledge sources, ideas and knowledge of the local histories, stories, folklore, practice, beliefs, traditional management practices help in having a better understanding of the local communities from diverse angles. Such sources help in understanding the background of a local community in terms of its culture, socio-economic, political and ecological trends. The participatory methods described in chapters 4, 5, 6, 7, 8 and 9 include both indirect methods supportive of PRA/PLA and those that involve direct participation of the local communities. Participatory methods, tools and techniques differ with regard to their nature, application, and opportunity for group participation and focus. Some participatory methods are relatively simple to apply as compared to others. Participatory mapping is one method, which is relatively simple and its process can help in involving the local people at different stages. For example, when a local group is preparing a map of a locality it is relatively easy for others to join the mapping process at any point of time and contribute. However for the participatory methods like matrix scoring/ranking participants need to be present throughout the entire process for continuity and relative comparisons. Those joining at a later stage may find it difficult to understand and follow the discussions. This is especially true for matrix scoring on a large scale, involving multiple variables and criteria and on-going revisions and changes in the output.

Some methods are better for rapport building, for instance, DIY, while others can be applied at a later stage once effective rapport building has been established, for example, application of Venn diagrams are generally better once rapport has been established. Methods also influence the number of participants. Whereas, in the application of vector scoring there can be many active participants doing the scoring, wealth ranking involves selected number of informants thus posing a limit to the size of participation. Wealth/poverty grouping of households on social mapping by communities is more participatory and open. This is less threatening as compared to wealth ranking of households, in which each household is ranked as per the local criteria by key informants. Some participatory methods have inherent limitations of scale/size and hence application of such methods can become limited by the size of the locality under consideration, for example, social mapping. Social mapping involving a large number of households may be time-consuming and not practicable.

Application of participatory methods depends on the objective at hand. If the objective is to study food security of a the local community in question then application of a method like food-livelihood calendar is more appropriate for such probing. The facilitation skills required also vary from method to method. The volume and kinds of data generated through social mapping may be much more than that of Venn diagramming. Visually, technical, socio-economic and ecological data can be generated through mapping whereas mostly socio-economic data tend to emerge through Venn diagramming.

10.1.1 Comparative Strengths of "Visual" Methods

The strengths of the "visual" methods such as mapping, matrix scoring, vector scoring and others in comparison to "verbal" methods such as semi-structured interviews are listed below:

- The "visual" methods encourage participation by providing a "visual" basis, which stimulates the thought process and encourages the local people to offer their views. It makes individual participants think, compare and contrast their views with others. A "visual" basis also encourages informal assessment by others to point out errors and omissions, additions, deletions and alterations.
- They help in facilitating discussions by means of "visual" medium. By seeing it visually, different people are able to focus on different aspects of the topic under discussion and can inter-link them easily. Perceptions on different aspects can be easily represented/recorded visually which opens up opportunities for further discussion.
- They allow more information at a glance than an interview. The information is retained in the "visual" output and can be referred as and when required as compared to information retained mentally or summarised in notebooks. They help in comparing and contrasting different aspects of a topic under discussion.

- The "visual" methods are accessible to literate, semi-literate and illiterate as they involve either mapping, scoring or diagramming as ways of expression. An illiterate or a semi-literate person can draw a mental map of the locality concerned, make diagrams and sketches to depict different things and score and rank while making comparisons. The items for such mapping, diagramming, scoring and ranking can be shown through different symbols to highlight criteria and items.
- "Visual" methods help in cross-checking information from interviews and secondary sources and validate them.
- "Visual" methods can be used anywhere, any location, on ground or paper involving relatively a large number of people. Such methods can be used either individually or with groups.
- "Visual" methods help in consensus building especially in the case of group output. Different aspects of a topic are illustrated visually to the members participating in a session and are left open for alteration, addition and deletion. Such methods help in projection of different viewpoints and resolving of differences to arrive at a consensus.
- "Visual" methods are flexible and help to make issues precise and objective and make things explicit and, hence, require less explanation.
- Application of "visual" methods helps in cumulative build-up of knowledge. As information is retained and recorded through the visual method it is possible to generate more and more information on that basis.
- "Visual" methods provide a logical framework for description, analysis, project planning and appraisal. Sequencing of these methods builds up a causal chain of analysis for in-depth probing.

"Visual" methods provide a basis for discussion and they need to be supplemented and complemented by "verbal" methods, for example, semi-structured interviews for probing and analysis. "Visual" and "verbal" methods go hand in hand and both can be used for PRA/PLA-type sessions depending on their relevance and strength.

10.2 Types of PRA/ PLA Activities

There are different types of PRA/PLA-type activities undertaken for different purposes. They include the following:

(a) Participatory programme/project formulation
(b) Participatory needs assessment
(c) Participatory planning and action
(d) Participatory monitoring
(e) Participatory evaluation/impact assessment
(f) Participatory action research
(g) Participatory questionnaire-survey

10.2.1 PRA/PLA for Programme/Project Formulation

PRA/PLA used in all stages of a project cycle can make projects more adaptable to the local needs. If the local communities or groups are involved in a project right from its initiation the sustainability of the project increases. As shown by experience, if a project is exogenously set up in a locality, the chances of its success are low. The risk bearing inclination of the project participants is expected to be higher in all cases where those who are the intended participants of a project have a voice in decision-making and project activities. In this context, it may be mentioned that different projects, if planned by the local community with their local knowledge, are likely to be in harmony amongst themselves and together their net effect on the local natural and social capital can be favourable.

A case study describing attempts at formulating a community empowerment programme in Bangladesh provides interesting insights into the relevance of PRA/PLA type approaches, the steps and the field lessons in such formulation. The case study is based on the field notes of the author.

Participatory Programme Formulation in Bangladesh

The United Nations Development Programme (UNDP), Bangladesh, in collaboration with the Government of Bangladesh (GoB) adopted PRA/PLA-type activities for fielding two sets of Community Empowerment Programme (CEP), which involved direct participation of the local communities in decision-making and implementation processes of projects concerning them. The CEP Formulation Mission of UNDP, Bangladesh, was on a fast track with its scheduled period of about two months in mid-1997 with an agenda for preparing 6 project documents and 2 concept papers at the national level. The CEP Mission for project formulation was a sequel to the earlier work on Human Development Report, Volume 3, that the UNDP, Bangladesh, did in 1996, where, a PRA team interacted with more than three thousand poor women, men and children of Bangladesh and presented their views and analysis as expressed by them.

Focusing on two primary objectives, capacity building of the poorest and facilitating developmental collaboration between the community and other agencies, the CEP Formulation Mission aimed at consultation with the poor community, with GoB and other development agencies for preparation of 6 project documents on the following areas/ communities:

— Urban poor in "pourashavas" (town municipality areas)
— "Adivasi" (tribal groups)
— Rural poor
— Garment workers
— Commercial sex workers
— Street children

and 2 project concept papers related to

— Inland fisherfolk community
— Traders in the informal sector

A survey of literature on the project formulation by different agencies showed that little was available regarding community participation at the stage of project formulation, when such projects get identified and prepared as compared to that of planning and implementation stages. The challenge facing the Formulation Mission was two-fold, one to find appropriate ways to enable the communities to broadly identify and design projects based on their "worldview" and the other was that of matching community "reality" with other stakeholders' "reality", the latter included the experts, UNDP, government and non-governmental organisations.

A quick variation of Participatory Rural Appraisal (PRA) called Participatory Rapid Rural Appraisal (PRRA) was applied for consultation with the local communities. The different phases of the programme formulation Mission were as follows. Phase 1 was on review Assignment with experts/government departments/non-governmental organisations/Mission team for the background information on the sub-sector, the areas to be visited and checklist of themes/issues, if any.

Phase 2 was an exploratory round of participatory interaction/ consultation with the community using PRRA and leading to preliminary community design. Phase 3 was one where consultants prepared individual project concept papers based on such design and other primary data and made presentations. In Phase 4 there were stakeholders' workshops held for validation, feasibility of options and linking up. Phase 5 was based on participatory interactions and consultations for topical round of field investigation/community interaction. In Phase 6, the consultants revised proposals while validation/negotiations continued. In Phase 7, project documents were submitted by respective consultants for appraisal and acceptance.

Of the 6 proposed projects, only 3 of them (those on rural poor, tribals, urban poor of pourashavas) covered stage 5 while others skipped it for want of time, and, only one proposed project (that on the commercial sex workers) slowed down due to slower process of consultation and ownership issues. Of the 2 project proposals, one (informal traders) was completed in stage 3 while the other (inland fisherfolk community) reached stage 4 to be revised for the subsequent stage. In the field, PRRA methods were used with key informants for sampling of thanas and villages. PRRA was conducted not with the purpose of having representative results from the community but for providing broad indications of the major issues in a community and also providing an overview. It was based on a selection of communities covering different criteria such as interior villages, poor/other groups, groups having/not having interventions etc. The sampling was made random within the poor groups of women and men.

The local communities were met in small groups of women and men, at different locations. The groups initially described their state of poverty, conditions of existence, their concept of empowerment, ways to overcome poverty and their own ways of justifying the proposed project concerning them. The communities also identified their problem set, scored/ranked them, listed their coping strategies, suggested project activities and proposed roles of themselves and developmental agencies. For each proposed project, the results of community interactions in different locations were organised into two large matrices. Matrix 1 was organised around the grassroots concept of poverty and empowerment with the sub-headings shown on next page.

Matrix-2 was organised around the problem-domain as described by the communities and their suggested strategies and actions. It had the sub-headings as shown on next page.

Matrix 1: Grassroots Concept of Poverty and Empowerment

Name of project, community, location	State of poverty and conditions of existence	Concept of empowerment and strengthening linkages	Ways to overcome/ reduce poverty	Reasons for project justification

Matrix 2: Community Problem-Domain, Suggested Strategies and Actions

Name of project, Community and Location	No. of sessions and size of group interactions	Nature and process of poverty	Major problem domain as described by poor	Coping strategies, including seasonal ones	Suggested actions and community contribution proposed	Expected project impact and other remarks

Matrix 1 was significant because it reflected the community perspective on poverty and empowerment, which was as important as the other stakeholders' perspectives including that of donors and other agencies. It also provided the conceptual basis of the community perspective leading to Matrix 2. Matrix 2, on the other hand, helped in preserving community made project designs and also inputting into the logical framework analysis of project documents as required by UNDP.

Some Field Lessons in CEP Formulation

Some field lessons of the Mission are described below. The poor group/s participated in the preliminary design of the projects at an initial stage of project formulation by identifying their problem set, qualifying their problem and describing major components/activities to overcome many of the problems. This is quite different from those projects where the community gets involved in the later stages of planning and implementing, once project formulation is over. However, though the local communities were ready to contribute in their own way, they expected other stakeholders to come up with a range of options on problems that they found difficult to solve. Again, there were limited answers to many of their problems even from the other stakeholders' side, for example, ways of dealing with outsiders' attitudinal problems as raised by the street children. Different groups of poor people contributed their "reality" on different themes, in their own way and the issue was to organise them and project them upstream for basic project design to emerge. Output from such field-based sessions was organised into large matrices, which made comparisons possible. Based on scoring/ranking of problems as done by the community simple indices were constructed of issues raised by communities and their prioritisation of such issues.

Matching community's "reality" with "reality" of other stakeholders/institutions was not that easy. There were both social and political parameters within which a project had to be adapted. For example, commercial sex workers of Tangail expressed one of their priority needs as that of gaining social recognition for which they used fresh white flowers to symbolise it on the ground and also score it amongst other priorities. Little did they realise that they were considered "outcastes" and "threat to society's moral fabric", and hence their stated priority was totally contrary to that of many other stakeholders. In stakeholders' workshops, some also raised questions about the technical validity and legitimacy of the community perspective. The question was related to the legitimacy of communities projecting their "reality" in their own way and with their own emphasis. It was not easy to handle such issues. Some stakeholders of the CEP failed to take cognisance of the fact that there was an intense participatory process to arrive at the final programme formulation. The underlying participatory process, though not obvious to many, was the mainstay of such programme formulation Mission.

10.2.2 Participatory Needs Assessment

PRA/PLA can be applied for making need assessment of participants for any topic under consideration, for example, needs assessed for training purposes. Application of participatory methods helps in arriving at a portfolio of needs of the participants for whose needs assessment is being made. At the local level, such need assessment helps in focusing on the relevant topics, setting goals and objectives and making action plans. Need assessment at the local level by the local participants is a starting point for identifying a basket of the local needs and appropriate activities to suit those needs. The methodology adopted for participatory training needs' assessment for China Wetland Bio-diversity Conservation Project is described below.

Participatory Training Needs Assessment in China

Training is a major project component in the China Wetlands Project. The objective was to do comprehensive training needs analysis and design of "training packages" for selected National Nature Reserves and their associate offices including the central project office. Training needs assessment was to improve the current capability for managing wetlands for biodiversity conservation and sustainable use. For meeting the objectives of the Project a field inquiry was undertaken for interaction with different groups of participants towards the last quarter of 2000. One main approach was training needs assessment made by the participants themselves. Participatory needs assessment done by the participants was approached in three different ways:

— Organisational needs assessment by meeting-discussions with different tiers of personnel in different organisations.
— Group needs assessment by meeting small groups of women

and men at the local level from the local communities living in and around wetlands.

— Individual needs assessment by interviewing individual participants and the responding to a small set of informal questions.

In general, the process for interactive sessions with different groups was as follows. After explaining the Project objectives and the objectives of the training needs assessment to different groups of stakeholders in the project semi-structured interviews were held on different issues related to wetlands conservation and management and the scope for appropriate training. In most meetings only the leaders were vocal and it was difficult to learn about the views of others present. One way was adopted to overcome this constraint by requesting the participants in a group to answer a small set of questions in writing. This created space for participants to express their own views. They were personal views, which were frank stating individual perspectives and positions. For interacting with the local communities/groups of women and men, participatory methods such as semi-structured interviews, mapping, listing of issues, etc., were used within limited time periods keeping in view that the groups were quite busy due to the harvesting season. The sessions were conducted separately with women and men groups at different places keeping gender considerations in view.

On the basis of training gaps identified through interactive sessions, as above there emerged a vector of training needs and accordingly the participants suggested topics for future training. This vector was joined together with the types of training programme/s suitable for meeting project objectives of the China wetland project.

10.2.3 Participatory Planning and Action

Increasingly development projects are adopting participatory approaches to its planning, implementation, monitoring and evaluation. This is recognition of the significance of PRA/PLA-type activities. The "open-ended" approach and methodological innovations in PRA/PLA have opened new vistas on the developmental scene. PRA/PLA-type activities help the local communities in identifying problems and opportunities and planning on the basis of the local resources. The following is a case study on participatory micro planning based on the field notes of the author

Participatory Micro Planning in Vietnam

Ha Giang Province is situated in the northern part of Vietnam bordering China with relatively lower level of literacy, especially in its remote areas. The Province has ethnic minorities as inhabitants, who are multi-cultural and multi-lingual living in the mountainous terrain under difficult living conditions. Three basic workshops on PRA/PLA micro planning for project officials and members of Farmers' Union and Women's Union were held at Ha Giang, where the workshop participants undertook facilitation of the local-level micro planning in areas with low literacy and those with high literacy. It was also important to identify ways of influencing the conventional "top down" commune-level planning.

Participatory micro planning in areas having a high literacy rate was not much of a challenge. They took relatively less time with both the local women and men groups participating in making of such micro plans. However, such micro planning in villages with low literacy was tried in ways more than one.

- That of utilising the services of a literate person in the village to be the scribe where other villagers participated in the planning process by word of mouth.
- That of villagers using different symbols to represent the issues that they raised and then scoring them as per their preference.
- That of villagers drawing objects on paper and making pictorial plans with scoring/ranking of their priorities.
- That of villagers using picture cards to do their plans.
- In some villages, villagers adapted different combinations of the 4 ways of micro planning as given above. Ways adopted in areas with low literacy were more diverse than those with high literacy.

One main objective of the workshops was to demonstrate ways of influencing commune-type planning from "bottom up" where individual village plans would lead to commune-level plan. Influencing the commune planning process was visualised as a three-step approach, though in actual practice, it was not possible to cover the third step during the workshop period.

- First step was that both women and men groups of villagers made their own plans and presented and validated them in their own villages;

— Second step was holding of commune-level meeting-discussion where villagers from each village shared and discussed their plans; and

— Third step was to put together all the micro plans to arrive at a commune plan where the resources, time, etc., would get matched for the commune-level plan to be ready for implementation.

These steps as above were in sharp contrast to the normal practice at the commune level, where the decisions from the "top" would get passed to the provinces, districts and then to the communes with pre-determined funds, targets and time. As for the making of village micro plans prepared during the workshops, it was possible to cover only 6 villages out of 10 villages of Phuong Do commune due to paucity of time. Commune-level presentations, organised on that basis were scheduled for half a day in which farmers from different villages, both women and men, made short presentations on their micro plans for different project components. All micro plans were exhibited at the presentation hall for the others to see and discuss. Farmers' presentations were preceded by an "overview" by the chairman of the commune with the help of a sketch map of the commune, a "visual" problem chart and basic statistics relating to the commune. The presentations were followed by a question-answer session on the issues raised. Though only 6 villages were covered from 10 villages of Phuong Do commune, one basic objective was achieved in terms of initiating and demonstrating a participatory process to influence commune-level plans. For the third step, which involved arriving at an overall commune plan, finding ways of putting together the PLA micro plans was important. However, the aggregation of PLA micro plans was not that simple since such plans were diverse and any one format for aggregation would limit such diversity. This was overcome to some extent by suggesting formats for componentwise aggregation of the village plans for administrative and financial convenience. Since, only 6 villages out of 10 villages were covered in Phuong Do commune the aggregation of PLA micro plans was incomplete to that extent.

The field work in low literacy areas showed how pictorials could be used for planning. The micro plans done by the villagers were done through the pictorials made by them. Only those villagers willing to draw pictures helped with the pictorial plans while others discussed and watched the process. With many pictures drawn by farmers, it was suggested that the project office could select a range of them and print them to make copies for distribution to the project staff for use by farmers for micro planning. Such pictures drawn by farmers were of different kinds such as those of pigs, buffalo, field, trees, duck, hen, school, irrigation canal, water tap, disease, crops, forest, farmer, attitude, behaviour, etc. Another lesson learnt was that it was better to go for relatively simple plans, which could be understood and validated easily. PLA-type micro plans in low literacy areas were simple ones with 2 rows, where one showed the problems while the other showed the solutions. Sometimes a utility matrix on the topic concerned also preceded such plans. Pictorial planning took time where each pictorial required additions and alteration as suggested by the farmers. Often the farmers were reluctant to draw and motivating them required time and patience. The micro plans prepared by the villagers, both literate and non-literate, were returned to the village communities. The village communities in many villages wanted to retain the plans for future use whether by the project or other development agencies.

Amongst the limitation of such participatory pictorial planning it was difficult to copy pictorial plans for official report writing. The participants faced problems in retaining copies of pictorial plans for future use. Since many plans were made on large sized chart papers, photocopying of pictorial plans was not easy. Often longer time and imagination were required for making micro plans for low literacy areas, which was not thought convenient for the stipulated time frame of the project. There was a limit to pictorials for each activity. The farmers were also busy throughout the year. At the commune-level presentation, only a few farmers from each village could be accommodated for lack of space. Broad-basing of face-to-face participation was not easy at the commune level, especially because the commune was of big size. The larger the village/commune size, the greater can be the time taken for presentation and discussion. Planning for too many components and activities took time and their presentation by and with busy farmers, in village/commune, was also not easy to organise.

10.2.4 Participatory Monitoring

Monitoring shows progressive trends in a project/programme, whether partial or total. It helps in checking, setting up warning systems and keeping records. In participatory monitoring the local people are directly involved in such monitoring processes. For purposes of monitoring the local people evolve a set of local indicators to guide effective implementation of a project. In the case of a problematic situation PRA/ PLA-type monitoring activities help in resolving conflicts. In a monitoring process, the local people are in a good position to identify gaps between expected and actual results. Their views can also help in improving upon the working of the project as far as practicable. Different kinds of impacts of the project such as socio-economic, ecological, both short-run and long-run, can be examined and analysed by the local communities and the outside team for the purposes of impact monitoring. The flexibility in PRA/PLA methods adds to the flexibility in monitoring and helps in improving the performance of the project. Participatory monitoring is generally based on both qualitative and quantitative information. The steps in setting up a participatory monitoring system at IFFDC's project at Pratapgarh, Rajasthan, is briefly described in Box 10.1. Such field experience shows that it is possible to develop such a compact system based on the local people's knowledge and experience.

Box 10.1: Setting up Participatory Monitoring System

At IFFDC, Pratapgarh in Udaipur, Rajasthan, Western India Rain-fed Project sponsored by DFID, a total of 8 workshops were held over time for setting up and operationalising a participatory monitoring system consisting of output and impact monitoring based on the locally evolved indicators. The process adopted for constructing the monitoring system was a series of workshops with the local people and project team so as to evolve the whole system from the grassroots. Such workshops helped in clarifying concepts and issues related to participatory monitoring, project objectives, activities and output, building criteria based on the local perspectives, customising system and making it focused, integrated and comprehensive. The monitoring indicators were evolved in the workshops with participants from the local communities and project team, including both women and men. All workshops held ensured participation of grassroot actors in the project and encouraged group-work, field visits, shared learning and ownership. In setting up a participatory monitoring system based on PRA/PLA, indicators were evolved with the help of the local people. The processes encouraged through the workshops were as follows:

— Moving from open-ended inquiry to more focused

(Contd.)

approaches and systems adapted to the local context.

— Participation of the local key informants and project team members to set up customised monitoring system and testing it under field conditions for further improvement.
— Understanding of micro-meso-macro linkages in sustainable rural livelihoods.
— Combining quantitative and qualitative indicators to build monitoring systems.
— Combining PRA methods with the conventional methods like enumeration purposes.

Some lessons learnt in the process are that the local knowledge and experience are essential for building up a localised monitoring system for output and impact monitoring. Follow-up activities from time to time help in improving the system and making it more responsive to the local needs.

Source: From field notes of Neela Mukherjee on WIRFP, Pratapgarh, Rajasthan (India).

10.2.5 Participatory Impact Assessment/Evaluation

Participatory evaluation of any project/programme is a learning activity for both the local people and outside team to take stock of the past, reflect on processes, activities and outputs and learn in order to improve future decision-making. Impact assessment/evaluation can be conducted by the project implementation agency or by an external organisation for assessing appropriateness of design, implementation methods for achieving objectives and the objectives themselves. In participatory evaluation the local people are directly involved in the evaluation process and in designing and carrying out the evaluation, analysing information and presenting evaluation results. Outsiders facilitate such evaluation by assisting the local people in planning and conducting the evaluation. Besides the qualitative impact, such evaluation may also involve participatory assessment such as fixing value, estimate and other quantifications and assessment of performance in relation to overall and immediate objectives/targets. When objectives and activities are re-examined, re-considered and revised, some aspects of the participatory review get included in participatory evaluation. Participatory evaluation helps in better decision-making by the local people, better understanding of the issues concerned, improved communication of the outside team with the local people, mutual sharing of results and ensures relevance of project activities and objectives.

PRA/PLA-type activities can help in participatory impact assessment/evaluation of project/programme. With the participants' evaluation, lessons can be learnt, problems identified, assessments made and solutions offered for improving project activities and objectives. Operation of projects can be better informed and problems can be resolved through PRA/PLA. Participatory impact assessment/evaluation is a frontier research area in participatory approaches. It is in striking contrast to the conventional approach, where the job of evaluation is mostly specialised with emphasis on "numbers", "materials" and "targets". Such emphasis fails to capture the nuances of the development process, and the "worldview" of project beneficiaries that participatory evaluation can account for. Box 10.2 is on the participatory impact assessment/evaluation in which a participatory method by the name of "Project Benefit-Impact Matrix" (PBI Matrix) was applied to evaluate Nhilandhe Integrated Atoll Development (NIAD) Project of United Nations Development Programme (UNDP) at Maldives for conducting the ex-post evaluation.

10.2.6 Participatory Action Research (PAR)

From field experience one finds that such PAR is initiated either by "insider" (the people) or by "outsider" (practitioner) or by both collaborating as a team. The objectives can be varied for undertaking PAR and it is important to mention in this context that it is possible for an action researcher to engage in some form of self-development in addition to larger objectives. Another issue is whether the tools, techniques and process adopted for such research are participatory thereby creating enough space for the people to be actively involved in such research. It is important that the poor, women, aged and marginalized groups are included as participants apart from the rest of the group/community. The more they "own" the research process, the more they can influence the outcome and the greater is the degree of participation. So PAR covers a broad spectrum where the degree of participation can range from one end of the spectrum to another depending on the way of involving the local people.

In PAR, it is also possible that the community is actively participating of its own choice and is setting the research agenda and

Box 10.2: Participatory Evaluation at Maldives

Maldives, a classic case of dual economy, has 200 inhabited small islands where the resort islands are prosperous tourist economies while the traditional island communities are relatively deprived, considerably remote and are vulnerable to shortages of food, water and basic services. In the post-project evaluation at Maldives, the evaluation team members visited 8 traditional island communities of a total of 13, in the two administrative atolls of Faafu and Dhaalu and facilitated the local people to do their own evaluation through impact. The PBI matrix, a "visual" participatory method (for illustration see Chapter 7 of this book) was applied, which is a combination of listing and scoring of criteria coupled with card sorting.

As facilitators, one practical limitation of the participatory evaluation was that with large groups of participants there arose many views where consensus building became a time-consuming process. Another point observed by the outside team was that the group recall of project activities took time since the project was no longer running. Since both women and men groups were approached separately for participatory evaluation, the results showed clear differences in gender-based perspectives. Again since, most participants were literate, they wrote their points on small paper cards. Some strengths of such participatory evaluation were as follows. The PRA/PLA-type sessions with the local people provide enough flexibility for compact evaluation of the project. They help in evaluation being both transparent and flexible by enabling participants to be open-minded and evaluate project activities as a group, and change their scores and views as and when required. To encourage wider participation each participant can be involved in group discussions and "visual" PRA/PLA methods.

Source: From field notes of Neela Mukherjee on NIAD Project, Maldives.

the issues to be covered (White:1999). The larger agenda for action research covers both insiders and outsiders' agenda and has both direct and indirect impact on the different levels of policy and practice. The research results are generally of relevance to the local people but may or may not be practicable depending on the availability of resources. In the absence of appropriate resources, it often leads to rising of community expectations (though not always) followed by inaction/disappointment. Hence, clarification of objective/s from the very start is an important component of PAR. Another question relevant to PAR is "how do we improve upon what we are doing?" The core of the research rests on "participatory action", which is in the "driver's seat" and such research informs practice. PAR is a powerful method in the hands of research facilitators and needs to be used with care so as not to become "extractive". The challenge of PAR lies in not mere involvement of communities as passive objects of research but in their active involvement in the research process. It implies involvement of the local communities in discussion and deliberation of the research agenda, analysis of issues, ownership of processes and concomitant action.

Development activities are complex and decision-making is not a simple task. Often the forces determining developmental activities are too intricate and not easy to decipher. Generally speaking, there are no "blueprints" available for participatory development and there is dearth of availability of definite answers or customised solutions to issues in such a process. Hence, there are many "empty boxes" in the sphere of participatory development, which PAR can help to answer by exploring possible ways of filling such boxes. It is important to have activities on a pilot basis and trial runs on a smaller scale before attempting activities on a larger basis. PAR as a part of any pilot project can provide clues for addressing unknown issues in the terrain of development activities. It helps in confidence building for undertaking new areas of activities/action and new challenges. Sometimes in order to influence policy-making and key decisions, results/evidence from PAR can be crucial. Based on such PAR, new policy parameters can be framed and implemented.

PAR is useful in validating experimental and innovative efforts and creates a base for "scaling up" and replication of process. It helps in diagnostic analysis and in highlighting and verifying issues. It helps in better understanding and preparation for undertaking/sustaining project-related activities. It creates space for serving the local communities based on such experience. PAR is a way of focusing on selected issues and bringing about improvement in practice. It makes learning-by-doing possible. It helps in undertaking mid-way corrections and to improve upon the process of individual/group learning. Such action research can lead to the formation of a self-critical community.

Participatory Action Research—An Illustration

A participatory action research project on "community perspectives on agriculture and air pollution" was conducted during 1998-2000 in the peri-urban areas of Faridabad and Varanasi with the objective of learning about livelihood strategies of the local communities in the study areas and the role and importance of agriculture and whether air pollution was recognised by the local communities as a serious constraint on agricultural production (Mukherjee *et al.*:2001). This was part of a collaborative research with scientists investigating the scientific aspects of crop yields and agriculture, the social researchers interacting with the local communities and the policy researchers inquiring into policy implications. The field lessons from such research were shared with the local communities and extension agents through face-to-face workshops in a few villages and peer review workshops were also held for wider dissemination. The results of the project were also shared with the policy-makers and widely disseminated through professional and popular writings to highlight community perspectives on the topic inquired.

The methods and principles of PRA were the basis of the field research. The participatory methods included sketch mapping, group discussion, seasonal analysis, problem tree, benefit-cost matrix, criteria listing, scoring/ranking, do-it-yourself, lend-a-helping-hand, time line/oral history, card sorting, wealth grouping, etc. Such research had two parts—exploratory and topical. For all field sessions it was important to start with "warming up" and rapport-building exercises with the local communities and groups which also included an explanation of the project objectives without raising expectations. The exploratory part of the field research entailed a general approach towards exploring the objectives of the project under consideration, for example, household livelihood strategies in general or livestock problems, in general, for having an overview of the issues concerned. This was followed by a topical round of research for focusing on selected issues, for example, constraints related to wheat crop or issues in women's empowerment and livelihood. There was the additional issue that people did/did not recognise, such as the direct and indirect impact of air pollution on crop production. The fact that it was "invisible" meant it was not widely recognised as a "problem" by farmers. The field researchers in consultation with the scientific research team selected villages/hamlets in Faridabad and Varanasi for conducting participatory research. Such selection was refined and amended in consultation with the local communities. The social researchers also provided feedback to the community on research findings and cross-checked field output through application of different participatory methods, interacting with different groups at different places and times and also through peer group discussions.

For interacting with farmers, often a common meeting place was chosen as the place for discussion. When farmers were busy in the field, group discussions and interactive sessions were held near the field to the extent possible. PRA-type sessions were mostly held in separate groups of women and men, in which some mixed groups were also interacted with. This helped in cross-checking. The participants also did an oral analysis, which was recorded by the facilitators. Though it wasn't envisaged at the beginning, village-based field research had to be staggered for creating space for additional rounds of field inquiry in the same villages. The local groups/communities expressed their opinion on the issue of agricultural constraints and strongly suggested that researchers re-visit them for topical investigation related to agricultural constraints such as weeds/insects/disease/others. Staggered visits over the crop cycle helped in generating in-depth discussion, more clarity and mutual understanding of issues (Mukherjee *et al.*:2001).

10.2.7 Participatory Questionnaire-Survey

PRA/PLA methods are used to complement questionnaire-survey. Such use can be multiple and diverse as given below:

- to design questionnaire/to re-design it
- to determine bases for stratification and sampling
- to clarify questionnaire-survey results
- to validate questionnaire-survey results through in-depth studies
- to estimate selected parameters
- to reduce non-sampling errors

Both PRA/PLA-type inquiry and questionnaire-survey can complement each other depending on the nature of inquiry. If the method in question is the conventional survey then use of PRA/PLA can help in different stages of such surveys. At each stage of a survey, PRA/PLA is of assistance in making the learning process iterative, meaningful and clarifying issues so as to attain the objectives of the concerned study in a better manner (Mukherjee:1995). The two types of inquiry under discussion have different operational procedures. For example, a questionnaire-survey with a fixed set of questions is operationalised through field enumerators, whereas a PRA/PLA-type inquiry normally involves a multi-disciplinary team where pre-set questions are discouraged. There are selected aspects of questionnaire-survey as discussed below for which application of PRA/PLA-type inquiry can make for improved design of a questionnaire-survey, its better canvassing and higher quality of output.

Appropriate Adoption

The questionnaire design is often problematic and the worst executed stage of survey preparation. Some problems of questionnaire survey in developing countries have been neatly summed up by Gill (1993) such as :

— questionnaires being inefficient due to the people in developing countries not appropriately trained in designing it;
— questionnaires normally written in another language and translated before or during the interview;
— respondents not familiar with the rationale behind surveys and the tendency to give answers, which respondent thinks are wanted;
— respondents not literate cannot correct any mistakes or misunderstandings; and
— enumerators having very different socio-economic backgrounds from the respondents.

It is here that PRA/PLA-type inquiry can overcome the shortcomings of questionnaire-survey where pilot studies through PRA/PLA can be undertaken for framing of a questionnaire and its field-testing can also be complemented and supplemented with PRA/PLA. This can help in identifying the gaps in language, content and direction of questionnaires to be used for undertaking any survey. Orone's (1993) study shows how PRA helped in redesigning of a questionnaire on ground water resource management to make it more appropriate to field situation.

Informalising Interview

The aim of questionnaire-survey is to attain uniformity in asking of questions and recording of answers. Hence the researchers and the enumerators seek standardisation of the interview process. Such a method may not yield appropriate answers, whereas informal interviewing can produce better results because of its flexibility and openness (Joachim Ziche:1991). PRA method can help in framing questionnaires on the basis of informal interviews, which are semi-structured. For better results Shah's (1993) experience brings home lessons of making questionnaires informal and visually interactive.

Questions to Anticipate

Questionnaires are based on the assumption that the questions framed for the survey are sufficient to collect the requisite information. Beebe (1985), while defining informal survey/Rapid Rural Appraisal took it as a starting point for understanding a local situation. This was based on information collected in advance, direct observation and interviews because it was assumed that all relevant questions were not identifiable in advance. PRA/PLA-type sessions in advance of survey, based on checklists, can complement in framing of a questionnaire for conducting a survey.

Varied Response to Identical Questions

It is essential that the respondent must understand the questions. It is most likely that the definition the respondent will have in mind will be different from what the survey seeks to investigate. There lies the possibility of wide variations in the definitions adopted by different respondents and also the same respondents at different times, if the survey involves more than one interview. PRA sessions can clarify issues and also check for the responses.

Such sessions can lend flexibility in adopting the local terminology, appreciation of the local perspectives and cross-checking of responses.

Analysis of Difference

One of the ideas behind surveys is to give an average picture or a general trend whereas an intensive study of a the local community can present analysis of difference based on the local diversity.

Complex Inter-relationships

For the study of complex inter-relationships amongst variables, conventional methods like questionnaire-survey with its emphasis on numerical figures has the inherent danger of being elementary and simplistic. It is difficult to anticipate all relevant questions for arriving at such inter-relationships. For certain aspects of a socio-economic change in the localities measurement is a simple matter and there are no serious debates regarding ambiguity of issues or rapport-building with the villagers, for instance, data on the availability of roads, its kinds, number of school buildings, hospitals, etc. Large-scale surveys can be designed to collect data on such aspects. They can map the direction and rate of change in terms of selected indicators. However, a survey by nature is constrained to unravel factors and processes underlying these changes and their relationships (Vaidyanathan:1989). And it is at this point that we need to complement with other types of approaches such as PRA/PLA.

Improving Degree of Accuracy

In a questionnaire-survey, the respondent can be asked to answer a question that is impossible to answer accurately, either because the answer is not known to the respondent or too much is expected of the respondent's memory or the respondent is unwilling to answer. For instance, it may be difficult to find appropriate answers from respondents in the rural areas about gross crop areas or average milk yields per head of cattle, or about the net income from informal business, or weight of the food consumed. Direct responses to questions would vary from place to place and indirect means of approaching such issues will have to be devised on the spot, otherwise the accuracy of the responses can be affected in the process.

Group Interaction

Questionnaire-survey can enrich itself by means of group interactions as in PRA/PLA where group views are solicited in addition to answers given by individual respondents. Such group interactions with selected groups are also useful either as a self-contained means of collecting data or as a supplement to both quantitative and qualitative methods. Such data and insights would be less accessible without the interaction found in a group. Apart from quantitative data, group interaction combine merits of two important means of collecting qualitative data in social sciences, namely, the individual interviews and the participant observation (Morgan:1988).

10.3 Reflections on PRA/PLA

Each PRA/PLA-type of exercise can be unique in its own way since there is no "blueprint" involved and structured sessions go against the basic principles of PRA/PLA. No methodology, however, is perfect and PRA/PLA is no exception to this general rule. PRA/PLA-type approaches have their own share of imperfections. There are two issues in this context : one, how big are the imperfections and two, can they be overcome, and if so, to what extent. Much depends on what the imperfections are and whether there are ways to minimise the imperfections in order to achieve better quality of work.

The lessons have been grouped into the following generic clusters :

- — Selected issues from the field
- — Selected issues in capacity building
- — Selected issues in epistemology and policy-making
- — Selected issues in participatory research

10.3.1 Selected Issues from the Field

There are a host of issues from the field, which need to be kept in mind while doing participatory inquiry. It is important to listen and learn from other people's field experience, however, it is not possible to formulate hard and fast rules about approaching the local community for PRA/PLA-type activities. Some issues in this regard are discussed below.

Approaching Local Community for PRA/PLA

The process of rapport building with the local communities can itself be a lengthy one. Proper rapport building with communities and explanation of the objectives of the interactive process are important. One simple way is to help them in their daily work and/or by generally getting to know them while chatting. Not always can issues/themes under inquiry be broached in a direct manner. Depending on the situation different ways need to be adopted for approaching the localities for PRA/PLA-type exercises.

PRA/PLA-type sessions need not be easy to conduct. There are many variables in a participatory process and efforts at interacting with the local people need not result in an effective session with them.

Sometimes rapport building with the local people may not even happen or it may take unduly long to happen. It may not be possible to initiate a PRA/PLA-type exercise for reasons more than one. One may be due to the problems in the behaviour of outsiders while another reason may be that the people are not willing to participate. It is often difficult to motivate the poor villagers, who tend to be elusive. They do not wish to participate and share their views and experience. There are social power relations in a locality, which may keep the poor away from participating. Such aspects make PRA/PLA-type exercise all the more challenging. One may face many difficulties in facilitating local-level participation. However, one need not be unnecessarily pessimistic and need not give up easily. The point is that there can be large variations in attempts at initiating a participatory process. There is no clear-cut formula in which participation can be guaranteed. Each PRA/PLA-type exercise is a process of learning for the outside team.

Lending a Helping Hand

The local community members are often busy throughout the year eking out livelihoods from different sources. One way out is to help them in their work as much as possible and in the process learn from them. This helps in establishing some goodwill and mutual trust between the outside team and the local community members/group interacted with. Such gestures like lending a helping hand to the daily lives of the local communities help in building social bridges with participants. Building personal/group rapport is important for acceptability and credibility and for opening channels of communication. The community, in the process, is able to appreciate the objective/s of the visit by the outside team.

Often during the initial visits to the local community the outside team is treated with suspicion and resistance. In the sowing/harvesting season, the agriculture-based villages become quite busy. However, for example, if the outside team's focus is on issues related to agriculture at the sowing/harvesting stage then it is important to interact with the local farmers concurrently at that stage. Lending a helping hand for sowing helps in breaking ice and in forming a constructive relationship.

One-off visits to the local communities do not help in sustaining rapport. Credibility and honesty of the outside team needs to be proved over time by multiple visits and stay in the village. In a village near Varanasi in Uttar Pradesh, an outside team was mistaken as income tax officials from the government who had come for assessment purposes.

This apprehension made the households shut their doors and the local people were reluctant to meet the outsiders. Gradually, with much effort made for establishing contact and rapport over time such initial apprehension transformed into a constructive relationship, which improved over time by re-visiting the village communities. The bonds got even stronger when some members of the outside team also followed up by sending mails/notes to the community members. This helped in maintaining contact with the community over time.

Learning from the Local Community

In PRA/PLA-type activities it is important that the local people are able to appreciate the objectives of field visits of outside teams and agree to participate. Gaining the confidence of the local community members is important though not at the cost of raising their expectations. Hence, listening to the community members and going by their advice help in better learning from the community. An outside team studying agricultural constraints of the local farmers at Faridabad in Haryana was advised by the latter to repeat visits for a better understanding of the crop constraints and problems in different seasons. Based on their advice the outside team undertook rounds of visits to the farmers in those seasons/periods, which the farmers thought as important. The farmers indicated that most of their problems were seasonal and such seasonal dimensions were best explained and understood when visits were made as and when such problems occurred. One lesson learnt in the process was that the outside team undertaking field inquiry requires enough flexibility so as to base their activities on the local people's advice. This helps the activities to become more grassroots-oriented and practical and also helps in strengthening relationship with the local communities.

Another lesson learnt is that socio-biophysical resources are better understood in their relevant context as and when they actually occur. They are understood properly through joint observation and mutual discussion with the local participants who are the repository of the local knowledge. For example, in a participatory action research project, it was observed that impacts of air pollution on crops often have a large "visual" element (for example, leaf injury or dust deposit on crops) and learning about it *in situ* enables the local people to explain it vividly on the spot. Sometimes "word" or verbal explanation falls far short of the "visual" features of the problem under description. For this joint walks and joint observation with the local participants helps in a realistic analysis.

Keeping Pace with Community

The local communities are generally busy throughout the year in different activities whether farming or non/off-farming. However, time is an important factor for both "breadth" and "depth" of PRA/PLA-type activities. And for process-oriented participatory interactions it is necessary to spend time with the community especially the deprived groups. With limited time at hand it is important to make effective use of time. It is better to have staggered interactions with the community over time rather than one-off interactions.

Box 10.3: PLA facilitators' comments from Vietnam

"Farmers are not familiar with such PRA/PLA approaches (nobody has asked them ever their perspective). Farmers' time depends on whether crops are growing or it is harvest time. Customs vary across communities and farmers have varying educational levels, where some are literate, others semi-literate and few illiterate. Usually farmers list out too many problems."

Source: Field notes, PLA facilitator group, Quang Binh, Vietnam.

Drawing from the field notes of a social motivator of a project in the Doon Valley, Dehradun, interactive sessions with the local participants were for short durations since both women and men were busy in different activities. As a result, once rapport was built and the project objectives were explained to the community, PRA/PLA-type sessions progressed at a slow pace given the willingness of community members to participate. All interactive sessions were undertaken during the time convenient to the local community. One important lesson from the project experience is that it is important to keep pace with the way of life of the community. Such pace varies across the local communities, so do the local perspectives. Appreciating and learning about different perspectives helps in the analysis of difference, which is important to PRA/PLA.

Conducting Field Inquiry

One lesson learnt from the project is related to the way of doing in-depth topical PRA/PLA, for example, on agriculture. For best results, It is important to conduct staggered rounds of interactive sessions in line with the agricultural crop cycle. It enables the local community to describe their priority issues *in situ* to external facilitators. It also helps in a mutual discussion amongst themselves in order to identify the related issues and arrive at a group consensus. As for outside team, such staggered rounds of field interactions help in locating problems/constraints faced by the local communities, better appreciation of live issues by closely observing them, understanding them and conducting in-depth discussions with the concerned community/groups.

Participatory interactions, both exploratory and topical, are important from the point of view of any field inquiry. "Overviews" provided at the exploratory stage are important for learning about the local issues whereas topical inquiry on selected issues helps in deeper inquiry see Box 10.4. Since both exploratory and topical dimensions help in building blocks for future action, it is important to both "broaden" and "deepen" such PRA/PLA-type exercises as required.

Appropriate methods are important to be sorted out and flexibility in methods is the crux of PRA/PLA-type approaches. In PRA/PLA there is a large inventory of methods. Appropriate selection of methods and their sequencing help in better field inquiry and enable the local participants to analyse and act. "Visual" methods create an environment for group participation, make participants interested in analysis of their own problems and help in generating discussion on related issues, which the participants deliberate upon. One lesson from the vast field experience related to PRA/PLA is about the limits posed by a verbal discussion. Some of the problems and issues raised by the local communities can be quite complicated and verbal description may not be that effective. In such cases the alternative is to have a "visual" description and inquiry into the real conditions/objects and initiate discussions on that basis.

Quality of Interactive Process

Quality of interactive process at the field level is often more important than quantity since it is a major determinant of the kind of the local involvement and the kind of information generated in the process. Quality of information is related to the process adopted. The better the rapport building and interactions with the community, the better is the quality of information and its depth. The local groups of women and men feel free to speak, express their views and engage in the deeper analysis. They are withdrawn in their approach when community-based interactions are superficial with the community not having much confidence in the outside team.

Box 10.4: Participant farmers' comment from Quang Binh, Vietnam

" PLA helps in assessing situations properly. PLA-based micro plans are highly feasible; they meet the aspirations of communities and are democratically made where all can express their opinions. Such plans also help in exploiting potential sources in the locality."

Whereas, multiple interactions with the local community members through staggered visits help in assuring the community about the perseverance, transparency and seriousness of outside team members and help in building mutual relationship, confidence and trust. Sheer quantity of information adds little value to the process of PRA/PLA-type activities.

Box 10.5: Our trampling habits die hard

"We began the exercise around 11.30 in the morning and it was already 5.00 p.m. The time lost in the early hours was vital. People got restless and began to leave. We called it a day. We paid the price for not respecting their time....

Once the mapping was completed, we sat down for introspection and reflection. The following was our realisation. One, that the habit we have of trampling things, not belonging to us stuck on to us. We did this during the practice session in APARD and despite repeated realisation and discussion that this should not be done; we kept on doing it both in APARD and once again in the village. This had led to loss of time and confusion in the minds of the community. We were trampling on space (and things) by habit. We did this despite the best of intentions and despite all our resolve to be on our best behaviour and being all the time conscious of the fact that we ought to give primacy to the villagers, as we were learners. Habits are as important as attitude and behaviour. Someone said, 'habit is second nature'. For PLA it is necessary to have good habits. It is necessary to have good nature."

Source: From the field notes of Amitava Mukherjee on village Gundlapally, Kosgi Mandal, District Mehbubnagar, Andhra Pradesh (India).

PRA/PLA and Sensitive Issues

Some topics are sensitive in nature and questions related to them can create conflict. In such cases it is better that the local groups themselves find opportunities to raise issues without leading questions being posed by PA researchers. Topics like impacts of the local industrial pollution are often sensitive, bearing a background of the local grievance and conflict of polluters and those polluted. In such cases it is important to have a feel of the issues, which are the locally sensitive and observe the local "do's" and "don'ts" in the discussion of such issues. This helps in discussions to take place in congenial and constructive environments. Potential areas of conflict need to be handled with care and tact. Hence, the way questions get posed is important. The locally sensitive issues, if tackled in a non-threatening manner, help community/groups to think in a positive manner and look for ways of resolving conflict and mutual confidence building.

Sensitive issues need to be handled carefully in a PRA/PLA-type exercise. Surfacing of such issues through PRA/PLA-type interactive sessions can lead to tensions and difficult situations. The opinions expressed by one group may clash with those expressed by another group in heterogeneous communities having large socio-economic and political differences. One for example of sensitive issues can be communal feelings in stratified societies, which need to be handled carefully for they can create problems for such a participatory session.

PRA/PLA-type exercises can be used in a constructive manner for conflict resolution of different problems facing the local communities. An important determinant of which is the external team and the local participants. Their ability to handle an issue in a positive manner can resolve conflicts and help in diffusing explosive situations. At all stages, however, the cooperation and participation of the local participants is an important requirement.

Managing People's Expectations

A PRA/PLA can be conducted in such a manner that it can raise expectations at the local level of positive things to happen. If expectations at the local level are raised unnecessarily and nothing happens then such a PRA/PLA-type session hits against the ethical issue of "extractive" interactions. Apart from this problems can crop up at the field level for future participation in the absence of earlier promises not being fulfilled. Hence, it is essential that, at all times, objective/s of a PRA/PLA exercise should be explained clearly to the local people and on that basis voluntary participation sought. For instance, if a PRA/PLA exercise is being conducted for the purpose of training an outside team or for the purpose of some research objectives then the same needs to be explained to the local people whose participation is being sought.

Development agencies, conducting PRA/PLA-type activities, should exercise caution in not raising unnecessary expectations. People can easily get frustrated when they spend their time doing their own analysis yet no change comes about and *status quo* is maintained (Action Aid-Ethiopia/IIED:1989). In case expectations are raised then genuine attempts at fulfilling such expectations can help the local people to have hope in the development strategy and process.

In a participatory action research project, social researchers at Varanasi in Uttar Pradesh were in a continuous dialogue with the scientists (engaged in doing research under the project) and gave them feedback from the local community and *vice versa*. For the villages in Faridabad in Haryana selected agricultural issues as expressed by the local farmers were communicated to the government departments, especially the State extension department and extension workshops were held with farmers, while some social issues were resolved through a mutual discussion of social researchers with the local groups.

Enthusiasm can wither off easily

After the initial PRA/PLA-type exercise, sustaining enthusiasm of the local people for implementation of their own plans can sometimes pose problems. It has been experienced that the initial enthusiasm is high as a result of PRA/PLA but easily withers off over time. PRA/PLA needs to aim at long-term mobilisation of community (Ford & Lelo:1991).

Assigning Responsibilities

In a village planning process through PRA/PLA, experience (Ford & Lelo:1991) shows that precision is required in assigning responsibilities for different kinds of work to be done including finding of those people who will be responsible for finding external inputs such as building materials, etc. Ways to find external resources by the local people in a PRA process is also not easy. This may mean approaching the government, NGOs or donor agencies by the local communities for external inputs. It has been pointed out that the community leaders often lack the skills to use PRA data for formulating project proposals and procure external funds (Ford & Lelo:1991). Hence even when the local people do their own planning they can face difficulties in implementing their own plans and programmes. This indicates that help by development agencies to support implementation of the local plans through PRA can constitute a critical input.

Making Process Culturally Compatible

Often women in conservative societies have problems talking to men facilitators from outside. Such conversations may not be culturally convenient given the cultural framework and similar can be the case for women facilitators talking to men. Hence such gender bias can be offset in PRA/PLA-type activities by having the outside team with both women and men. Offsetting "dominance" of men and the local leaders is another aspect, which requires tact and deft handling by an outside team. One lesson learnt in this regard is from a PRA/PLA session in a hamlet at Varanasi in Uttar Pradesh where men influenced priority issues of women group/s. It implied further probing with the women group and finding ways of avoiding the presence of men. One way was to politely ask those men present during PRA/PLA sessions to let women take the initiative and talk. Or alternatively, keep men engaged in separate sessions while interacting with women groups. In case of learning about gender perspectives it is often desirable to have separate interactions with women and men groups to the extent possible.

10.3.2 Selected Issues in Capacity Building

Some issues in capacity building integral to PRA/PLA-type activities are discussed below. These relate to changes to be brought about in "our" mindsets, "our" commitment and spirit, "our" understanding of the local process and issues related to capacity building and its scale.

Changing "our" Attitude

"Our" problem starts from changing of attitude towards the local people in order to appreciate the importance of their participation in decision-making and be willing to learn from them. This, however, is not so easy to happen see Box 10.5. It is possible to influence attitudinal changes through appropriate training and learning from field-level PRA/PLA-type sessions. Where large bureaucracies are involved in PRA/PLA-type activities, initiating attitudinal changes about the poor people and their capabilities is a mammoth task and requires training of numerous functionaries in government and non-government organisations.

"Our" Commitment and Spirit

It is important to have team members with commitment and quality and not necessarily large teams for doing participatory inquiry. Such large teams become a crowd in any locality and can disturb the rhythm of a participatory process and interactions. At any point, a committed and dedicated team small in size is in a better position to establish effective communication with the focus groups as compared to a large team, though the latter helps in a larger coverage of groups/communities. It is spending quality-time with the community where appropriate attitude and behaviour help in establishing effective communication with the local groups. This, if done by a small team, helps in improving the quality of relationship over time.

Understanding Local Development Process

Kaplan (1996) writes that in the process of the local development there are different forms of practice depending on the stage/phase of development that a group/the local community has reached. Examples of such roles are facilitating individuals and groups; facilitating development of organisations and their institutional capacities; facilitating social transformation, access to resources, access to larger societal functioning, etc. Often due to lack of a conceptual framework of development process, development practitioners are unable to differentiate between different roles of outsiders, which such processes envisage. This directly affects the understanding of their changing roles in such a process.

Training and Its Scale

PRA/PLA-type activities can fail to give its best results if outside team members are not trained properly, they are inexperienced or unskilled with a difficult attitude and have a tendency to rush the process

(Messerschmidt:1991). Team members need training in the right kind of approach to initiate participation, application of methods, facilitation, supportive skills and a clear understanding of context and purpose. The greater the speed at which PRA/PLA spreads, the greater is the need for good trainers to conduct training at different levels. Experience shows that at the local level, it is important to create an inventory of the local facilitators who are capable of organising community participation to handle the PRA planning process starting from data collection to implementation (Ford & Lelo:1991).

10.3.3 Selected Issues in Epistemology and Policy-making

It has been often remarked that we miss the larger picture in PRA/PLA-type activities, hence miss out on one crucial variable for sustainability of the local development process. Some issues raised in this context are discussed below.

Romanticising "the local"

There is a tendency to romanticise "the local" implying downplaying of the local social inequalities and power relations. Mohan and Stokke (2000) write that instead of romanticising the role of the locals we need to examine the political use of the "local" by various actors such as State, donor agencies and NGOs. Many aid-receiving governments are doing it because it is high on the donor's agenda. Many NGOs are "top-down" and bureaucratic in their approach yet doing it for similar reasons. It is important to be aware of such a complex reality.

Consensual Approach and Local People

There is an implicit assumption that the local communities which are harmonious in PRA/PLA-type activities tend to promote a consensual approach (Goebel:1998). While the poor are set against "elite" or "non-poor" where the former operate through ties such as kinship, ethnic group while the latter through modern methods, State supported (Brown:1994; Brass: 1995). Such categorisation of "poor" and "non-poor" undermine PRA's principle of seeking diversity. Nelson and Wright observe that the concept of "community" is a concept used more by the "outsiders" than the people themselves. PRA promotes a consensual view thereby ignoring interests of the power groups in a community. Not all community members are equally likely to speak out in group interviews. If likelihood of participation is positively related to the education level and wealth (Grootaert: 1998) then a small number of community interviews can miss the important under-privileged sub-population (Smith *et al.*:2000). Such criticisms have been tackled at the community level by identifying the heterogeneous character of any community by the people themselves and also the people analysing gendered differences.

The "Insider" and "Outsider"

It has been pointed out that the "insider" and "outsider", "the local" and "the non-local" are treated as separate entities and knowledge flow and advice/lecture from the "outsider" are to be avoided. All these tend to block a two-way dialogue and learning in a PRA/PLA situation.

Isolated View of the "Local"

There is a tendency to view the "local" in isolation from the broader economic and political picture. In development practice the move towards the local participatory approaches and empowerment has led to under-emphasis of national and global economic and political forces. With the focus on "the local" the importance of State has dwindled. It is crucial to look at issues of scale between "local", "national" and "global" and the inter-connections between the three. Even with the people's participation the systems and structure that determine power and resource allocation remain intact. The issue is how to influence the larger picture. Recent initiatives through development projects towards scaling up and linking up with external institutions have shown results, though on a limited scale. However such recent initiatives for influencing policy planning and decision-making at different levels hold promise.

Local Knowledge and Participatory Development

The emphasis on local knowledge and less reliance on "expert" knowledge is the starting point for creating space for the local knowledge and for development strategies and processes to be locally determined. The role of the local knowledge generation in improving policy-making helps in empowerment of the local communities and also in interpretation of the local needs. Indigenous Technical Knowledge (ITK)—the political nature of participation is debated and also the role of knowledge generation. Development practitioners assume that the local knowledge will reverse the damage done by the earlier "top-down" approach to development, which treat the local people as passive. For some ITK is important for improving policy-making. However, just recognising and respecting the validity of traditional knowledge is not enough for development especially where the local people are not aware of the significance of their knowledge and the outsiders lack practical ideas to adapt the knowledge for improving practice. Many of the local people tend to look at outsiders knowledge, technology and gadgets with awe thinking that they are of a superior nature.

Communication Linkages with PRA/PLA Practitioners

Communication linkages of PRA/PLA practitioners with scientists and experts in other fields are important because they can be mutually supportive. But there exists a huge gap in communication between the two sets of people and both remain worlds apart governed by different paradigms. Such communication helps both the social and technical world, for example, communication with scientists, helps in mutual sharing. They help PRA practitioners to appreciate the larger picture of scientific and environmental issues and keep abreast of scientific research and *vice versa* and to see the relationship from an inter-disciplinary point of view. It also helps them to raise further queries on the subject with the local communities. Such participatory interactions can help in exploring the societal basis of scientific and environmental phenomena. The local groups are also benefited in the process. This actually happened in a participatory action research project at Varanasi in Uttar Pradesh where the scientific team from the Banaras Hindu University and Imperial College, U.K., took considerable interest in participatory research output and responded to some of the feedback from the local community and shared their scientific results.

Process of Empowerment

One aspect of PRA/PLA-type activities is the process of empowerment where the local communities do decision-making for their own development. However, PRA/PLA-type approaches do not go well with every institutional framework. PRA/PLA implies the people's empowerment, which need not fit in with the socio-political parameters existing in the institutions of many countries and regions. PRA may not be meaningful in repressive conditions. In such conditions, people may not be willing to reveal their perceptions or tell the truth. An ideal institutional setting for PRA is one which is congenial to participation, a setting which is not only open but one in which there is provision for decision-making to start from the bottom.

The "PRA/PLA" Type

There are instances of projects, where PRA/PLA is undertaken for favouring donor-driven agenda, which imply quick funds and quick results. Going by the hype created by the name of "PRA/PLA" some are tempted to adopt it in a quick fashion without realising what it involves and its complexities in terms of adapting it, thus overlooking the integral participatory processes of decision-making and the local-level empowerment. At the end of the day it is they who are frustrated by the PRA/PLA methodology and often blame it for all ills without ever understanding it in its true sense.

10.3.4 Selected Issues in Participatory Research

Selected issues in participatory research are discussed below. It is a flexible methodology, which incorporates a host of methods, which are both qualitative and quantitative. For example, secondary data review from conventional methods help outside teams in doing their groundwork. PRA/PLA encourages participation between outsiders and the local people as well as within the local people themselves. Apart from quantitative data the strength of PRA lies in generation of qualitative data which numerical measures are not capable of reflecting.

Some research issues discussed below relate to rapid generation of data, approaching research frontiers, cultural compatibility of PRA/PLA and recognising the role of PRA/PLA more as an approach than as a final solution.

"Rapidity" and PRA

This is a criticism associated with the feature of rapid data generation with PRA/PLA methods. Some doubts have been raised whether methods involving "rapid appraisal" are appropriate for understanding contemporary social change. Some have expressed concern that the practice of rapid appraisal can become popular because of its rapid results and can be frequently used and so may go out of control (Pottier: 1991).

It is thought that PRA/PLA can help in accessing indigenous world (e.g. technical knowledge, rural perceptions, decision-making) relatively quickly. The basic idea is that "the data are out there to be collected, objectively and quickly" (Pottier:1991) and this can be done by asking the local people and using some commonsense. The presumption of PRA is that friendly interaction can bring out the local people's knowledge and perceptions. However, critics are of the opinion that the scope for discrepancy between response of informants and what they actually do or think may be quite different, which an outside team may not be able to comprehend without entering into a discourse of a given culture which is not rapid but a slow and painful approach (Pottier:1991). Though there is some truth in the above argument the context in which PRA/PLA is being emphasised is quite different. The "rapid" feature of PRA/PLA needs to be appreciated in comparison to a method like survey, which is the accepted method for official data collection. It is in this context that the relatively "quick" and participatory nature of PRA/PLA would yield better quality of information, which is relatively cost-effective as well.

Approaching Research Frontiers

New areas/topics for field research based on PRA/PLA, which are generally under-researched, require time for carrying them out. Technical issues in research require a fair amount of technical knowledge and understanding. It is also important to build communication channels with technical person/experts for a better clarification of the technical problems raised by community/group/researchers. Scientific briefing of PRA/PLA team (assuming that many have social science background) becomes important for those technical topics, which are relatively new and normally not researched. Only those scientists would be effective in briefing social science researchers who can de-mystify the terms, jargons, processes, technical facts, etc., and explain them in simple language. In this respect, those scientists are better equipped who are in a position to appreciate the significance of community perspective in field research. It is not always easy to find many of them as and when required for supporting participatory action research.

Is PRA/PLA Superficial?

Some anthropologists tend to believe that semi-structured interviews are one-off attempts to capture "real" life worlds at the local levels, which need not be realistic. According to them, there are no short-cut ways for knowing a given culture. An understanding of rural realities is time-consuming and involves learning of the local language, culture and gradually making one's physical presence unobtrusive. Learning a culture, its subtleties, sensitiveness and other details are against rapidity. At best, rapid appraisals can be polite conversations (Pottier:1991). Only long-term field work can make an anthropologist competent for assessing the circumstances under which interviews can take place. Long-term residence and language familiarity can check the danger of a significant bias creeping into the interview. To gain from an interview a researcher must understand the participants' modes of thought, their socially constructed values, their attitudes towards interviews, their ways of manipulating interviews and others. Insights into such areas can be gained only from long-term field work (Pottier:1991). In this context, it is important to point out that in order to be realistic, there is a need for a methodology which helps in collecting relevant data in less time than long-term anthropological studies and is relatively quicker than sample surveys. And it is this gap, which PRA/PLA can fill in the narrow sense as compared to the broad role, which PRA/PLA plays in community empowerment.

It has also been pointed out that visual representations, which are integral to PRA/PLA/RRA can be alien to many societies and hence the responses, comments and interpretations of such representations can vary across groups and the localities, different from what the researchers think they are getting. Venn diagrams are not of any use to villagers since they are descriptive showing interactions or lack of the same between institutions/individuals. They do not help in analysing how institutional problems can be resolved.

In answer to the points raised above it may be said that "visual" representations make points simple to understand and outside team members can take care of the discrepancies in the local perceptions and their interpretations through relevant discussions, use of different methods and other sources of the local knowledge. As for Venn diagrams the presentation of "visual" relationships of individuals/institutions is itself important to understand the local-level realities. Analysis of such relationships and bringing about changes in them is a separate issue.

No Final Answer

No approach or methodology can promise to guarantee any final answer. The same is with PRA/PLA-type approaches, which are not expected to provide the final solutions to the local problems. Such approaches should be looked upon as approaches towards a better understanding of the local problems, the local views and preferences rather than providing final answers. Some local problems are too complex to be dealt with at the local level and hence, even with PRA/PLA-type approaches no satisfactory answers may emerge.

PRA/PLA induces participation and brings to the fore the local knowledge and involvement of the local people and these are considered to be the core elements in search of improved solutions. The views and opinions of the local people can give indications of their possible involvement, the limitations of their indigenous solutions and the extent to which their initiative in approaching a problem. These are far more important as initial steps in approaching the local problems rather than having the local communities sitting as passive onlookers.

PRA/PLA is a powerful methodology for the local development and it is important that its limitations are recognised and understood so as to use PRA/PLA for maximum benefit in terms of the local development. It is important to remember that PRA/PLA is not a final answer to the local development, it is an approach to seek an answer.

REFERENCES

Action Aid-Ethiopia/IIED (1989), *Action Aid in The Local Partnership, an Experiment with Rapid Rural Appraisal in Ethiopia*, Sustainable Agriculture Programme, International Institute for Environment and Development, London.

Anonymous, "Can Rural Appraisal Really Be Rapid?", a critical assessment by a group of "slow" researchers and practitioners, typescript.

Beebe J., (1985), Rapid Rural Appraisal; the critical first step in a farming systems approach to research, Farming Systems Support Project, Networking Paper No. 5, 36 pages.

Brass, T. (1995), "Old Conservatism in "new" clothes", *The Journal of Peasant Studies*, 22(3), pp. 516-540.

Brown, D., (1994) "Seeking the consensus: populist tendencies at the interface between research and consultancy" paper presented at the workshop "From Consultancy to Research", University of Wales, Swansea.

Chambers Robert. (1983), *Rural Development: Putting the Last First*. London, Longman

Chambers Robert, (1986), "Poverty in India: Concepts, Research and Reality—an exploration", typescript, Institute of Development Studies, University of Sussex, Brighton, 22nd July.

Chambers Robert, (1991), "Shortcut and Participatory Methods for gaining Social Information for Projects" in Cernea Michael M. (ed.) *Putting People First, Sociological Variables in Rural Development*, Oxford University Press.

Chambers Robert, (1993), Extract from Draft Paper "Participatory Rural Appraisal (PRA): Analysis of Experience", Institute of Development Studies, Sussex, July.

Chambers Robert, (1993), "Participatory Rural Appraisal (PRA): Challenges, Potential and Paradigm", Institute of Development Studies, Sussex, July.

Ford Richard and Lelo Francis (1991), Evaluating participatory rural appraisal: Listening to Village Leaders in Kakuyuni Location, *Forests, Trees and People, Newsletter* No.13, June.

Gill Gerard J., (1992), *Policy Analysis for Agricultural Resource Management in Nepal: A Comparison of Conventional and Participatory Approaches*, Research Support Series, Number 9, HMG Ministry of Agriculture/Winrock International Policy Analysis in Agriculture and Related Resource Management, July.

Goebel, A. (1998), "Process, perception and power!" Notes from participatory research in a Zimbabwean resettlement area, *Development and Change*, 29, pp. 277-305.

Grootaert, C. (1998), *Social Capital and Household Poverty in Indonesia*, World Bank mimeo, Washington D.C.

Lanjouw Peter & Stern Nicholas, (1991), "Poverty in Palanpur", *The World Bank Economic Review*, Vol. 5, No.1: 23-55, The World Bank.

Messerschmidt Donald A. (1991), Rapid Appraisal for Community Forestry: The RA Process and Rapid Diagnostic Tools, Institute of Forestry Project, *Technical Paper* No. TP 91/2, IOF Project, Pokhara, Nepal.

Mohan, Giles, and Kristian, Stokke, (2000), "Participatory Development and Empowerment: The Dangers of the Localism", *Third World Quarterly*, Volume 21, No. 2, pp. 247-268.

Morgan David, (1988), *Focus Groups as Qualitative Research* (Sage University Paper Series on Qualitative Research Methods, Vol.16), Beverly Hills, CA, Sage.

Mukherjee, Neela, (1993), *Participatory Rural Appraisal, Methodology & Applications*, Concept Publishing Co., Delhi.

Mukherjee, Neela, (1995), *Participatory Rural Appraisal & Questionnaire Survey: Comparative Field Experience & Methodological Innovations*, Concept Publishing Co., Delhi.

Mukherjee, Neela, with Meera Jayaswal, Bratindi Jena, Sudipta Ray and Amitava Mukherjee (2001), *Alternative Perspectives on Livelihoods, Agriculture and Air Pollution (Agriculture in urban and peri-urban areas in a developing country)*, Ashgate Publishing Ltd., Hampshire, (Forthcoming).

Orone Patrick, (Pers. comm. 1993), Makerere Institute of Social Research, PO Box 16022, Kampala, Uganda.

Pottier Johan (1991), Representation and Accountability: Understanding Social Change Through Rapid Appraisal, with reference to Northern Zambia, typescript, Department of Social Anthropology, S.O.A.S., University of London, April.

Smith Kevin, Barrett Christopher B. and Box Paul W. (2000), Participatory Risk

Mapping for Targeting Research and Assistance: With an example from East African Pastoralists, *World Development*, Vol. 28, No.11, 1945-1959.

Shah Parmesh, (1993), "Questionnaires: Participatory, Reliable and Interesting ?" A note prepared for IIED/IDS workshop on "Alternatives to Questionnaire Surveys" on 26th October.

Vaidyanathan A., (1989), "Macro and Micro Approaches to Studying Rural Economic Change: Some Pointers from Indian Experience in Bardhan Pranab (ed.), *Conversations between Economists and Anthropologists*, Oxford University Press, Oxford.

Ziche Joachim, (1990), "Some Critical Aspects in Gathering Socio-Economic Data in Rural Areas of Non-Western Societies in Hoeper Bernhard (compiled) (1990), *Qualitative versus Quantitative Approaches in Applied Empirical Research in Rural Development*, Zed Publishers, Bonn.

BIBLIOGRAPHY

Action Aid-Ethiopia/IIED (1989), *Action Aid in Local Partnership, an Experiment with Rapid Rural Appraisal in Ethiopia*, Sustainable Agriculture Programme, International Institute for Environment and Development, London.

Anonymous, 'Can Rural Appraisal Really Be Rapid?', a critical assessment by a group of 'slow' researchers and practitioners, typescript.

Beebe, J., (1985), Rapid Rural Appraisal; the critical first step in a farming systems approach to research, Farming Systems Support Project, Networking Paper No.5, 36 pages.

Brass, T. (1995), 'Old Conservatism in 'new' clothes', *The Journal of Peasant Studies*, 22(3), pp. 516-540.

Brown, D., (1994) 'Seeking the consensus: populist tendencies at the interface between research and consultancy, Paper presented at the workshop 'From Consultancy to Research', University of Wales, Swansea.

Brown, Andrew and Paul, Dowling, (1998), *Doing Research/ Reading Research: A Mode of Interrogation for Education*, The Falmer Press, London.

Burgess, Robert G., (1990), *In the Field, An Introduction to Field Research*, Contemporary Social Research Series, General Editor: Martin Bulmer, Routeledge, London.

Chambers, Robert, (1981),"Rapid Rural Appraisal: Rationale and Repertoire", *IDS Discussion Paper* No.155, Institute of Development Studies, Sussex.

Chambers, Robert, (1983), *Rural Development: Putting the last First*, London, Longman.

Chambers, Robert, (1986), 'Poverty in India: Concepts, Research and Reality—an exploration', typescript, Institute of Development Studies, University of Sussex, Brighton, 22nd July.

Chambers, Robert, (1990), *Microenvironments Unobserved*, Gatekeeper Series No.22, Sustainable Agriculture Programme, International Institute for Environment and Development, London.

Chambers, Robert, (1991), 'Shortcut and Participatory Methods for Gaining Social Information for Projects, in Cernea, Michael M. (ed.*), Putting People First, Sociological Variables in Rural Development*, published for the World Bank, Oxford University Press.

Chambers, Robert, (1992), Rural Appraisal: Rapid, Relaxed and Participatory, *IDS Discussion Paper* 311, Institute of Development Studies, October, Sussex.

Chambers, Robert, (1993), Challenging the Professions frontiers for rural development, Intermediate Technology Publications, London.

Chambers, Robert, (1993), Extract from draft Paper 'Participatory Rural Appraisal (PRA): Analysis of Experience', Institute of Development Studies, Sussex, July.

Chambers, Robert, (1993), 'Participatory Rural Appraisal (PRA): Challenges, Potential and Paradigm', Institute of Development Studies, Sussex, July.

Chambers, Robert, (1994), 'Participatory Rural Appraisal (PRA): Analysis of Experience', *World Development*, Vol.22, No.9, pp.1253-1268.

Chambers, Robert, (1997), Whose Reality Counts? Putting the first last, IT Publications, London.

Conway, G.R. (1985), Agroecosystem Analysis, *Agricultural Administration*, 20 (1), 31.

Conway, G.R. (1986), Agroecosystem Analysis for Research and Development, Winrock International Institute for Agricultural Development, Bangkok, Thailand.

Conway, G.R., Mian, A., Alam, Z., Yar, M., and Husain, T. (1987), Agroecosystem Zoning of the Hunza Valley: First Iteration—May 1987, Draft Report, International Institute for Environment and Development, London.

Conway Gordan, (1988),'Editorial- What's in a name', *RRA Notes* No.1, June.

Collinson, M.P. (1981), 'The Exploratory Survey Content, Methods and Detailed Guidelines, for Discussions with farmers', in CIMMYT eastern Africa Economic Programme Farming Systems Newsletter, April-June.

Dewees, Peter, (1989), 'Aerial Photography and Household Studies in Kenya', *RRA Notes*, Number 7, September, IIED, London.

Epstein, T. Scarlett, Suryanarayana, A.P. and Thimmegowda, T., (1998), *Village Voices, Forty Years of Rural Transformation in South India*, Sage Publications, New Delhi.

Freire, Paulo (1970), *Pedagogy of the Oppressed*, The Seabury Press, New York.

Ford, Richard and Lelo, Francis (1991), Evaluating participatory rural appraisal: Listening to Village Leaders in Kakuyuni Location, *Forests, Trees and People*, Newsletter No.13, June.

Gill, Gerard J., (1992), Policy Analysis for Agricultural Resource Management in Nepal: A Comparison of Conventional and Participatory Approaches, Research Support Series, Number 9, HMG Ministry of Agriculture/Winrock International Policy Analysis in Agriculture and Realted Resource Management, July.

Goebel, A. (1998), 'Process, perception and power! Notes from participatory research in a Zimbabwean resettlement area, *Development and Change*, 29, pp. 277-305.

Grandin, Barbara, (1988), *Wealth Ranking in Smallholder Communities: a field manual*, Intermediate Technology Publications, London.

Grootaert, C. (1998), *Social, Capital and Household Poverty in Indonesia*, World Bank mimeo, Washington D.C.

Guba, Egon G. (ed.) (1990), *The Paradigm Dialog*, Sage, California.

Guijt, Irene and Pretty, Jules (1992), *Participatory Rural Appraisal for Farmer Participatory Research in Punjab*, Pakistan, IIED, London.

Hallowell, Edward M. (1999), 'The Human Moment at Work', *Harvard Business Review*, January-February, pp. 58-66.

Hildebrand, P.E.(1981), Combining Disciplines in rapid Appraisal: The Sondeo Approach, *Agricultural Administration* 8 (6), 423.

Jayakaran, Ravi, (1991), 'PRA Camp at Mahilong, Bihar, 27-30, November, 1990: Krishi Gram Vikas Kendra', *RRA Notes*,

Number 13, August, IIED, London.

Kaplan, Allan, (1996), *The Development Practitioners' Handbook*, Pluto Press, London.

Kanji, Gopal K. & Mike Asher, (1996), *100 Methods for Total Quality Management*, Response Books, New Delhi.

Khon Kaen University,(1987), *Proceedings of 1985 International Conference on Rapid Rural Appraisal*, Rural Systems Research and Farming Systems Research Projects, Khon Kaen University, Khon Kaen, Thailand.

Kloos, Peter, (1998), 'Restudies in Anthropology, Modalities, Limitations and Alternatives', in Breman Jan *et al* (ed.) *The Village in Asia Revisited*, Oxford University Press, Delhi.

Lanjouw, Peter & Stern, Nicholas, (1991), 'Poverty in Palanpur', *The World Bank Economic Review*, Vol. 5, No.1: 23-55, The World Bank.

Mascarenhas, Jimmy & Prem Kumar, P.D., (1991), 'Participatory Mapping and Modelling: Users' Notes', *RRA Notes*, Number 12, July, IIED, London.

Massarik, Fred (1981), "The interviewing process re-examined", in Reason Peter *et al* (ed.) *Human Inquiry, A Sourcebook of New Paradigm Research*, John Wiley & Sons, Chichester.

Mathema, S.B. and Galt, D.L. (1987), 'The Samuhik Brahman Process in Nepal: A Multidisciplinary Group Activity to Approach Farmers', Paper presented at the Workshop on Farmers and Agricultural Research: Complementary Methods, Institute of Development Studies, England 26-31 July.

Max-Neef, A. Manfred, Antonio, Elizalde and Martin, Hopenhayn, (1991), *Human Scale Development, Conception, Application and Further Reflections*, The Apex Press, New York.

McCracken, Jennifer, Pretty, Jules and Conway, Gordon,(1988), *An Introduction to Rapid Rural Appraisal*, Sustainable Agriculture Department, I.I.E.D., London.

McCracken, Jennifer, (1989), 'Diagrams for Participatory RRA', *RRA Notes*, September, IIED, London.

Mearns, Robin, (1988), 'On Oral History and Local Calendars: Experiences in the Field in Papua New Guinea', *RRA Notes*,

Number 3, IIED, London.

Mearns, Robin, (1989), 'Aerial Photographs in Rapid Land Resource Appraisal, Papua New Guinea', *RRA Notes*, Number 7, September, IIED, London.

Messerschmidt, Donald A. (1991), Rapid Appraisal for Community Forestry: The RA Process and Rapid Diagnostic Tools, Institute of Forestry Project *Technical Paper* No. TP 91/2, IOF Project, Pokhara, Nepal.

Mohan, Giles, and Kristian, Stokke, (2000), "Participatory Development and Empowerment: the dangers of localism", *Third World Quarterly*, Volume 21, No.2, pp.247-268.

Morgan David, (1988), *Focus Groups As Qualitative Research* (Sage University Paper Series on qualitative Research Methods, Vol.16), Beverly Hills, CA, Sage.

Mukherjee, Amitava,(ed.), (1995), *Participatory Rural Appraisal, Methods and Applications in Rural Planning*, Vikas Publishing House Private Ltd., Delhi.

Mukherjee, Neela (1992), 'Villagers' Perceptions of Rural Poverty Through the Mapping method of PRA', *RRA Notes* no.15. IIED, London.

Mukherjee, Neela,(1993), *Participatory Rural Appraisal: Methodology and Applications*, Concept Publishing Co., Delhi.

Mukherjee, Neela,(1995), *Participatory Rural Appraisal & Questionnaire Survey: Comparative Field Experience & Methodological Innovations*, Concept Publishing Co., Delhi.

Mukherjee, Neela, (1997), *Participatory Appraisal of Natural Resources*, Concept Publishing Company, New Delhi.

Mukherjee, Neela, Mohammed Zahid, Aminath Lateefa and Mohammed Rasheed, (1999), Project benefit-impact matrix from the Maldives—a method for participatory evaluation, *PLA Notes*, 34, February.

Mukherjee, Neela, with Amitava Mukherjee, Meera, Jayaswal, Bratindi, Jena and Sudipta, Ray (2001), *Alternative Perspectives on Livelihoods, Agriculture and Air Pollution (Agriculture in urban and peri-urban areas in a developing country)*, Ashgate Publishing Ltd., Hampshire.

Narayan, Deepa, Raj Patel, Kai Schafft, Anne Rademacher and Sarah Koch-Schulte (2000), *Voices of the Poor, Can Anyone Hear Us*? Published by Oxford University Press for the World Bank, New York.

Orone, Patrick, (Pers. comm. 1993), Makerere Institute of Social Research, PO Box 16022, Kampala, Uganda.

Pretty, Jules, (1988), 'Portraits and Stories', *RRA Notes* Number 3, IIED, London.

Pretty, Jules, (1993), "Alternative Systems of Inquiry for a Sustainable Agriculture", Sustainable Agriculture Programme, International Institute for Environment and Development, London, 10th December.

Pretty, Jules, Irene Guijt, Ian Scoones and John, Thompson, (1995), *A Trainer's Guide*, International Institute for Environment and Development, London.

Pottier, Johan (1991), Representation and Accountability: Understanding Social Change Through Rapid Appraisal, with reference to Northern Zambia, typescript, Department of Social Anthropology, S.O.A.S., University of London, April.

Raintree, J.B. and Young, A. (1983), Guidelines for Agro-forestry Diagnosis and Design, *ICRAF Working Paper* No.6, Nairobi.

Reason, Peter and John Rowan (ed.) (1981), *Human Inquiry, A Sourcebook of New Paradigm Research*, John Wiley & Sons, Chichester.

Reddy, Ratna V., (1999), "Wealth Ranking in Socio-Economic Research: Substitute or Complement?", Research Notes, *Indian Journal of Agricultural Economics*, Volume 54, No. 1, January-March.

Rhoades, Robert E. (1979), The Art of the Informal Agricultural Survey, Social Science Department Training Document, International Potato Centre, Lima, Peru.

Rhoades, Robert E. (1987), 'Basic Field Techniques for Rapid Rural Appraisal', *Proceedings of 1985 International Conference on Rapid Rural Appraisal, Rural Systems Research and Farming Systems Research Projects*, Khon Kaen University, Khon Kaen, Thailand.

Richardson, S.A., Dohrenwend, B.A. and Klein, D. (1965),

Interviewing Its Forms and Functions, Basic Book, New York.

RRA Notes, (1991), Number 13, August, IIED, London.

RRA Notes/PLA Notes, various issues, Sustainable Agriculture Programme, International Institute for Environment & Development.

Sainath, P. (1996), *Everybody Loves a Good Drought, Stories from India's Poorest Districts*, Penguin Books, New Delhi.

Sandford, Dick, (1989), 'A Note on the Use of Aerial Photographs for Landuse Planning on a Settlement Site in Ethiopia', *RRA Notes*, Number 6, IIED, June.

Schwandt, Thomas R. (1990), 'Paths to Inquiry in the Social Disciplines—Scientific, Constructivist and Critical Theory Methodologies', in Guba Egon G. (ed.) *The Paradigm Dialog*, Sage, California.

Scoones, Ian, (1988), 'Learning About Wealth: A Example from Zimbabwe, *RRA Notes*, Number 2, October, IIED, London.

Scoones, Ian, (1992), 'Wealth ranking: Insights into patterns of Rural Differentiation in Southern Zimbabwe', typescript, Sustainable Agriculture Programme, IIED, London.

Shah, Parmesh, Bharadwaj, Girish & Ambastha, Ranjit, (1991), 'Farmers as Analysts and Facilitators in Participatory Rural Appraisal and Planning', *RRA Notes*, Number 13, IIED, London.

Shah, Parmesh, (1993), 'Questionnaires: Participatory, Reliable and Interesting ?' A note prepared for IIED/IDS workshop on 'Alternatives to Questionnaire Surveys' on 26th October.

Shaner, W.W., Philipp, P.F., and Schmehl, W.R.,(1982), *Farming Systems Research and Development: Guidelines for Developing Countries*, Westview Press, Boulder, Colorado.

Smith, Kevin, Barrett Christopher, B. and Box, Paul W. (2000), Participatory Risk Mapping for Targeting Research and Assistance: With an Example from East African Pastoralists, *World Development*, Vol. 28, No.11, 1945-1959.

Theis, Joachim & Grady Heather M., (1991) *Participatory Rapid Appraisal for Community Development, A Training Manual* Based on Experiences in the Middle East and North Africa, IIED & Save the Children Federation

UNDP, 1996, *UNDP's 1996 Report on Human Development in Bangladesh A Pro-Poor Agenda, Poor People's Perspectives*, UNDP, Dhaka, Bangladesh.

UNDP, *Who are the Question Makers? A Participatory Evaluation Handbook*, United Nations Development Programme, New York.

Vaidyanathan, A., (1989), 'Macro and Micro Approaches to Studying Rural Economic Change: Some Pointers from Indian Experience in Bardhan Pranab (ed.), *Conversations between Economists and Anthropologists*, Oxford University Press, Oxford.

Valadez Joseph and Bamberger, Michael (1994), *Monitoring and Evaluating Social Programs in Developing Countries: A Handbook for Policy-makers, Managers and Researchers*, EDI Development Studies, Economic Development Institute of the World Bank, The World Bank, Washington D.C.

Ziche, Joachim, (1990), 'Some Critical Aspects in Gathering Socio-Economic Data in Rural Areas of Non-Western Societies in Hoeper Bernhard (compiled) (1990) *Qualitative versus Quantitative Approaches in Applied Empirical Research in Rural Development*, Zed Publishers, Bonn.

INDEX